Madame Bovary on Trial

Emile Durkheim: Sociologist and Philosopher
A Preface to Sartre

Madame Bovary on Trial

Dominick LaCapra

Cornell University Press

ITHACA AND LONDON

Copyright © 1982 by Cornell University Press

All rights reserved. Except for brief quotations in a review, this book, or parts thereof, mut not be reproduced in any form without permission in writing from the publisher. For information address Cornell University Press, 124 Roberts Place, Ithaca, New York 14850.

First published 1982 by Cornell University Press.
Published in the United Kingdom by Cornell University Press Ltd.,
Ely House, 37 Dover Street, London W1X 4HQ.

Quotations from *Madame Bovary* by Gustave Flaubert, tr. by Paul de Man, A Norton Critical Edition, are reprinted by permission of W. W. Norton & Company, Inc. Copyright © 1965 by W. W. Norton & Company, Inc.

International Standard Book Number 0-8014-1477-6
Library of Congress Catalog Number 81-70714
Printed in the United States of America
Librarians: Library of Congress cataloging information
appears on the last page of the book.

The paper in this book is acid-free, and meets the guidelines for permanence and durability of the Committee on Production Guidelines for Book Longevity of the Council on Library Resources.

Contents

For then I go blind, blood veils my eyes and I hear what the great Gustave heard, the benches cracking in the court of assizes.

Samuel Beckett, *Molloy*

Preface

In recent years much attention has been focused on the reception or reading of texts as a way of renewing our understanding of literary history. This focus indicates an obvious point where intellectual history and literary history converge, for intellectual history is profoundly concerned with the interaction between texts and their various contexts. One particularly fruitful approach to the study of reception is to examine the reading or interpretation texts receive at trials. For a trial is a locus of social reading that brings out conventions of interpretation in a key institution—the judicial system—and the way a text is read at a trial has decisive significance for the "literary" and the "ordinary" life of the writer. At times the trials of important writers provide special insight into the complex way "literature" is a contestatory force in modern culture—a force that may even have political implications.

In light of these considerations, it is surprising that so little has been written about the famous trial of Flaubert in 1857 for outrage to public morality and religion. The trial posed a mystery at the time of its occurrence—what were its real grounds? —and it has continued to do so ever since. In this book I argue that the trial processed as ordinary crime what was, in significant and special ways, ideological or political "crime." *Madame Bovary* was ideologically criminal in that it placed in question the very grounds of the trial by rendering radically problematic its founding assumptions: the validity, in the context common to the novel and the trial, of norms relating to the family and religion, as well as the tenability of a belief in the central identity of the subject of narration and judgment. Thus, while the trial was "reading" the novel in one way, the novel may be argued to have read the trial in a rather different way.

To elucidate how the novel confronted the trial, I turn to a discussion of Flaubert's projects in writing as he enunciated them in his letters. I argue that the project of art for art's sake, emphasized in Jean-Paul Sartre's interpretation, is supplemented by another crucial project—carnivalization of literary traditions and of contemporary social reality—and, further, that the two projects interact in complex fashion in *Madame Bovary* as a text. Far from being a straightforward exemplification of the ideology of pure art, *Madame Bovary,* as "ideological crime," is at the intersection of the traditional and the modern novel in that it simultaneously invokes conventional expectations (such as those operative at the trial) and places them in subversive, possibly regenerative, question. Indeed, to the extent that the novel, or any mode of discourse, breaks contact with conventional expectations, it threatens to lose its role as an ideological challenge and to fall into the realm of formal or technical experimentation. *Madame Bovary's* very threshold position between the traditional and the modern, I believe, gives it a conjoined ideological and formal significance, a status and function to which the trial paid indirect homage.

In the later sections of this book, I inquire into the precise ways the novel might be said to "read" the trial, notably with reference to the key issue of the roles of the family, religion, and the narrative subject in the modern context. Here a particularly intricate problem is that of how Flaubert's multiplication of the positions of the narrative subject situates his so-called "free indirect style" and brings out the limitations of conceptions of his writing in terms of unity of point of view. My effort stems from the conviction that only a detailed analysis of the structure and functioning of the novel can substantiate my contention about the nature of the reading at the trial, for only it can disclose the specific manner in which the novel constituted a variant of ideological crime.

My approach, moreover, rests on the larger claim that the study of a text's reception should be combined with an attempted critical reading of the text that provides intellectual and historical perspective on processes of reception. This claim does not assume that the intellectual historian is in a position to provide a definitive interpretation of a text, stilling all controversy and disagreement. On the contrary, it questions the plausibility and even the desirability of this goal. And it takes its distance from the kind of neopositivistic formalism that attempts to detach inquiry from substantive argument and to confine it to the empirical delineation of actual processes of reception, the systematic elucidation of conventions or codes that control the production and reception of texts, and a general semiology that integrates these endeavors in a comprehensive program of research. The project for a general semiology is an important one, and it has significant consequences for the reconstruction of intellectual history. In elaborating the conditions of possibility that prefigure a given range of interpretations, it specifies the shared assumptions that may underlie divergent conclusions or emphases. But it should, I think, be supplemented and contested by attempts at critical reading that actively enter the lists of interpretative argument with all the risks and the political implications this mode of argument entails. The danger of semiotics is the confinement of critical inquiry to metacriticism that politically and socially neutralizes itself by placing the analyst in a deceptive position above the conflict of interpretations. Yet it is only by entering this conflict in a critical and self-critical way that we can revise our idea of what constitutes a valid or at least a valuable interpretation—one that extends empirical and systematic research to allow for debate that is committed without being fanatical or dogmatic. Indeed, insofar as one rejects both a rigid dualism between convention and usage and the belief that convention simply determines usage (with variations having the status of mere subjective epiphenomena), then acts of interpretation become necessary modes of enacting and testing the conventions that inform one's own readings in critical dialogue with other possible readings.

I have tried elsewhere to articulate the ways in which contemporary theorizing in literary criticism and philosophy is relevant to historical understanding—indeed to an attempt to rethink our very conception of intellectual history.[1] I am tempted

1. "Rethinking Intellectual History and Reading Texts," *History and Theory* 19 (1980), 245–76. Reprinted with a few changes and additions in *Modern Euro-*

to reformulate R. G. Collingwood's famous dictum and assert that there is either intellectual or anti-intellectual history— either history that makes some attempt to reexamine its own assumptions or history that remains securely, perhaps complacently, tied to the traditional procedures of the craft. Here the historian may have something of value to learn from Flaubert himself. As the study of Flaubert should demonstrate, however, the relation between tradition and its critical reworking cannot be comprehended in terms of a categorical either-or choice. Flaubert became a patron saint of "modernists." But the modernist myth of a total rupture with tradition finds relatively little in his work to sustain it. The goal of a "postmodern" reading of Flaubert may be precisely to undo the deadly dichotomy between tradition and its critique and, in the process, to reopen the question of the relation between continuity and discontinuity over time.

No study of Flaubert written today can avoid coming to terms with Jean-Paul Sartre's massive *L'Idiot de la famille.*[2] In the work that follows, Sartre—or his memory—is often a principal interlocutory "voice." This book is a supplement to *L'Idiot* in that Sartre himself provides neither a discussion of Flaubert's trial nor anything approximating a "reading" of *Madame Bovary*. In other ways, it is an argument with Sartre's approach that I hope is well mannered enough to qualify as a tribute to his memory, for it is in part addressed to the question of what is alive and what is dead in *L'Idiot de la famille*. It should also go without saying that this book will raise many more questions than it can hope to answer, a fact that may be taken as another indirect tribute to Sartre and to the mode of interrogation that is perhaps his greatest legacy. For the point of an interchange with Sartre is not to agree with his conclusions but to experience the urgency of his way of questioning even when one disagrees with him.

---

pean Intellectual History: New Perspectives ed. Dominick LaCapra and Steven L. Kaplan (Ithaca: Cornell University Press, forthcoming). The present work may be seen as a test case that tries to redirect intellectual history along paths sketched out in this programmatic essay.

2. Paris: Gallimard, 1971–72, 3 vols. My practice in referring to *L'Idiot de la famille* is to give volume and page number in parentheses.

In another sense, this book may be read as a companion piece to Jonathan Culler's *Flaubert: The Uses of Uncertainty*.[3] There are many parallels between Culler's work and my own. But I focus upon a given text rather than apply the combination of fragmentation and thematic analysis that Culler invokes to explore the corpus of Flaubert's writings. And I try to take inquiry in directions that at times diverge from the emphases and specific interpretations of Culler's excellent book. Geoffrey Hartman recently risked a definition of literature that helps to identify the tendency to which Flaubert, in Culler's understanding of him, made a decisive contribution: "Literature destabilizes, by overdetermination or indeterminacy—by what seems to be an excess (figurality) or a defect (equivocation)—the 'real character' of communication."[4] I shall attempt to make a contribution to our understanding of the applicability and limitations of this definition with reference to *Madame Bovary*. I also explore the issue of the social functions or effects of this kind of literature (or, perhaps, dimension of literature), an issue that has become increasingly insistent in the recent past. Here a central concern is the interaction among symptomatic, critical, and transformative forces in the relationship between literature and society. To some degree, this large and rather intractable concern is crystallized in the question of how the trial "read" *Madame Bovary* and how the text may be argued to have "read" the trial.

Given the various editions of Flaubert's letters and the absence of the second volume of Jean Bruneau's Pléiade edition of the *Correspondance*, I have decided to refer by date alone to letters from which I quote. When possible, I have checked my translations against those of Francis Steegmuller, *The Letters of Gustave Flaubert 1830–1857* (Cambridge, Mass.: Harvard University Press, 1980). All references to *Madame Bovary* by page number are to Paul de Man's "substantially new" translation and critical edition (New York: Norton, 1965). De Man's edition also contains translated selections from *Madame Bovary, Nouvelle version précédée de scenarios inédits* (New Version Pre-

3. Ithaca: Cornell University Press, 1974.
4. Geoffrey Hartman, ed., *Psychoanalysis and the Question of the Text* (Baltimore: Johns Hopkins University Press, 1978), viii.

ceded by Unpublished Scenarios), edited by Jean Pommier and Gabrielle Leleu (Paris: Librairie José Corti, 1949). (This title is, of course, something of a misnomer since the "new version" is an amalgamation of drafts for the book that Flaubert decided not to write.) De Man also provides an excellent collection of critical essays and selections from books on *Madame Bovary* and Flaubert. The only deficiency of this edition is its failure to conform to standard French editions in one respect: it does not include the trial. A translation of the trial by Evelyn Gendel may be found in *Madame Bovary*, A New Translation by Mildred Marmur, foreword by Mary McCarthy (New York: New American Library, 1964). My own page references to the trial are to the Pléiade edition of Albert Thibaudet and René Dumesnil, *Flaubert Oeuvres I* (Paris: Gallimard, 1951), 615–683, and translations are my own.

DOMINICK LACAPRA

Ithaca, New York

Madame Bovary on Trial

1

A Problem in Reading

> The police have blundered. They thought they were attacking a run-of-the-mill novel and some ordinary little scribbler; whereas now (in part thanks to the prosecution) my novel is looked on as a masterpiece; as for the author, he has for defenders a number of what used to be called "*grandes dames*"; the Empress, among others, has twice spoken in my favor; the Emperor said, the first time, "They should leave him alone"; and despite all that the case was taken up again. Why? There begins the mystery. . . . It's all so stupid that I have come to enjoy it greatly.
>
> Flaubert, Letter of January 20, 1857

Flaubert wrote the letter from which the above excerpt is taken ten days before his trial. Over a hundred years after the trial, the mystery still remains. Little has been done to dispel or even to understand this mystery, for the trial of Flaubert has in the interim received relatively scant historical and critical attention. Jean-Paul Sartre, for example, despite the fact that he devotes an entire volume of his *Idiot de la famille* to the historical context of Flaubert, curiously omits any significant discussion of the trial.

The relative neglect of Flaubert's trial is unfortunate given its status as an important event in its own right and as a crucial instance of the reception of a major text: *Madame Bovary*. Trials in general are of course noteworthy instances of the social reception of cultural phenomena. They attest to the way these phenomena are read or interpreted in a decisive social institution and to the hermeneutic conventions operative therein. They tell us something about the way lawyers and judges are trained to read. And, to the extent that forensic rhetoric is based upon an accurate appreciation of the expectations of an audience that lawyers attempt to convince or to persuade, a trial may also be an index of conventions or norms of reading in the larger public, at least on an "official" level of conscious-ness. At times there are even remarkable congruences between the conventions or unspoken assumptions operative in a trial and those at work in important approaches to interpretation in literary criticism itself. In any event, a trial enables one to be somewhat more precise in investigating a *"mentalité"* or "climate of opinion." It is also a telling case of the way in which the reading or interpretation of a text has real or material con-sequences for the "ordinary" and the "literary" life of an author. A trial indicates not only the manner in which an author is held responsible for what he or she has written; it also affects how he or she shall approach later works, for it crystallizes risks and, in the event of a first conviction, it may involve even greater penalties to come. At the very least, a trial is a force for intimidation and perhaps, in the case of a very self-conscious writer, it may be the occasion for a qualified experience of *Schadenfreude*. All these factors were at play in Flaubert's trial, where the author was not permitted to speak but was made to listen to the prosecution, the defense, and the judgment of the court. Indeed one of the more disquieting features of this trial was that the author did not speak in his own "voice" or behalf but had to defer to others' views of what he meant to say. Thus he was placed in the position in which authors generally find themselves only after their death.

The immediate reasons why Flaubert was brought to trial are not my principal concern. Rather I focus upon an analysis of the trial and upon a critical reading of *Madame Bovary* that attempts to explore the tension between the trial and the text. In this way, I think, one may get at more fundamental issues of interpretation and perhaps of motivation. But the immediate and explicit reasons for the judicial proceedings have some relation to the modes of reading employed during the trial. It is especially significant that these reasons are not altogether clear. One can bring together a number of plausible or possible reasons, but they do not add up to a fully convincing explana-tion of why Flaubert was tried for what he had written. There

A Problem in Reading

even seemed to have been forceful grounds for the dismissal of the case. I would suggest that this lack of conclusive reasons of a more apparent type is one sign that factors were operative at the trial that were not fully conscious, and may even have been repressed, at the trial itself. In other words, *Madame Bovary* was experienced as somehow unsettling or disorienting by its readers, but the reasons explicitly given for discomfort do not adequately account for the unsettling, even uncanny, effect of the text. A number of seemingly anomalous aspects of the pretrial and posttrial context help to lend credence to this point, notably in the case of the prosecuting attorney, Ernest Pinard.

The trial has most often been seen by commentators as it was seen at the time by Flaubert and others—as a simple pretext for the government to attack the *Revue de Paris,* the periodical in which *Madame Bovary* first appeared in serial form. Flaubert himself commented: "I am a pretext. The government is out to destroy the *Revue de Paris,* and I have been chosen as its instrument" (December 31, 1856). This understanding of the trial as a pretext is one reason why the trial has not been accorded greater importance and more extended treatment in the Flaubert literature. No doubt, the trial was in part a pretext for the government to exercise authority over an unruly periodical. But this more narrowly *Realpolitik* function of the trial hardly exhausts its meaning and significance. Indeed Flaubert's own conception of the trial as a pretext for a governmental attack upon the *Revue de Paris* was itself related to his firm belief, as much as two weeks before the trial, that his case would never come to court. In a letter whose probable date is January 16, 1857, he changed his mind about his role as a pretext and indicated his puzzlement over the course of events:

I have not written to you, my dear Achille [Flaubert's brother] because I believed the affair to be completely ended. . . . There is in all this *something,* someone invisible and relentless [*acharné*]. At first I was only a pretext, and now I believe that the *Revue de Paris* is itself only a pretext. Perhaps there is a grudge against one of my protectors? They have been considerable, even more in terms of their quality than of their quantity.

Everyone passes the buck and says: "It is not me; it is not me." What is certain is that the prosecution was stopped, then taken up again. Where does this turn-about come from?

Censorship was formally strict but often haphazardly administered during the Second Empire. As F. W. J. Hemmings observes: "If the Second Empire provided a discouraging climate for literature and the arts, this was more because of the philistinism of the general public than in consequence of the repressive measures that were put into force after the *coup d'état*."[1] Works of a manifestly pornographic or "lascivious" nature were not the objects of prosecution, as Sénard, Flaubert's defense attorney, himself pointed out at the trial. The fact that a work of the highest artistic merit, such as *Madame Bovary,* was brought to trial was a cause of some surprise at the time, and more recent reactions have often been similar. Yet this fact should not, at least in one sense, occasion surprise. For a "great" work of art may be a contestatory and partially subversive force in ways that cannot be fully accounted for in terms of its presumed deviance from existing moral or legal norms. I shall try to argue that the trial attempts to process exclusively as ordinary crime—crime involving standard forms of deviation from established norms or values—what may in some sense be "ideological" or political crime—"crime" that places in question the very grounds of the trial itself. In other words, the text may raise radical doubts about the validity of important norms and categories in the context which is common to its world and the ordinary world which is the setting for the trial of its author. It must, however, be acknowledged that the nature of "ideological crime" conveyed by a novel is difficult to define even outside the context of a trial, for the political and social protest at issue does not fall squarely within established categories of either ordinary deviance (for example, theft) or subversion (for example, treason or armed rebellion).

The type of "ideological crime" in which a novel may be implicated involves the use of language. A regime based on censorship is not constrained by the rules that operate in a

---

1. *Culture and Society in France 1848–1898* (London: Batsford, 1972), 52.

polity legally recognizing civil liberties. But the questions raised by Flaubert's trial tend to transcend or to undercut this important consideration, for they would also raise difficulties with respect to more conventional tests concerning freedom of speech and of the press. (These questions came to a head with reference to the family, religion, and the status of the narrative subject.) In general, the use of language has a problematic relation to the distinction between thought and action, and the complex problems it generates induce a displacement of attention onto narrower and more easily negotiable considerations (for example, that of whether a novel serves "prurient" or "lascivious" interests or has "redeeming social value"). The use of language is a practice mutually related to other practices in culture and society. And significant changes in it may be related to social and cultural issues in ways that give "stylistic" innovations a political significance, thus taking them beyond the range of purely "formal" concern. Perhaps the largest question related to these issues—one that is pertinent to the reading of *Madame Bovary* at Flaubert's trial but that also goes beyond it to engage broader interpretative matters—is the extent to which the novel conforms to (or is symptomatic of) its context, is critical of it, and initiates processes that cannot be contained within the categories of the symptomatic and the critical but are nonetheless bound up with sociocultural transformation in its most comprehensive sense.[2]

2. Some definitions are in order here. The term "symptomatic" refers to a process of reinforcement or "legitimation" of the given—a process that cannot be reduced to mere mirroring because it is also productive and reproductive of the given. The ordinary meaning of "symptomatic" in pathology carries with it a negative connotation that is not altogether misplaced in the present instance, for Flaubert himself saw certain major characteristics of society and culture as strongly negative in nature. I am primarily concerned with the relation of *Madame Bovary* to these characteristics (as is, in another vein, Jean-Paul Sartre in *L'Idiot de la famille*). "Critical" might seem self-explanatory, but it becomes more complicated in its relation to the transformative. The transformative does not entirely transcend the symptomatic or negate the critical, but it does situate both in a larger frame of reference where they interact with forces and possibilities that are not fully comprehended by their ordinary meanings. Thus, while certain crises or situations open to criticism may conceivably be overcome through sociocultural transformation (those dependent upon the economic system in the narrow sense, for example), other modes of crisis and the critical function itself may be resituated and given significantly different objects and roles. This is the case with the crisis (or hysteresis) provoked by what Jacques

Madame Bovary *on Trial*

Before turning to the larger questions I have evoked, I shall explore the degree to which Flaubert's trial was indeed a pretext for the government to "crack down" on the *Revue de Paris.* Enid Starkie, in her useful biography of Flaubert, has summarized the evidence well.[3]

The *Revue de Paris* was known to authorities of the Second Empire as a periodical purveying objectionably liberal, repub-

Derrida terms the "instituted trace"—a crisis that is related to the problems of language, the narrative subject, undecidability or indeterminacy of voice, the uncanny, and the carnivalesque. The uncanny (*unheimlich*) in Freud signals the return of the repressed, and it is related to the problematization of the boundary or limit between the real and the imaginary. For Freud, our feeling of the uncanny is bound up with the recurrence of what we have once repressed, and the compulsion to repeat engenders anxiety or even a sense of the demonic, for the once-familiar repressed thing has been estranged by repression. The repetitive workings of the unconscious are also uncanny or strangely disconcerting in the way they exceed the limits of control by the individual subject (including reality-testing) and thereby raise the problem of possible transgression of norms and founding categories or oppositions. (See especially Sigmund Freud, "The Uncanny" [1919], trans. Alix Strachey, in *Studies in Parapsychology*, ed. Philip Rieff [New York: Cromwell-Collier, 1963].) The transindividual dimension of language approximates it to the unconscious. But the more specific and dynamic relation of language and the unconscious may be located in repression that renders certain things or desires silent or "unsayable." The undecidable in Derrida designates what cannot be placed squarely on one side or the other of a divide but partakes (variably) of both poles of an opposition: its status is liminal and transgressive with reference to pure "founding" oppositions. It engages the problem or process of differing and deferment, for it is subject not to final solutions but to repeated (or iterated) alterations. One might suggest that, in this sense, it points to the interaction of repression and displacement, for the disclosure or articulation of one repressed force or desire comes with the occlusion or concealment of another. Total enlightenment on this view becomes an ideal or virtual object itself continually deferred. Carnivalization might be seen as an affirmative or joyful manner of playing out undecidable or uncanny relations in the face of anxiety which is never entirely transcended. Yet it involves a life-and-death struggle or "contest" between contending forces. In Flaubert, uncanny effects are often produced by extreme indeterminacy or undecidability of voice, and I shall attempt to relate them in part to the role of the canivalesque in his writing. This complex set of problems may reopen the question of what is at issue in basic sociocultural transformation. For the broadest question thus broached is that of the actual and the desirable relations among the given, what is critical of the given, and what eludes the standard opposition between the given and the critical without being simply dissociated from this opposition. Needless to add, what constitutes the given in any comprehensive interpretative sense is itself contestable, and its determination cannot be divorced from processes of signification or from critical and transformative apprehensions.

3. *Flaubert: The Making of the Master* (London: Weidenfeld and Nicolson, 1967).

lican, and generally "advanced" views. Maxime Du Camp, who had earlier been a very close friend of Flaubert, persistently urged the reluctant Flaubert to publish something and thereby to assume his proper place among the recognized elite of *belles lettres*. Du Camp was anxious to have *Madame Bovary* appear in the pages of the *Revue*. But, along with the other editors, he feared, upon reading the novel, that it would prove to be the occasion for censorship that the government sought. Indeed the way the editors themselves read the text had remarkable similarities to the way it was read at the trial. Aesthetic judgment, combined with political caution and moral reservations, led the editors to suppress portions of the novel. Here one has a first sign of the strange alliance between stylistic and ethico-political considerations in the trial of Flaubert.

Du Camp reports that he and Laurent Pichat arrived without prior consultation at nearly identical conclusions about the need for excisions in the novel. In a letter to Flaubert of July 14, 1856, Du Camp exhorted Flaubert to allow the editors of the *Revue* to be the "masters" of the novel and to make the cuts they deemed indispensable for its aesthetic success and political safety: "Be courageous, close your eyes during the operation and trust, if not our talent, then the experience which we have acquired in this kind of business and our affection for you. You've buried your novel under a heap of well-made but useless things, and one can't see it clearly; it is only a question of cleaning it up." On the back of this rather impertinent letter, Flaubert wrote "*gigantesque.*" On November 18, 1856, Du Camp wrote Flaubert: "It's no joking matter. Your scene in the cab [Part III, Chapter II] is impossible." The cab or fiacre scene was the first segment of the novel to be cut, and Flaubert demanded that an explanatory note be inserted in the *Revue* attributing this action to the editors. As we shall see, Sénard, in his defense of Flaubert, provided an interpretation of this series of events that many commentators have followed, for he saw Flaubert's action as itself instrumental in attracting the attention of the censors.

In his *Misères et grandeurs littéraires*, Louis Ulbach, another editor of the *Revue*, offered this account of why the novel caused him concern:

First I was very much alarmed when, after a first reading, I recognized that we were about to publish a strange and daring work, cynical in its negation of everything, unreasonable by dint of reason, false on account of too much truth in detail, badly observed on account of the crumbling, so to speak, of observation. *Madame Bovary* offended my artistic taste more than my modesty as a reader, but I was afraid lest it provide a pretext for those who might be looking for one to get the review suppressed.[4]

Ulbach's retrospective account weights the aesthetic, ethical, and political factors in his own way, but what seems clear is that the editors of the review were moved to precensorship because of some combination of these factors. (At the trial itself, all mention of the political factor would of course be bracketed, and the prosecution and defense would reach a limited agreement on the aesthetic quality of the novel. But they would relate the aesthetic to the moral and the legal in a manner that indicated both shared assumptions and different conclusions, for the art that was an inducement to evil for the one became an incitement to virtue for the other.)

Flaubert refused to accede to the demands of the editors, but they went ahead with their decision to cut certain passages. Flaubert begrudgingly allowed the sacrifice of the fiacre scene in the first installment of the novel, but when cuts were made in the second installment without his being consulted, he became irate. He demanded that the manuscript be returned to him and wrote to Pichat on October 2, 1856: "You attack details but you should go for the whole work. The brutal element is deep down in the work, and not on the surface. One can't whiten negroes, and one can't change the blood of a book; one can only impoverish it, that is all."

Flaubert at first refused to have more of the novel printed. But he relented and accepted the editors' offer to append a note announcing that the editors had removed passages from the work and disclaiming Flaubert's responsibility for the text as it appeared in the *Revue*. The reader was asked to consider it as a fragment of a larger work.

4. Quoted in Starkie, *Flaubert*, 245–46.

The arguments over the cuts embittered Flaubert. It is conceivable that his own response helped to attract the initial notice of the authorities, although it does not fully explain why they persevered in the effort to put him on trial. What Flaubert apparently did after the publication of the novel in the *Revue* was, in the opinion of Enid Starkie, even more likely to bring censorship upon him:

> Flaubert, in order to vent his annoyance against *La Revue de Paris,* did something very foolish; he ransacked the review to find passages which he considered as worthy of censure as his own book. Maxime Du Camp declares that he collected any odd sentences, or words, any possibly licentious passages— one came from Du Camp himself—and gave the dossier to a journalist who made an article from it, in which he asked how it came about the editors who could write such things themselves could be so prudish for others. This was all very unwise as it drew the attention of the government to the review. The article was noticed by the authorities; it was brought to the attention of the Emperor; it was sent to the Minister of the Interior; and, finally, it reached the Public Prosecutor. Flaubert's contributions to *La Revue de Paris* were gone through with a fine tooth comb and many things were found in them which made it possible, according to the laws of the day, to charge the author, the editor and the printer of the review with an offence against public morality. Thus Flaubert was, himself, largely responsible for the prosecution of his book.[5]

It should be remarked, however, that Starkie's account is an amalgamation of Du Camp's reconstructions, which were typically colored to cast a pleasant light upon himself, and the partially fictionalized and strategically situated narration of Sénard at the trial. It would, however, have been entirely in character for Flaubert to do something seemingly "foolish" in quixotic defense of a principle and even to be proud of it, but there are no references to the putative event of the dossier in his letters. In any case, this occurrence is still on the level of occasions for the trial; it accounts neither for the decision to proceed with

5. Ibid., 250.

the trial nor for the nature of the reading given the novel in court.

Considerations on the level of *la petite histoire* certainly have their "real-life" importance. Indeed, that they often have excessive importance may be one of the "lessons" to be derived from reading Flaubert. But they should not be made to supersede larger issues in interpretation. Both at the trial and in one's own attempt to relate the trial to a critical reading of the novel, the pretext is partially transcended as the text itself becomes a problem. It would be historically shortsighted to make the views of agents in the past concerning the proximate causes of events become one's own pretext for arresting inquiry at a superficial level of description and analysis.

In a certain sense, *Madame Bovary* and Flaubert himself do indeed seem to have been taken as scapegoats at the trial. But the obvious question is: scapegoats for what? To see the trial as a mere pretext is unambiguously to locate the scapegoat's "referent" in the *Revue de Paris*. My own commentary will suggest that, if a process of scapegoating occurred, the "referent" of the process is less easy to find, and it may be situated on a level that is not altogether literal. Scapegoating involves the substitution of one "object" for many others who feel polluted by, or implicated in, a larger scandal or evil which they would like to localize and purge. Scapegoating is an extreme response to an extreme situation: the anxiety-ridden sense that an event or series of events constitutes a fundamental challenge to the norms, values, and ways of life assuring the solidarity of the group.[6] Through scapegoating, a ritual of purification is enacted so that the concentration of "guilt" or, in less moral terms, of contamination upon an "other," who is somehow expelled from the group, cleanses the group, safeguards it from radical disorientation, and returns it to social and ritual order. When norms and values are themselves in doubt, scapegoating may become especially irrational and violent, for the state of at least relative innocence and order to which it promises return is itself elusory—and this exacerbates the need for assurance and

6. For a discussion of the scapegoat mechanism, as well as a speculative theory about its role in culture, see René Girard, *Violence and the Sacred* (Baltimore: The Johns Hopkins University Press, 1977).

security. Flaubert's trial was to some extent a secularized ritual process in a context where at least a significant segment of the intellectual and artistic elite—that dangerous supplement in any modern society—had severe doubts about the viability of the dominant society and culture. And the force of their ambivalent "gifts" to the cultural heritage was to place society itself on trial, at times in ways that challenged the role of the scapegoating mechanism. One of the disconcerting effects of *Madame Bovary* is to unsettle the secure oppositions upon which the trial depended and which a scapegoating process is functional in generating or preserving. In this way, the "referent" for which a scapegoat was substituted became indeterminate, for it included the society that legally constituted itself as judge of the novel. That the novel may have invited this displacement or transference of guilt upon itself is part of its complexity.

There are two partial exceptions, of extremely different natures, to the critical and historical tendency to be satisfied with the idea that the trial was a pretext and that it held little interest beyond this circumscribed status. One is to be found in Hans Robert Jauss's "Literary History as a Challenge to Literary Theory."[7] In his insistence upon the importance of an aesthetics of reception, Jauss has noted the significance of Flaubert's trial. We shall defer a discussion of his stimulating comments to a later chapter.[8]

A second exception to the reduction of the trial to a mere pretext is the curious and fascinating pamphlet of André Pasquet, *Ernest Pinard et le procès de Madame Bovary.*[9] Pasquet does not offer anything that might be called a critical reading of the novel in relation to the issues raised at the trial. But he does insist that the prosecution of Flaubert was not a simple instrument in the government's attack upon the *Revue de Paris*. He makes his case in an effort to show how the prosecuting attorney, Pinard, responded to the novel, and his larger design is to rehabilitate Pinard whom he sees as an unjustly maligned figure. For Pasquet, literary critics have largely accepted the idea that Sénard's defense was eloquent and cogent and that

7. *New Literary History* II, no. 1 (1970), 7–37.
8. See Chapter 3.
9. Paris: Editions Savoir Vouloir Pouvoir, 1949.

Pinard's presentation was mediocre—a view, be it noted, that Flaubert himself was the first to put forth: "Maître Sénard's speech was splendid. He crushed the attorney from the Ministry of Justice, who writhed in his seat and made no rebuttal. We flattened him with quotations from Bossuet and Massillon, smutty passages from Montesquieu, etc. . . . Sénard spoke for four hours. It was a triumph for him and for me" (January 30, 1857). Here Flaubert goes so far as to create the impression that Sénard was fully authorized to speak in Flaubert's own voice. To say this is to indicate that an author may subscribe to, or even enunciate, interpretations of his work that may be radically called into question by the way his writing may be argued to function.

Pasquet challenges the more or less canonical version of events which elevates Sénard only to degrade Pinard. His own conclusions cap an argument that serves to bring out a number of questions: Was Pinard motivated by concerns that exceeded the desire to clamp down on the *Revue de Paris?* Did Pinard make a number of points that a critical reading must take into account? Was Sénard's argument if anything more "naive" and rhetorically flatulent than that of his adversary?

These are, of course, not the terms in which Pasquet frames his discussion. His own approach is most relevant to the first question specified above, concerning Pinard's motivations. Pasquet argues that, in his prosecution, the lawyer was motivated by the ideals which informed his exemplary career: the defense of Christian morality—and not of mere bourgeois convention. The possibility that the two may intermingle in certain contexts is apparently beyond Pasquet's purview. And he omits mention of something that caused Flaubert bitter amusement in retrospect: Pinard, later in life, published a book of obscene verse. (For Flaubert's reaction, see his letter of April 16, 1879.)

For Pasquet, as for Pinard, art is not a law unto itself. It is subject to the higher law of Christian morality which, according to Pasquet, Pinard had every right to invoke. It offered the only way to find secure orientation in the world out of joint depicted in *Madame Bovary.*

Before reaching this apologetic conclusion, Pasquet makes a number of other observations that are worth mentioning. He

notes that there are no fully conclusive reasons of a more obvious sort that explain why Flaubert's case came to trial. The
use of Flaubert as a pretext, excisions in the *Revue* that attracted the censor's attention, the ambitions of the young
Pinard (only thirty-five at the time), and the putative role of
Christian morality in motivating the honorable prosecutor—
these are contributing "causes" that do not amount to a total
explanation of the trial. Flaubert's attempts to get the case dis-
missed seemed at the time to Flaubert himself to be sure of
success. Pasquet, despite inconsistencies in his account (for
example, his insistence that Pinard was not responsible for
having the case come to trial but was only doing his duty in
contrast to his observation that Pinard adamantly refused to be
replaced as prosecutor), is most suggestive in touching upon
Pinard's less obvious motives and psychological investments in
the case. He states: "How can one know, moreover, Pinard's
deep feelings [*le sentiment profond*] about *Madame Bovary*? Did
he not undergo its penetrating charm? And did he not consider that in it there were all the elements of a subtle temptation, of a dangerous seduction, against which one had to fortify
and protect souls?"[10]

What Pasquet senses is that Pinard was disturbed by the
novel in a way that Sénard refused to be disturbed. He seemed
open to the temptation of a narcissistic, hysterical, and beautiful woman whose existence was imaginary but whose effects
might be real. Sénard's interpretation, as we shall see, made the
novel out to be altogether conventional in nature. Pinard, on
the contrary, experienced its insinuations and unsettling potential despite his effort to construe it in terms of simple deviance
from established norms. Indeed, at times he did broach issues
of a broader nature. At the very least, Pinard may have been
"poisoned" or contaminated by the "painting of passion" in the
novel and, himself facing temptation, may have set out in a
self-preservative quest to find a legal antidote to Flaubert's
writing.

Pinard himself discussed his role in the trial in his *Journal*
of 1892, and Pasquet notes what might be called the bizarre

---

10. Pasquet, *Ernest Pinard*, 13.

anomalies in Pinard's account—anomalies so glaring that they suggest not simple errors but evasion and repression:

> The novel *Madame Bovary* reveals a true talent; but the description of certain scenes goes beyond all bounds [*toute mesure*]; if we close our eyes, Flaubert will have many imitators, who will go even further in the same direction. In addition, the *Chambre correctionnelle* had just condemned Baudelaire's *Les Fleurs du mal*; it inflicted a fine upon the author and ordered the suppression of certain passages. If we abstain, one will say that we are easy on the strong and the heads of schools and that we are accommodating toward our own but inflexible for opponents. Baudelaire had many friends in the camp of the republicans while Flaubert was an assiduous, feted guest in the salons of Princess Mathilde.[11]

This after-the-fact rationale of Pinard's is astounding. Pasquet does not doubt Pinard's attempt to forestall the possibility of mimetic contagion that would result if Flaubert's novel were disseminated. But Pasquet comments: "Ernest Pinard's memory betrayed him in an extreme way. It is difficult to accumulate more errors in a few lines."[12] What were these errors? First, the condemnation of Baudelaire could not have influenced Pinard's decision because Baudelaire's *Fleurs du mal*, which appeared on June 25, 1857, was condemned on August 20 of that year, six months after the trial of Flaubert. Second, Flaubert's relations with the Princess Mathilde began only in 1860, three years after the trial. Third, Flaubert at the time of the trial was hardly a powerful *chef d'école*. He had published nothing. (He became a figurehead for "realists" and "naturalists," much to his dismay, only after the trial.) Fourth, those responsible for the trial probably did not know of the social importance of Flaubert's family, a point which Flaubert commented upon in his letters and which Sénard would make much of at the trial. (One might add that Baudelaire's stepfather, General Aupick, had a national prominence greater than the more regional fame of Doctor Flaubert and that the aesthetic views of Baude-

11. Quoted in Pasquet, *Ernest Pinard*, 10.
12. Ibid., 11.

laire and Flaubert were quite similar—as they both immediately recognized.) Pasquet notes that Pinard's prosecution of Baudelaire, in spite of its "successful" outcome (Baudelaire was convicted), was more moderate than his treatment of Flaubert, and Pasquet speculates that this was so because "there subsisted in Baudelaire powerful spiritualistic and Christian vestiges that had completely disappeared from the soul of Flaubert."[13] This may have been what Pinard felt, but the question of "Christian vestiges" and their relation to "subversive" tendencies is, of course, more intricate in the cases of both Baudelaire and Flaubert. Flaubert's practice of art has itself, with some reason, been seen as a form of secularized Christian asceticism.

Pasquet does not relate these "tricks" of memory to the ambivalence in Pinard's response to the novel. In any event, they add another dimension of mystery to the trial. For they may also be referred to the problem of the manner in which the novel provoked responses that cannot be accounted for either in terms of the trial as pretext or in terms of the more explicit reasons for trial offered at the trial itself.

13. Ibid., 13–14.

2

The Trial

La vérité sortira de l'examen sérieux du livre. [Truth will emerge from a serious examination of the book.]
Sénard for the defense

Every notary carries within himself the debris of a poet.
Flaubert, Madame Bovary

How does the trial "read" the novel? Indeed how can a trial, given the framework in which it operates, read a novel? What sort of truth can emerge from the "serious examination" of a literary text at a trial?

One may initially approach these questions by attempting to specify the assumptions shared by the prosecution and the defense, for these were in crucial respects the conditions of possibility for the reading of the novel at the trial. Then one may look more closely at the arguments which led the two to opposite conclusions. Finally, one may examine the judgment of the court which, confronting problems peculiar to itself, indicated further difficulties in the reading at the trial. One may also note in passing that the trial followed a highly stylized format: the speech for the prosecution, the speech for the defense, and the judgment of the court. The monologues of the prosecution and the defense are of course marked by an internalized awareness of how the other might respond to certain points, and the court strains to arrive at some resolution of the issues in its decision. More direct dialogue is limited to a few brief interruptions or interjections on the part of the prosecutor during the speech of the defense. There is no direct questioning of witnesses or cross-examination in this judicial proceeding.[1]

1. As noted in the Preface, all page references concerning the trial are to the Pléiade edition of Albert Thibaudet and René Dumesnil, *Flaubert Oeuvres* I (Paris: Gallimard, 1951).

On one level, the prosecution and the defense share a great deal, and what they share is perhaps more important than what divides them. To be able to function in accordance with standard operating procedures, the trial had to rely on certain tacit assumptions which the novel both elicits and renders radically problematic. The trial does not, and perhaps cannot, explicitly recognize these assumptions or the way the novel treats them. All those participating in the trial—prosecution, defense, and the court in its judgment—tend to read the novel in an extremely restricted way. This reading is not simply wrong, for it is invited by one level on which the novel itself operates or functions: the level of conventional expectations about how things make sense. What does not register at the trial is the manner in which the novel renders this first level of understanding and expectation highly questionable in its world and, at least by implication, in the larger social world in which the trial takes place. Only at certain points, especially in the speech of the prosecutor, are these larger issues—issues that cannot be confined to conformity or deviance in relation to established norms—touched upon. At these points, the conventional framework of the trial itself threatens to explode, for then the question becomes that of the validity of the norms, categories, and criteria tacitly assumed by the trial as its basis of understanding and judgment. Here the standard relation between text and context tends to be reversed; it is no longer the context that provides determinate boundaries for interpreting and evaluating the text. Rather the text comes to challenge its context and the adequacy of its framing or boundary-marking devices, for it questions the viability of criteria of understanding and evaluation as they function within that context or others sufficiently analogous to it. What is of course not made evident at the trial is that, at these points, the issue can no longer be that of ordinary crime or failure to conform but must in some sense be that of political or "ideological" crime. The profound difficulty, however, is that "crime" of this sort is not amenable to more or less regular judicial proceedings because it contests the very right of the trial to judge it—and in ways that are extremely difficult to define, especially within the terms of a trial. If the challenge to the rules of the existing order is scandalous or disconcerting enough, scapegoating becomes an alluring option for those who wish to maintain that the established system is basically just. But so does the attempt to show that the challenge is not a challenge at all, since what constitutes a challenge may be construed as reinforcing the status quo. Thus one has the possibility that different conclusions will be reached by those who share the assumption that what exists is fundamentally legitimate.[2]

The assumption that the society that forms the larger context for the novel is itself in a fundamentally healthy, normal, or legitimate state is, of course, never explicitly formulated or critically scrutinized at the trial. It constitutes the "unthought" ground of the trial—its unexamined preunderstanding of the nature of things through which the text is read. On its basis, the text may be understood and evaluated exclusively in terms of conformity to, or deviance from, established norms and values, for these norms and values are assumed to exist in a solid and unproblematic state within the larger sociopolitical and cultural context.

At the trial, the most significant explicit norms and values relate to the family and religion, and they permit one to draw a clear-cut opposition between marriage and adultery, the sacred and the profane. Since marriage is itself a sacrament in a Christian context, the two concerns may coalesce to give rise to the question of whether the novel conforms to, or deviates from, the image of the modern family as a holy family. In order that the novel may be processed in terms of this conventional but elevated "ideological" image, what must be more or less sys-

---

2. Beyond the confines of the literal trial, matters become even more intricate. For those who do not accept the legitimacy of the status quo may nonetheless accept the arguments of its most complacent defender concerning the conservative, merely symptomatic, or even aggravating functions of the text, in part because of an unwillingness to recognize and explore what the text does and what implications it may have—especially when these considerations complicate the problems of interpretation, criticism, and change. Certain of Sartre's arguments, for example, resemble those of Sénard, while others—notably with respect to Flaubert's nihilism and escapism—approximate those of Pinard. More generally, the combination in modern Marxism of presumed sociopolitical radicalism and cultural or epistemological conservatism (for example, in the quest for a "totalizing" dialectic and a securely unified narrative of the historical process) requires extensive investigation.

tematically suppressed, repressed, or avoided at the trial is the way *Madame Bovary* places in question the relevance of this image in the modern world and, with it, the fundamental assumptions about reading, understanding, and evaluation operative at the trial. Needless to add, the suppression of "evidence" in the novel for this kind of questioning cannot explicitly register at the trial. If it did register, those at the trial would be forced to engage in processes of self-reflection and self-criticism that would, to say the least, be difficult to accommodate within the parameters of the trial. For it becomes more difficult and complicated to judge when one senses that the grounds of judgment have become unstable. Indeed the very question of judgment tends to be displaced from the application of a standard in a case to the applicability of certain standards in a larger sociocultural context. A question of this sort does not facilitate standard operating procedures or routine processes of judgment. And chances are that it would be deemed irrelevant to the "normal" course of a trial. At this level, the trial and the novel may be at cross-purposes, or—to use a phrase of Karl Mannheim—the two may "talk past one another," because the differences are so extreme that they tend to jeopardize the existence of a common *habitus* or frame of reference in terms of which they may be adjudicated.

The fact that common assumptions structure the arguments of the prosecution and the defense often makes them appear as inverted mirror images of one another—almost like alter egos in a Flaubert novel. Discussion and decision turn on a simple binary choice of a positive or a negative answer to a set of shared questions. But there are a number of noteworthy variations in the way common assumptions and questions are employed, and it is worth mentioning them before treating in more detail the arguments of the prosecution and the defense.

The difference between the lengths of the speeches is the most obvious one. The prosecutor's speech covers nineteen pages of text in the Pléiade edition, while that of the defense attorney takes up forty-seven pages. The defense's presentation took over four hours to deliver, as Flaubert himself observed. The disproportionate size of the defense attorney's speech, along with what may have been a more effective mode of delivery, apparently gave it a greater rhetorical weight. A trial is one instance among numerous others in which oral presentation does make a difference. In the printed version of the trial, however, the prosecutor's speech appears to be more neatly argued, and it does succeed in raising a few points that even an attempted "critical" reading of the novel must confront.

Another difference between prosecution and defense is that between outrage and complacency. Sénard for the defense is unflappably complacent both in his thought and in his mode of presentation. He simply refuses to be bothered by certain questions. His interpretation is in one sense more narrowly conservative than that of the prosecutor, for—despite his apparently "liberal" conclusion—he construes the novel as a simple, clear, and distinct confirmation of existing morality and society. For Sénard, the author-narrator is a fully reliable guide in telling the sorry tale of Emma Bovary's fall and deserved punishment. The intention or spirit informing the novel is unmistakably one of moral condemnation attesting to the full rectitude of the narrator's (and the reader's) position. Only at rare points, which he does not notice, does Sénard's argument raise problems for the frame of reference in which it comfortably takes shape. Morality for Sénard is virtually identical with the existing order of society, and the moral of the novel is for him one of conservative adaptation within the status quo.

The relevant context for Pinard is Christian morality which is seen as the "foundation of modern civilizations" (633). This view provides at least the possibility that existing society may deviate from its moral and religious foundation. Pinard himself does not note this implication or draw conclusions from it. He is concerned only with the presumed deviation of Flaubert's novel. But his sense of outrage at the enormity of this deviation threatens at times to carry him beyond the restricted framework of conformity or deviance vis-à-vis established and socially contextualized norms and values. He can be shocked by certain aspects of the novel that the defense attorney must try to interpret in fully conventionalizing terms.

A further difference may be mentioned in a preliminary way. Pinard's understanding of the intention or "thought" of the author is in keeping with his focus upon the text of the novel. For him, intention is fully "embodied": it is what the author means to say in the text. Pinard will supplement this concern by a brief appeal to a fragment of another text by Flaubert, *The Temptation of Saint Anthony*, only to find in it the same "color" as that which prevails in *Madame Bovary*. (This "lascivious" color brings about the demoralization of the reader.) The defense, by contrast, understands intention in a broader and less discriminating way, for it merges in his account with general questions of motivation and character. Indeed the defense will turn to the text of *Madame Bovary* only toward the very end of his speech, and at that point his understanding of it is entirely predetermined by his prior discussion of its authorial and literary lineage—its "precedents" in biography or sources and its status in the eyes of reputable character witnesses who are not questioned but invoked. For both the prosecution and the defense, reading and evaluation are very much constitutive of a *procès d'intention*, and it is assumed that the functioning of the text is essentially identical with the intention or "thought" of the author.

A final difference bears upon the way Pinard and Sénard relate to Emma Bovary and see her role in the novel. Both assume that she is the central character and that the reader's relation to her will be one of identification or recognition. But for Pinard, she serves as a positive identity and thus lures the reader into the same temptations and immoral forms of behavior to which she succumbed. Emma herself is not so much a scapegoat of society as a temptress who gets her way with men and who dies for purely contingent reasons devoid of moral import. For him, the novel does not present her suicide as punishment for her immorality. One might almost say that, for Pinard, Emma should be more of a scapegoat than she is, for she gets away with too much. For Sénard, Emma serves as a negative identity, providing the reader with an object (and an abject) lesson in what he or—more decidedly—she must avoid. She is a scapegrace who fully gets what she deserves.

Pinard and Sénard tend to become two more of Emma's men, and their drastically opposed but largely unqualified judgments concerning the way Emma is presented in the novel are in concert with their approaches to reading *Madame Bo-*

vary as a whole. Another variation, however, occurs in this respect as well. Pinard will assume the role of the reader, but he will never directly assume that of the author—although he will interpret the novel as a function of his own understanding of the author's true "thought." Sénard blends the role of the reader and a rhetorical identification with that of the author, and he will even go so far as either to speak in the author's voice or to become a somewhat paternal underwriter or patron of Flaubert. Pinard thus identifies with Emma in ambivalent revulsion but refuses direct identification with Flaubert; Sénard refuses identification with Emma but securely substitutes himself for Flaubert.

Pinard begins his prosecution by noting a difficulty that he does not wish to dissimulate. The charge of offense to public morality and religion is "a little vague and a little elastic, and it is necessary to specify it." But this is not the difficulty that concerns him, for "upright and practical minds" will find it "easy to reach an understanding in this respect." The difficulty is rather that this charge is brought against "a novel in its entirety." A novel of some length, published in six installments in a periodical, poses problems distinct from those of an article that may readily be read to the court. The only solution in the case of a long work is "to narrate [*raconter*] the entire novel without reading from it" and then to incriminate the novel by quoting passages from the text. Thus Pinard justifies the method of paraphrase and synoptic content analysis, subsequently illustrated by quotation, by pointing to a simple difficulty in reading. He must replace Flaubert's extended narration with his own more condensed or economical one (616).

Pinard's next step is to query the title in the attempt to arrive at the text's core or synoptic meaning. The title and subtitle provided by Flaubert—*Madame Bovary: Moeurs de province*—do not, for him, explain the "thought" of the author; only the subtitle gives a presentiment of it. The author wanted to provide tableaux or pictures: the language of the novel is a "picturesque" one, and it depends upon the "colors" of the picture for its effects. While the portrait of the husband begins and ends the novel, "it is evidently [the portrait] of Madame Bovary" that is the most "serious" one in the novel, the one that "illuminates" all the others (616). For Pinard, Emma is the sun of this literary system.

Pinard then proceeds to a plot summary following the outline of the four principal scenes he will later use as frames for his quotations: (1) Emma's "fall" with Rodolphe, (2) the religious transition between the two adulteries, (3) the "fall" with Léon, (4) the death of Emma. On the basis of this summary, he feels justified in offering a new title, a précis of the novel's meaning, and a delineation of its dominant "color."

The new and more accurate title is "The History of the Adulteries of a Provincial Woman" (618). The essential meaning is also the essential charge against the novel: "The offense to public morality is in the lascivious tableaux that I shall place before your eyes; the offense to religious morality is in the voluptuous images mingled with sacred things" (619). The "general color of the author . . . is the lascivious color, before, during, and after the falls" (619). The author, employing "all the wonders of his style," has used these colors to paint Madame Bovary, and the result is a glorification of adultery and an undermining of marriage. For "the beauty of Madame Bovary is a beauty of provocation" (621).

The genre or school to which this use of language belongs is the "realistic" one: "the genre which Monsieur Flaubert cultivates, that which he realizes without the circumspection of art but with all the resources of art, is the descriptive genre: it is realistic painting." Realism for Pinard seems to signify all that is upsetting in the art of Flaubert. But it is more specifically related to Flaubert's presumably "lascivious" colorations and to his lack of *mesure* or circumspection in art. Pinard will hark back to these complaints in his conclusion. At this point, he asserts that the fragments of *The Temptation of Saint Anthony* printed in the review, *L'Artiste*, reveal the same "color," the same "energy of the brush," and the same "vivacity of expression" as *Madame Bovary* (630).

In developing his argument, Pinard interrupts a quotation to interject a parenthetical expression of scandalized dismay. The phrase over which he stumbles and whose peculiar nature he senses is: "*les souillures du mariage et les désillusions de l'adultère*" [the defilements of marriage and the disillusions of adultery].

He notices the telling reversal of ordinary expectations that Flaubert effects with this phrase. "There are those who would have said: 'The disillusions of marriage and the defilements of adultery.'" And shortly thereafter, he repeats this complaint and adds: "Often when one is married, instead of the unclouded happiness one expected, one encounters sacrifices and bitterness. The word disillusion might be justified; that of defilement could never be" (625).

The effect of the novel on the reader—and perhaps the intention of the author—is for Pinard one of demoralization and corruption. The novel is literally poison. It is especially dangerous for its most probable readership:

> Who will read the novel of Monsieur Flaubert? Will it be men who busy themselves with political or social economy? No! The light pages of *Madame Bovary* will fall into even lighter hands— into the hands of young women, sometimes of married women. Well, when the imagination will have been seduced, when seduction will have descended into the heart, when the heart will have spoken to the senses, do you believe that a very cold reasoning will be very strong against this seduction of the senses and of sentiment? In addition, even men must not drape themselves too much in their force and virtue; men too harbor instincts from below and ideas from above and, with everyone alike, virtue is the consequence of effort, very often painful effort. Lascivious paintings generally have more influence than cold reasonings. [631–32]

Pinard thus restages a very old conflict in almost storybook fashion. The cold light of reason is weak in comparison with the heat of the imagination and passion. The language of art is the language of images and pictures that appeal to the lower faculties. The fatal declension from the imagination to the senses that it effects is especially dangerous for women, who are particularly prone to its allures. But men themselves may be feminized by literature, and their protective garments may be penetrated by its wiles. Man as he reads literature must also be provided with a safeguard to supplement his "force and virtue." Here one has the proper province of the laws as guardians of public morality and religion.

Drawing to a close, Pinard attempts to preempt an important line of defense. "One will say as a general objection: but, after all, the novel is fundamentally moral, because adultery is punished." For Pinard, even if the ending were moral, it would still not justify "lascivious" details in the book; if it did, anything would be justified by a moral ending. But even assuming that this end existed—an assumption Pinard denies—it would not justify the means. For "this would go against the rules of common sense. It would amount to putting poison in the reach of all and the antidote in the hands of a very small number, if indeed there were an antidote" (631).

The ending of *Madame Bovary* is not truly moral for Pinard. The death of Emma proves nothing. There is no moral connection between her adultery and death such that the latter counts as warranted punishment for the former. "She dies not because she is adulterous but because she wanted to die. She dies in all the splendor of youth and beauty" (632). Thus the poisoning of Madame Bovary is itself no antidote to the poisoning of the reader brought about by the way Emma and adultery are painted. Her self-poisoning is a willful event that resembles her adultery, thereby compounding her crime rather than serving as a punishment for it.

Pinard concludes with general reflections on the immorality of the novel "from a philosophical point of view" (632). Touching upon what later theorists would refer to as unreliable narration, he exclaims:

> Who can condemn this woman in the book? Nobody. Such is the conclusion. There is not in the book a character who can condemn her. If you find in it a wise character, if you find in it a single principle in virtue of which adultery may be stigmatized, then I'm wrong. Thus if in all the book there is not a character who can make her bend her head; if there is not an idea, a line in virtue of which adultery is scourged, then I am right: the book is immoral. . . . Would you condemn her in the name of the author's conscience? I do not know what the author's conscience thinks. [632–33]

Thus for Pinard there is no stable, secure, or reliable position within the novel from which to condemn Emma. Conjugal honor is represented by a benighted husband who literally hands his wife over to her lovers. Public opinion is "personified in a grotesque being, the pharmacist Homais, who is surrounded by ridiculous people whom this woman dominates." Religious sentiment is incarnated in the priest Bournisien, "a priest about as grotesque as the pharmacist, believing only in physical and never moral suffering, almost a materialist" (632). The author is an elusive presence at best whose position cannot be determined. What is left is the overpowering personality of Emma and the example she gives. Within the novel, "the only personage who dominates is Madame Bovary" (633).

For Pinard the fact that no one in the novel is in a position to throw the first stone leads to the conclusion that one must look outside the text to a larger and more certain text—that of "Christian morality, which is the foundation of our modern civilizations." In the light of the higher morality cast by this more certain sun, "everything becomes explained and clarified" (633). For this morality serves as the source of clear and absolute principles through which the novel and its characters may be judged. It alone is a force able to dominate Emma Bovary and put an end to her poisonous influence.

> In its name adultery is stigmatized and condemned not because it is an imprudence which exposes one to disillusionments and regrets but because it is a crime for the family. You stigmatize and condemn suicide not because it is an act of madness—the madman is not responsible, not because it is an act of cowardice—it at times demands a certain physical courage, but because it is the contempt for one's duty in the life which is ending and a cry of disbelief in the life that begins. This morality stigmatizes realistic literature not because it paints the passions: hatred, vengeance, love—the world lives on nothing else, and art must paint them—but when it paints them without brakes, without measure [*mesure*]. Art without rules is no longer art; it is like a woman who takes off all her clothes. To impose upon art the unique rule of public decency is not to subordinate it but to honor it. One can grow only in accordance with a rule. These are the principles which we profess; this is a doctrine which we defend conscientiously. [635]

Before turning from Pinard's forcefully imperious peroration to Sénard's defense, one may note an aspect of Pinard's argument to which Sénard does not respond for obvious reasons. It concerns degrees of guilt among author, publisher, and printer, and it casts an interesting light upon Pinard's conception of liability in publication.

For Pinard, the publisher and the printer have a secondorder responsibility, and one may show a certain leniency toward them. The publisher Pichat is to be held accountable not because he suppressed a few passages but because he should have suppressed more. The printer is placed by Pinard in a crucial position: "he is the advance sentinel against scandal." Printers must read what they print, and if they fail to read or to have others read what they commit to paper, they do so at their own risk and peril. "Printers are not machines; they have a privilege; they take an oath; they are in a special situation; and they are responsible." As advance sentinels, "if they let an infraction pass, it is as if they had let the enemy pass." But it is above all Flaubert who is "the principal culprit: for him the court must reserve all its severity" (631). Those with lesser degrees of responsibility may benefit from mitigating circumstances, but no mercy should be shown to the author whose responsibility is absolute.

Sénard's defense takes the tack that Pinard's sense of outrage is entirely misplaced. For the novel is not at all sacrilegious or nonconformist. On the contrary, it is the fully reputable and responsible confirmation of conventional morality.

Sénard begins by giving his own rendition of the intention or thought of the author. It is "an eminently moral and religious thought that can be translated by these words: the incitement to virtue through horror of vice [*l'incitation à la vertu par l'horreur du vice*]" (634). It is, however, curious that in striking his first note, Sénard seems to introduce a little dissonance. "Incitement" is a strange word to apply to virtue, for it is a word that would ordinarily be applied to vice. Indeed it is a rather "passionate" word. Sénard himself seems to get involved initially in a reversal of ordinary expectations that might be seen as an unintentional mimesis of Flaubert, for his phrase resembles Flaubert's "*les souillures du mariage et les désillusions de l'adul tère.*" Sénard's magisterial speech is not caught up by such a bagatelle. Indeed he does not notice any problem. His entire line of defense is one of insistent conventionalization of the novel, conducted with all the confirmed skill of forensic rhetoric. *Madame Bovary* becomes in his hands a provincial *Bildungsroman* or a *roman à thèse* leading on all levels to a resounding reaffirmation of existing morality and society.

Sénard engages Pinard in a battle of titles and the right thereto. He vehemently protests against Pinard's proposed subtitle for the novel. His own counter-title requires rather lengthy exposition of his understanding of the novel's essential meaning:

> No! The second title of this work is not *The Story of the Adulteries of a Provincial Wife*; it is, if you absolutely must have a second title, the story of the education too often given in the provinces; the story of the dangers to which it can lead; the story of degradation, of villainy, of a suicide seen as a consequence of an early transgression, and of a transgression that was itself induced by a first misstep into which a young woman is often led; it is a story of an education, the story of a deplorable life to which this sort of education is too often the preface. [636]

Madame Bovary becomes in Sénard's presentation the story of social maladjustment: a farmer's daughter, socially predestined to become the wife of a small-town *officier de santé*, receives an education inappropriate for her station in life. This discrepancy between social position and the illegitimate expectations created by education is the source of Emma's difficulties, and the lesson Sénard draws from it is socially and morally conservative.

> Oh! God knows, those of our young women who do not find enough in honest and elevated principles or in a strict religion to keep them steadfast in the performance of their duties as mothers, who do not find it above all in that resignation, that practical understanding of life that tells us that we must make the best of what we have, but who turn their reveries outside, these most honorable and pure young women who, in the

prosaic everydayness of their household, are sometimes tormented by what goes on around them—a book like this will, you can be sure, lead more than one of them to reflect. This is what Monsieur Flaubert has done. . . . The dénouement in favor of morality is found in every line of the book. [639]

Indeed, for Sénard, every line of the book poses the question: "Have you done all you should in the education of your daughters?" (677). To establish the exemplary morality of the novel, Sénard begins with an extensive discussion of Flaubert's character and family. "M. Gustave Flaubert is a man with a serious character, carried by his nature toward grave and serious things." His studies, "conforming to the nature of his spirit," were also serious and large, and "they included not only all branches of literature but also the law" (635). (Given Flaubert's intense hatred of his early legal studies, the last point is an especially nice touch.)

The defense of Flaubert is for Sénard a matter both of conscience and of friendship. Flaubert's father was his friend, and the good doctor's honorable son is the friend of Sénard's children.

His illustrious father was for more than thirty years surgeon-in-chief at the Hôtel Dieu of Rouen. He was the protector of Dupuytren. In giving his great teachings to science, he endowed it with great men of whom I need only cite a single one—Cloquet. He has not only himself left a great name to science, he has left great memories of immense services rendered to humanity. [634]

Thus Sénard establishes an impressive genealogy of moral respectability for his client. But he is himself the principal character witness, and he postulates both a personal responsibility for Flaubert's text and a privileged access to the mind of the author enabling him to speak in Flaubert's voice. He attempts to generate the most traditional kind of patron-client relationship between himself and the author of *Madame Bovary*: "I know his thought; I know his intentions; and the lawyer has the right to present himself as the personal bondsman [or bail —*caution*] for his client" (635).

Along with a personal genealogy, Sénard will also establish a literary lineage of impeccable respectability to which Flaubert is the rightful heir. From character references concerning the person of the author, he turns to precedents and opinions assuring the moral quality of the text. Flaubert's sources included not only past masters such as Bossuet and Massillon but (with reference to the scene of Emma's Extreme Unction) the *Rituel* of the Catholic Church itself. Indeed Sénard's ploy will be to attempt to show that the most unquestionably canonized of precedents in the literary tradition are more daring and explicit than *Madame Bovary* in treating the theme of sex. Far from being lascivious or *outre mesure*, the text is exceedingly chaste; it is also less disconcerting than the most anodyne classics in the Western heritage.

Early in his defense, Sénard mentions the phrase which caused Pinard difficulties: the seeming reversal of ordinary expectations in *"les souillures du mariage et les désillusions de l'adultère."* Sénard's strategy is to pass quickly over the first part of the phrase and to avoid the problem of reversal altogether. Instead he dwells on the second part of the phrase in pacified isolation, and he provides a thoroughly reassuring gloss of it, construing it as a testimony to the way in which adultery will not bring a hoped-for escape from the platitudes of marriage but only something worse:

> There where you expected to find love, you will find only libertinage. There where you expected to find happiness, you will find only bitterness. A husband who goes quietly about his affairs, who puts on his nightcap and eats his supper with you, is a prosaic husband who disgusts you. You dream of a man who loves you, who idolizes you, poor child! That man will be a libertine who will have taken you up for a moment to play with you. . . . The man of whom you dreamed will have lost all his glamour; you will have rediscovered in love the platitudes of marriage, and you will have rediscovered them with contempt and scorn, with disgust and piercing remorse. [638]

This apostrophe to Emma is intended to show how the novel brings out her foolishness and bad judgment.

44

Sénard peremptorily rejects Pinard's understanding of the genres or literary movements to which the text belongs. For him the novel is quite intelligible on grounds of common sense and without appeal to special categories of interpretation:

What is the frame he has chosen, what is his subject, and how has he treated it? My client is a person who belongs to none of the schools whose names I have just heard in the indictment. My God! He belongs to the realist school only in the sense that he is interested in the real nature of things. He belongs to the psychological school in the sense that he is prompted, not by the materiality of things, but by human sentiment and the development of passions in a given milieu. He belongs to the romantic school perhaps less than any other, for if romanticism does appear in his book, just as realism appears, it is only in a few ironic phrases, scattered here and there, which the public ministry has taken too seriously. What Monsieur Flaubert wanted above all was to take a subject of study from real life and to create or constitute true middle-class types, thereby arriving at a useful result. Yes, what has most preoccupied my client in this study to which he had dedicated himself is precisely this useful purpose, and he has pursued it by setting forth three or four characters from present-day society living in real-life circumstances, and by presenting to the reader's eye a true tableau of what most often happens in the world. [636]

As Hans Robert Jauss has noted, Sénard here touches upon the "mistake" of the prosecuting attorney in attributing opinions or views in passages written in the "free indirect style" directly to the author.[3] But the principal thrust of Sénard's comments is to show that the realism of the novel is a garden variety subordinated to a higher utilitarian purpose. The effect of the work on readers—especially that delicate class of readers referred to by Pinard—can only be a beneficial one. Sénard rhetorically asks: "Can this book, placed in the hands of a young girl, have the effect of drawing her toward easy pleasures, toward adultery, or will it on the contrary show the

3. "Literary History as a Challenge to Literary Theory," *New Literary History* II, no. 1 (1970), 35.

danger of the initial steps and make her tremble with horror?"
He later more than answers his question:

> My God! [a favorite exclamation of Sénard] There are nu-
> ances which may sometimes escape us given our habits, but
> they cannot escape women of great intelligence, of great
> purity, of great chastity. There are names that cannot be
> pronounced before the court, but if I were to tell you what
> has been said to Monsieur Flaubert, what has been said to me
> by mothers of families who read the book. . . . [642]

Thus the weak and susceptible vessels of Pinard become for
Sénard the exemplary recipients of the novel's true message.
And Sénard does proceed to tell the court of the reaction of
one reader special in his eyes—a highly poetical and sensitive
man.

> Nevertheless, among all these literary opinions there is one I
> wish to tell you of. Among them is a man respected for a fine
> and noble character, a man who fights courageously each day
> against adversity and suffering, a man famous not only for
> many deeds unnecessary to recall here, but famous as well for
> his literary works, which we must recall, for therein lies his
> authority—an authority all the greater for the purity and
> chasteness that exist in all of his writings—Lamartine.
> Lamartine was not acquainted with my client; he was unaware
> that he existed. Lamartine, at home in the country, had read
> *Madame Bovary* as it was published in each number of the
> *Revue de Paris*. Lamartine's impressions were so strong that
> they grew even greater with the events that I now describe.
> [642]

After this initial flourish of epideictic oratory, Sénard proceeds to tell a somewhat expurgated version of the story of how
Lamartine sent for Flaubert and told him of his admiration for
Madame Bovary, omitting Lamartine's failure to provide a promised letter to be used at the trial and the plausible grounds
for this failure. For Lamartine's was precisely the type of "romantic" work used ironically and parodically in *Madame Bovary*.
(As Flaubert, who was nonetheless upset by Lamartine's failure

to keep his word about the promised letter, wrote on January 25, 1857: "It was Lamartine who initiated the courtesies: that surprises me considerably—I would never have expected the bard of Elvire to conceive a passion for Homais." Lamartine appears in Flaubert's letters as an exemplar of the most saccharine romanticism.) But Sénard does, in bathetic tones, tell of Lamartine's one reservation about the novel—a reservation presumably attesting to Flaubert's moral rigor: "Lamartine only added: At the same time that I read you without reservation down to the last page, I reproached you for the last ones. You hurt me, you literally made me suffer! The expiation is literally out of proportion to the crime; you have created a frightful, a hideous death!" (642).

Sénard also informs the court that he has with him a "portfolio filled with opinions about the book in question by all the literary writers of our time, including the most distinguished, expressing the admiration they felt on reading this new work that is at once so moral and so useful" (643).

Given his account of the indubitably moral character of the novel, Sénard felt obliged to offer some explanation of the seemingly incredible fact that the work could ever have induced litigation. His own defense threatened to be self-defeating, for it made the legal system seem implausibly inept and foolish—almost like one of the more grotesque beings in Flaubert's novel. The explanation he offers is similar to that of many later commentators whose primary source of information he may well be. For he sees the grounds of trial as being almost entirely circumstantial. Thus the idea that the novel was a mere pretext arises in an apparent attempt of the defense attorney to explain away the problem of why Flaubert was placed on trial in the first place.

Sénard recounts that the excision of the scene in the fiacre or cab during the printing of the first installment of *Madame Bovary* led Flaubert to insist that the direction of the *Revue de Paris* insert a note explaining that they saw fit to suppress a passage.

Well! This unhappy suppression is [the cause of] the trial, that is, in the offices charged, with infinitely good reason, to exercise surveillance over all writings that might offend against

47

public morality, when they saw this cut, it put them on the alert. [The jumbled construction of this sentence by the usually careful Sénard may be significant here.] In those offices, they said: We must watch out for what comes next; when the following issue appeared, they fought over every syllable. These officials are not obliged to read everything, and when they saw it written that a woman had removed all her clothes, they took alarm without going any further. [646]

On the basis of this partially fictionalized reconstruction of the censor's reaction and in view of what he sees as an "excess of reserve" that induced precensorship on the part of the *Revue de Paris,* Sénard sees fit to read the entire fiacre scene to the court. The reading of "this fantastic ride" is to show how its excision gave rise to false expectations about its real content. People expected "something analogous to what you will be kind enough to read in one of the most marvelous novels to come from the pen of an honorable member of the French Academy, Monsieur Mérimée" (645). In *La Double Méprise,* Mérimée—in marked contrast to Flaubert—describes what goes on inside a cab, and he does so in terms that prevent Sénard from reading the passage aloud in court (645–46). And, aside from references to the poetry of André Chenier and *Les Lettres Persanes* of Montesquieu, Sénard tells the court that he has an entire collection of passages from the greats that make *Madame Bovary* seem prudish by comparison (666–67). Thus, far from liberating art from all rules and restraints, Flaubert has more *pudeur* than acknowledged and revered masters of the past.

The reading of the fiacre scene heralds Sénard's long deferred turn from character references, precedents, and context to the text itself. "The public ministry attacks the book; I must take up the book itself in order to defend it. I must complete the quotations he has made, and for each passage I must show the nullity of the accusation. This will be my whole defense" (648).

Sénard's procedure will be to argue that the prosecution quoted out of context and that his own response will simply be to quote more fully and in context. He alludes to his project of publishing with Flaubert a *Mémoire* that he himself would have signed with the author, composed of an annotated version of the entire text of *Madame Bovary* (647). Thus he was ready to underwrite with the authority of his own signature his belief in the respectability of the text. But an injunction was directed against the explanatory notes. Left with the text alone to defend, Sénard declares that he will not appeal to the "elevated, animated, and pathos-ridden appreciations" of the prosecutor. He will simply "cite the texts just as they are" (648). Sénard's earlier discussion of "extratextual" considerations had, of course, functioned to prefigure his discussion of the text. His exegesis will hold no surprises, for it will amount to variations on the theme of the novel's moral excellence. Indeed he immediately offers his overall understanding of the way the text will speak for itself. "First of all, I declare that nothing is more false than what was earlier said about the lascivious color" (648). Nothing in the book warrants this designation—neither the portrait of Emma nor the depiction of religion. To illustrate the way the novel has a salutary influence in revealing the dangers of the manner in which religion is often presented to the young, Sénard offers his own reactions as criteria of reader response. He does so in terms that both replicate the prosecutor's sentiments and go even further in providing what might be seen as an unself-conscious parody of Homais' own parody of Rousseau's Profession of Faith of a Savoyard Vicar:

As for myself, here is what I flatly declare: I know of nothing more beautiful, more useful, and more necessary to support us in the path of life [than religion]: not only for women, but also for men, who themselves have at times extremely painful trials to overcome. I know of nothing more useful and necessary, but the religious sentiment must be solemn and, allow me to add, it must be severe. I want my children to understand God, not a God in the abstractions of pantheism, but a Supreme Being with whom they are in harmony, to whom they raise themselves in prayer, and who, at the same time, helps them to grow and gives them strength. [649]

(Compare Homais who may here perhaps be credited with a greater frankness:

I have a religion, my religion, and I even have more than all these others with their mummeries and their juggling. I adore God, on the contrary. I believe in the Supreme Being, in a Creator, whatever he may be. I care little who has placed us here below to fulfill our duties as citizens and parents; but I don't need to go to church to kiss silver plates, and fatten out of my pocket, a lot of good-for-nothings who live better than we do. For one can know him as well in a wood, in a field, or even contemplating the ethereal heavens like the ancients. My God is the God of Socrates, of Franklin, of Voltaire, and of Béranger! I support the *Profession de Foi du Vicaire savoyard* and the immortal principles of '89! And I can't admit an old boy of a God who takes walks in his garden with a cane in his hand, who lodges his friends in the belly of whales, dies uttering a cry, and rises up again at the end of three days; things absurd in themselves, and completely opposed, moreover, to all physical laws, which proves to us, by the way, that priests have always wallowed in squalid ignorance, and tried to drag whole nations down after them.)[4]

Filling thirty pages in the Pléiade edition (650–80), Sénard engages the prosecutor in a war of quotations, and he clearly marshals the bigger battalions. As he mounts quote upon quote, his method of identifying himself with the voice of the author at times goes to histrionic extremes: "Ah! You have accused me of confounding the religious element with sensualism in my picture of modern society! Rather accuse the society in which we live; do not accuse the man who, like Bossuet, cries out: 'Awake and beware of the danger'" (650).

As Sénard literally becomes Flaubert's mouthpiece, one might notice a possible breach or diversion in his argument. The question of the manner in which the novel "accuse[s] the society in which we live" might lead to the problem of ideological crime. But this implication is not pursued, and the reference to society remains purely rhetorical in Sénard's presentation. Indeed the process of filling out the prosecutor's quotations can, for Sénard, lead inevitably to only one conclusion: "The reading of this book cannot produce in you an impres-

4. *Madame Bovary*, ed. and trans. Paul de Man (New York: Norton, 1965), 55. As noted in the Preface, all page references to *Madame Bovary* are to this edition.

sion other than that which it produced in us, that is, that this book is excellent as a whole and that its details are irreproachable" (680–81).

The verdict of the court constitutes a very weak dénouement to the trial. The Aristotelian might find it a highly implausible ending to the case. For the argument of the court seems up until the last minute to concur forcefully with the views of the prosecutor. But then an anticlimactic turning point is reached, and the court refuses to draw the apparent conclusion. Instead, almost in an incongruous aside, Flaubert is reprieved.

In the words of the court, Flaubert's work does "deserve stern censure, for the mission of literature must be to enrich and to refresh the spirit by improving the understanding and by perfecting the character, more than to instill a loathing of vice by offering a picture of the disorders that may exist in society." Indeed "it is not permitted, under pretext of painting local color, to reproduce in all their immorality the exploits and sayings of the characters the writer has made it his duty to paint, . . . such a system applied to the works of the mind as well as to the products of the fine arts would lead to a realism that would be the negation of the beautiful and the good, and that, in begetting works equally offensive to sight and mind, would be committing continual outrages against public morality and decency." Thus, for the court, the ideal and idealizing function of art itself condemns the putative "realism" practiced by Flaubert. What is significant is that the court itself affirms a stereotypically Platonic conception of art in order to censure Flaubert and, by implication, all "realists." In so doing, it provides evidence for the view that the official aesthetic ideology of the time was idealistic. Flaubert, in the eyes of the court, has "insufficiently understood" that "there are limits that even the most frivolous literature must not overstep." But the court nonetheless concludes that the charges against Flaubert have been insufficiently proved, not explaining how its own seemingly absolute judgments can be converted into a matter of degree. Evidence of rather nominal acquiescence by the author in the rituals of established society seems to be enough for the court. It is content to observe that Flaubert's novel was the product of much work, that the author affirms his respect for decency, and that his sole aim was not the gratification of the passions. "He has committed only the fault of sometimes losing sight of the rules that no self-respecting writer should ever infringe and of forgetting that literature, like art, if it is to achieve the good that it is called upon to produce, must be chaste and pure not only in its form but in its expression" (682–83). Thus the court will reprimand Flaubert, make him sit through a didactic lecture on art (in other circumstances a sufficient punishment for Flaubert), and release him without awarding him the costs of the trial.

3

From Trial to Text

To
Marie-Antoine-Jules Sénard
Member of the Paris Bar
Ex-President of the National Assembly, and
Former Minister of the Interior

Dear and Illustrious Friend,—

Permit me to inscribe your name at the head of this book, and above its dedication: for it is to you, before all, that I owe its publication. By becoming part of your magnificent defence, my work has acquired for myself, as it were, an unexpected authority. Accept, then, here, the homage of my gratitude, which, however great, will never attain to the level of your eloquence and your devotion.

Gustave Flaubert

Was Flaubert altogether serious in his dedication of *Madame Bovary* to Sénard? In the light of his genuine anxiety about the trial, his general views about the Sénards of the world, and the utterly conventional and moralizing nature of Sénard's reading of the novel, Flaubert's gesture would seem to be both serious and—whether intentionally or not—ironic. Paul de Man, in his "substantially new translation" of the novel, has introduced into the dedication six commas more than Flaubert himself used, thereby accentuating one's doubts about its intention. What is less open to doubt is the fact that Flaubert's dedication sets up an intertextual relation between the novel and the trial. Standard French editions of *Madame Bovary* include the trial as an appendix to the novel and thereby invite the reader to explore further the problem of their intertextuality. Indeed the supplementary position of the trial on the most literal level of the text induces the reader to extend to it the procedures and critical strategies engaged by the novel. The trial even seems like an anticlimactic scene in the novel itself. A knowledge of Flaubert's corpus might prompt the assertion that the trial, read in its implausibility as a literary text, goes beyond the measured experimentalism of *Madame Bovary* and approaches the more extreme overtures of *Bouvard and Pécuchet.* Yet it is, paradoxically, the very measured nature of *Madame Bovary's* experimentalism that makes the conventionalizing and didactic reading at the trial tempting and, indeed, even plausible on at least one level of reader response.

Yet the readers at the trial attempted adamantly to keep their interpretation confined to one level and resisted the ways their own lines of argument, turns of phrase, or suspicions seemed to open other possibilities in reading. I have already suggested that the trial, in its reading or reception of the novel, treated with reference to ordinary crime what was, in significant respects, ideological or political crime. It took as standard deviation from (or, in the case of the defense, as simple conformity to) the norm what tended to place in question the norm's viability in its larger sociohistorical and literary context. It thus reduced the radical negativity of the novel to manageable proportions either to condemn or to praise its author. On the basis of the trial alone, one may infer the existence of two related conventional expectations concerning what the novel should do: first, it should conform to certain rules or norms common to it and to the larger social world it inhabited—or, if it deviated from them, its deviation should be restricted to standard or recognizable forms; second, it should be narrated from a reliable and coherent perspective itself defined by established rules or norms. My contention that the novel was by contrast motivated by a subversive, scandalous, or "ideologically criminal" impetus that placed in jeopardy the very grounds of the trial must now be supported by an investigation of the novel itself.

In the world of *Madame Bovary* and, by disconcerting implication, in the social world it resembled enough to cause concern, the very opposition between marriage and adultery or between the sacred and the profane threatens to collapse. The terms of the opposition are rendered mutually convertible, and the contextualized norms that they subtend become insubstantial. This is evident with respect to plot and characterization alone, as Sénard himself seemed at times dangerously close to disclosing. Emma attempts to escape the banality of marriage through romance but finds in adultery only the replication of the platitudes of marriage—just as she married to escape the banality of her father's house but found only its deadly repetition. Her lovers in their mediocrity and inability to live up to her dreams have little to distinguish them from her husband. And, as Pinard noted, the priest to whom she goes for spiritual counsel turns out to be as much of a materialist as the pharmacist: he recommends something for her digestion. The final scene between the priest, Bournisien, and the pharmacist, Homais, shows them in a self-parodic act of reconciliation and mutual recognition: the ultimate loving couple, they eat and sleep together over Emma's coffin. In a manner more extreme than the mingling of erotic and religious desire in Emma herself, the final embrace of these two pseudo-antagonists reveals the opposition between the sacred and the profane—like that between marriage and adultery—to be a distinction without a difference.

The manner in which the novel subverted the specific oppositions basic to established familial and religious codes should—once it is pointed out—be fairly obvious. Equally obvious is the general relation of this process to the problem of the narrative subject. For the breakdown of the primary codes regulating religious and familial life increases the lability or uncertainty in the position of the subject. By contrast, the existence of strong and widely accepted codes in these areas of life helps to orient the subject, at times to the point of dogmatic fixation. Less obvious, however, is the precise manner in which the novel's testing or contestation of established categories and conventions is bound up with the problem of the status of the narrative subject.

What may also not be readily apparent is the way in which the problem of the narrative subject is itself related to broader political and ideological issues. This question has, of course, been taken up extensively in the works of recent French theorists such as Jacques Derrida, Michel Foucault, Julia Kristeva, and Jacques Lacan. A discussion of their thought which, to be useful, would have to attempt a delineation of the complex network of similarities and differences that link their initiatives, would be out of place here. Suffice it to say that the "*procès*" of the subject, involving its "decentering" and the entire matter of its constitution, engages a vast range of modern sociopolitical and cultural concerns. Most evident is the issue of the "bourgeois" individual who is presumed to have full moral and legal responsibility in his contractual relations with others. But, even more broadly, there is the problem of the autonomy of the individual subject, his relation to language and to social norms, and the extent to which his "liability" is limited by forces not entirely within his control. That this problem affects even "revolutionary" thought is abundantly documented in the works of Sartre, and it is one reason why he places such great emphasis upon the putative "passivity" or "pithiatism" of Flaubert in *L'Idiot de la famille*. The radical questioning or practical dislocation of the solid subject of judgment and action will, at the very least, force the rethinking of an interrelated set of assumptions basic to modern thought and behavior on levels that may even be, in certain respects, militantly opposed to one another. In these senses, the problem of the narrative subject in *Madame Bovary* has ideological dimensions that only narrow formalistic preconceptions can lead one to ignore.

At the trial itself, the prosecutor was manifestly disturbed by the absence of a clear and consistent moral principle, embodied in the author-narrator or in a character, by virtue of which Emma might be condemned. The novel seemed to depart from a convention shared by traditional narration in fiction and self-understanding in social life: the existence of a reliable center of value and judgment which integrated various aspects of experience in an intelligible and secure manner. Yet the way the novel departed from this conventional expectation is, as I have intimated, a moot issue even at the present time. Because this issue is crucial to one's comprehension of both the novel and the trial—especially with respect to the fashion in which the use of language in the novel constituted a specific mode of "ideological" crime—I shall now turn to an extended treatment of it and the ways in which it has been handled in recent criticism of Flaubert.

Let us start with the views of Hans Robert Jauss. In his elaboration of an aesthetics of reception, Jauss has pointed to the importance of Flaubert's trial and raised the question of its relation to the nature of the novel. Jauss locates the novel's disruptive "stylistic" change in its combination of impersonal, impassive narration with *erlebte Rede* (or *style indirect libre*), and he indicates certain of its effects on the reader. Both because they pinpoint significant issues and because they leave others indeterminate, Jauss's observations deserve to be quoted at length. The positive suggestions and the open questions of Jauss's account will preoccupy us in our own investigation of the ways in which the novel triggered processes whose effects made themselves felt at the trial but whose nature the readers at the trial did not, and perhaps could not, explicate.

The new literary form which forced Flaubert's readers to an unfamiliar perception of the "worn-out fable" [the tale of adultery in the provinces] was the principle of impersonal (or uninvolved) narration in conjunction with the so-called *"erlebte Rede,"* a stylistic device which Flaubert handled like a virtuoso and with a consistent perspective. What is meant by this can be seen in a description which the prosecuting attorney Pinard claimed in his indictment was immoral in the highest degree. In the novel it follows Emma's first "misstep" and tells how she looked at herself in a mirror:

> En s'appercevant dans la glace, elle s'étonna de son visage. Jamais elle n'avait eu les yeux si grands, si noirs, ni d'une telle profondeur. Quelque chose de subtil épandu sur sa personne la transfigurait.
> Elle se repétait: J'ai un amant! un amant! se délectant a cette idée comme à celle d'une autre puberté qui lui serait survenue. *Elle allait donc enfin posséder ces plaisirs de l'amour, cette fièvre de bonheur dont elle avait désespéré. Elle entrait dans quelque chose de merveilleux, où tout serait passion, extase, délire. . . .*

> [But when she saw herself in the mirror she wondered at her face. Never had her eyes been so large, so black, nor so deep. Something subtle about her being transfigured her.
> She repeated: "I have a lover! a lover!" delighting at

57

the idea as if a second puberty had come to her. So at last she was to know those joys of love, that fever of happiness of which she had despaired! She was entering upon a marvelous world where all would be passion, ecstasy, delirium. De Man, 117]

The prosecuting attorney regarded the last sentences as an objective description which included the judgment of the narrator and was upset over this "glorification of adultery" which he considered to be even more dangerous and immoral than the misstep itself. In this Flaubert's accuser fell victim to an error as the defense immediately pointed out. The incriminating sentences are not an objective determination of the narrator, which the reader can believe, but a subjective opinion of a person characterized by her feelings that are formed from novels. The scientific device consists in revealing the inner thoughts of this person without the signals of direct statement (*Je vais donc enfin posséder* . . .).[1]

Let us interrupt Jauss briefly here to note that he locates the essence of the free indirect style in the narratorial revelation of the "subjective opinion" or "inner thoughts" of a character without the use of the "signals of direct statement." I shall raise certain questions about this prevalent view at a later point. Jauss himself is especially concerned with the effect of stylistic innovation on the reader.

The effect is that the reader must decide for himself whether he should accept this sentence as a true statement or as an opinion characteristic of this person. . . . The consternating effect of the formal innovation in Flaubert's narrative style was obvious at the trial: the impersonal narrative form forces his readers not only to perceive things differently—"photographically exact" according to the judgment of the time—but it also forced them into an alienating insecurity about their judgment. Since the new stylistic device broke with an old novelistic convention—unequivocal description and well-founded moral judgment about the characters—*Madame Bovary* could radicalize or raise questions of life, which during the

1. Hans Robert Jauss, "Literary History as a Challenge to Literary Theory," *New Literary History* II, no. 1 (1970), 34–35.

trial caused the original motive for the accusation, alleged lasciviousness, to recede into the background.[2]

Jauss's useful commentary situates issues that seemed to register, if at all, in a largely displaced way at the trial, within the larger context of a critical reading of the novel. How does the so-called "free indirect style" function, and how is it related to the impersonal or uninvolved narration with which Jauss, somewhat curiously, seems to amalgamate it? What is the larger narrative and historical setting for the extreme problematization of existing norms and oppositions in *Madame Bovary*? How precisely, and with what implications, does *Madame Bovary* "radicalize or raise questions of life" or, as Jauss also puts it, "jolt the reader out of the belief that his moral judgment is self-evident and reopen the long-closed question of public morals"[3]? What in general are the relations among symptomatic, critical, and transformative effects in the way the novel comes to terms with its social and literary contexts? This complex of questions has of course been broached in a forceful manner by the interpretation offered by Jean-Paul Sartre in *L'Idiot de la famille*.

My own emphases will differ significantly from those of Jauss or Sartre, and it may be useful to anticipate them here. The disorienting nature of the novel, having both critical and more uncanny effects, derives from what I shall call its double writing or dual style: its ability to employ or refer to more traditional elements on one level and to sound them out or play havoc with them on other levels. Flaubert's "free indirect style" itself cannot be seen exclusively as a "free" technique to report indirectly a character's "subjective opinion" or "inner thought." It is itself a dual mode involving both proximity and distance—empathy and irony—in the relation of the narrator to the character or narrated object. This variable mingling of character and narrator, often in terms of a character's thoughts or feelings expressed in part through the narrator's language—with the inflexions in empathy and irony this makes possible—must

---

2. Ibid., 35.
3. Ibid., 36.

be seen in the context of shifts or modulations in narrative perspective or voice. These shifts seem natural and are glossed over by technical devices of transition which easily make them escape notice. But they can be drastic, and they are disconcerting even if they pass unnoticed on a conscious level. They create an indeterminacy of narrative voice that unsettles the moral security of the reader and renders decisive judgment about characters or story difficult to attain. They also raise the question of the relation between unifying and "decentering" forces in the position(s) of the narrating subject—among which impersonal or uninvolved narration is one relatively extreme position which cannot be identified with "free indirect style."

These variations in narrative perspective or position are related to other modes of "doubleness" (indeed multiplicity) in the novel whereby more conventional expectations are held out only to be critically tested and at times strangely dislocated. Here one has the way *Madame Bovary* is—or at least simulates— a "traditional" novel on one level and frustrates more conventional expectations on other levels. It invites conventional readings or (when autonomized) misreadings, such as those at the trial, only to reveal the limitations of those readings through processes engaged by the text. It is a novel on the very threshold between the conventional and the experimental—tradition and critique—and thus elicits responses (including the desire to read it simply as a story) which Flaubert's later novels, as well as novels inspired by his work, render less plausible if not gratuitous. *Madame Bovary* invites the kind of reading that *Bouvard and Pécuchet* manifestly repels or rewards with near total boredom. For while *Madame Bovary* is liminal, *Bouvard and Pécuchet* tends to be insistently beyond the fringe. It would probably never be brought to trial because its critical and disquieting effects would fail to register even on a subliminal level for the average reader, in part because the storyline that initially engages attention and emotional investment is so very thin, at least in conventional terms. It is an acquired taste, while *Madame Bovary* continues to be assigned in high schools and sold in railway stations or airports.

But a problem of the greatest difficulty which *Madame Bovary* poses to the reader is that of the relationship among the symptomatic (or reinforcing), the critical, and textual processes or movements not fully contained by these categories—processes Flaubert referred to as *l'indisable* (the unsayable). I have insisted that the trial resisted, repressed, or displaced the ways in which the novel constituted political or ideological crime. But it would be equally misleading to ignore the complex and at times intractable relations among the symptomatic elements of the text upon which Sartre insists, the critical effects that I have stressed, and the more uncanny or undecidable features which are significant without being of exclusive importance.

Another problem the novel raises is that of the relations between its textual processes and the more manifest intentions or projects of its author-writer. Before proceeding further in this respect, it may prove useful to distinguish among the roles of author, writer, and narrator, for the name "Flaubert" can be used to refer to all three roles. These distinctions tend inevitably to be blurred, especially when the narrator is neither a character nor defined as a distinctive or easily identifiable personality in the text. Yet a minimal note of caution is struck by the recognition that these roles are different aspects of the same "social individual" but that they are themselves not simply identical to one another. Indeed their relationship poses a problem. At the trial, both the prosecution and the defense tended simply to identify them with an ease and lack of self-consciousness that indicated the conventional nature of the identification. The prosecutor attributed not only the role of narrator but everything conveyed in the narration, including the contents of passages in "free indirect style," to authorial intention in the delimited sense of Flaubert's own authorial view or "voice." The defense attorney also identified the author with the narrator but insisted upon a differentiation between characters and author-narrator, and he, in at least a restricted fashion, noted the role of irony in the text. But he proceeded to construct a consistent moral position and identity for the narrator by piecing together various elements taken from Flaubert's life, the putative testimony of character witnesses, and fragments from the novel. It may further be observed that Sartre, with a more explicit awareness of what he is doing, insists on reading the text as an expression of its author's voice or at least of his profoundly "lived" if at times unarticulated intentions or projects.

The understanding of the relation among author, writer, and narrator as forming an overt or covert "expressive totality" is misleading, notably in the case of someone like Flaubert. It simply ignores crucial dimensions of his narrative practice, especially the nature of the "free indirect style" and its relations to other aspects of narration such as impersonality. This question of course did not arise at the trial. It is significant that it also does not arise in Sartre's *Idiot*. Sartre's insistence upon the relation of author and text is, I think, valid insofar as one attempts to relate life and writing and to attribute importance to personal responsibility in the act of writing. It was, one may observe, Flaubert as author of the text who was placed on trial. Yet the concept of author, as Foucault has convincingly argued, cannot be taken as an unproblematic center of interpretation.[4] It is in certain ways a historically specific concept with links to juridical, political, and cultural dimensions of the larger society. To the extent that the concept of author implies full authority or mastery over the workings of the text, it and the ambitions it signifies are resisted by the role of "writer." For the writer is always situated within a language and a history whose resources he does not entirely control. Even if one stops short of the more extreme critiques of "humanism" and anthropocentric interpretation, one may argue that the situation of the writer limits—but does not eliminate—the liability of the author and renders problematic—but not simply irrelevant—the relation between projects or intentions and what the text may be argued to do or to disclose. The liability of the writer-author is not total but it is considerable, and his intentions are essential in the estimation of his responsibility for what he does, even if those intentions do not entirely master writing and its effects.

The concept of narrator is situated more clearly as a component of the text. The narrator is in a sense a function of the writer's narrative practice which the text puts into play to bring about certain effects. The extent to which the narrator is a

4. Michel Foucault, "What Is an Author?" in Donald F. Bouchard, ed., *Language, Counter-Memory, Practice* (Ithaca: Cornell University Press, 1977), 113–38.

unified or personal presence, integrating various narrative perspectives or voices, varies with texts. One of the conventions of historical writing and at times of more traditional novels is that the narrator speak only in the author's voice or render the status of hypothetical statements altogether explicit. But one of the obvious freedoms of fiction is that the narrator need not be the mouthpiece of the author, and, as we shall see, one may raise certain questions about an absolute dichotomy between author-narrator and narrated object in historiography itself. A dictum of Flaubert's own "impersonal" style was that a work not be a *déversoir* (drainpipe) for its author, and while this dictum was qualified by the empathetic-ironic modulations of the "free indirect style" and by direct intrusions whose force is a function of their rarity, it was never simply dispensed with.

In summary form, one might suggest that, in a fictional text, the author is the role-specific person to whom responsibility is imputed; the narrator is the envoy to the imaginary or the delegate of the "social individual" in the text; and the writer is more of a threshold phenomenon, mediating and supplementing author and narrator with reference to the complex social individual and his or her relation to the writing process. Writing in the literal sense is one activity or practice of the social individual. Authorship is a role in which one attempts to control, and benefit from or be responsible for, the writing process. (It is one modality of what Freud termed the "ego" as executive agency of the person. Like the ego, it may be the object of illusory projections, notably the belief in total mastery of, and absolute responsibility for, the writing process or the workings of language.) And the narrator is situated in the text as a function of the narrative practice in part controlled by the author but also subject to processes he or she may not be entirely conscious of or fully master. On the narratorial level, "Flaubert" becomes a specular name or *"imago du nom propre"*— and it is this more imaginary persona to whom we often refer in discussing the novels or stories. Finally, the "social individual" is not simply the person designated by the mark of identity that is the proper name. He or she is the site where a scene is staged involving a more or less forceful desire for identity and heterogeneous tendencies, among which are various "roles."

While the subsequent discussion will not, and perhaps cannot, rigorously adhere to these distinctions, the problems to which they are related should at least be kept in mind. For the very movement—even the slippage—among terms is an indication of real problems in the object of study and in coming to terms with it.

I propose initially to focus on the question of Flaubert's "projects" and their relation to the functioning of the text, including its mode of narration or narrative practice. I shall follow the convention that the primary "source" for Flaubert's projects or intentions is his *Correspondance*. This convention requires an interchangeability of author and letter-writer that is open to question. For often it is not simply the author of *Madame Bovary* who writes the letters but a tired writer, an enthusiast, a *haut bourgeois,* a diplomat in the kingdom of love, a quasi-religious believer in art, an almost atheistic or perhaps clownish doubter in art, and so forth—who was also the author of *Madame Bovary.* The use of the letters as a source for projects also requires a directed reading that may at times ignore their status and functioning as complex texts in their own right. But their intricacy emerges even in the attempt to specify projects, for these are at times formulated in qualified and complicated— indeed internally contestatory—ways. The letters of Flaubert during the composition of *Madame Bovary* were of course not available at the trial to elicit the author's intentions or meanings. The correspondence of Flaubert is, by contrast, of paramount significance in the interpretation offered by Sartre. My own investigation of Flaubert's projects may be compared to the inferences drawn at the trial, and I shall attempt to situate it with reference to Sartre's views.

4

Flaubert's Projects: Pure Art and Carnivalization

"Not enough forms . . . ," said Flaubert. How is he to be understood? Does he wish to celebrate the other of form? The "too many things" which exceed and resist form? In praise of Dionysus? One is certain that this is not so. Flaubert, on the contrary, is sighing, "Alas! not enough forms." A religion of the work as form. . . . Nietzsche was not fooled: "Flaubert, a new edition of Pascal, but as an artist with the instinctive belief at heart: 'Flaubert est toujours haïssable, l'homme n'est rien, l'oeuvre est tout.'"

Jacques Derrida, Writing and Difference

Even in quarters where certainty is notoriously elusive, the conviction that Flaubert's project in writing was a formalistic quest for pure art has by now unseated earlier views of him as a realist or as a frustrated romantic. The entry for Flaubert in the *Petit Larousse* is an epitome of these earlier views:

> Prosateur soucieux de la perfection du style, il veut donner dans ses romans une image objective de la réalité mais garde quelques traits de l'imagination romantique.
>
> (Prose-writer concerned with the perfection of style, he wants to give in his novels an objective image of reality, but keeps some traits of the romantic imagination.)

The deficiencies of this overly pear-shaped conception of Flaubert should be evident, for they reduce him in *louis-philip-pard* fashion to an exemplar of the *juste milieu* in art. But it is still conceivable that views stressing his quest for pure art fail to account adequately for the manner in which realism and romanticism are pertinent reference points in his work. The understanding of Flaubert in terms of a formalist aesthetics nonetheless has a long and impressive lineage. Nietzsche condemned the nihilism implicit in Flaubert's asceticism and displaced Christianity, but Baudelaire sympathetically saw the true *gageure* in Flaubert's work as the attempt to create beauty from the most rebarbative materials. Henry James, with changing emphases, stressed the importance of Flaubert's dedication to *l'art pour l'art* and looked to him as "the novelist's novelist." Percy Lubbock, in his *Craft of Fiction*, codified James's more flexible principles and took *Madame Bovary* as a test case which he, plausibly but mistakenly, read as exhibiting the role of characters' consciousnesses as the unifying vehicle of narration. And André Gide took Flaubert's letters as a writer's bible whose value surpassed that of the novels themselves. Recently, of course, the image of Flaubert as the apostle of art has received a trenchant and critical formulation in Sartre's *Idiot* where the thesis is expanded to herculean proportions and developed with an intricacy attesting to the allure of the task and to Sartre's investment in it. Indeed it is significant that, despite differences in evaluative reactions, figures spanning the theoretical spectrum from Marxism to "high modernism" and beyond have in general agreed upon the understanding of Flaubert as the Christ of Art expounding a doctrine of secular redemption in the form of an ivory-tower, elitist escape from the modern crisis.

Much in Flaubert's letters justifies this image of him. But it is misleading to extract from the *Correspondance* the most lapidary formulations of the ideal of pure art, to identify them as *the* project of Flaubert, and to read the novels as the straightforward embodiment of this project. For this approach ignores at least two problems: the way the ideal of pure art is itself the object of multiple and at times contradictory "investments" in the letters; and the difficulty in relating a complex, often divided project to the actual functioning of a novel. In the light of these two related problems, let us inquire into the way Flaubert discusses art and its contexts in his letters, examine Sartre's interpretation, and raise the question of its adequacy with reference both to Flaubert's "projects" and to the reading or interpretation of *Madame Bovary*.

Flaubert offered a critique of bourgeois culture which blended imperceptibly into an indictment of humanity and the human condition in general. It was often difficult to distinguish between what was sociocultural and what was universal in his indictment. The bourgeoisie was not a class. It was a condition —the condition of those who thought basely and stupidly. In Flaubert's statements of this conception may be found both an inability to distinguish particular or class conditions from rash generalizations about *la condition humaine* and an ability to see how certain traits of *embourgeoisement* might reach further and further down the social scale in modern life. Modern times was the scene of "*avachissement universel*" (October 5, 1871).

> Mediocrity is creeping in everywhere; even stones are becoming stupid [*bêtes*], and highways too are stupefying [*stupides*]. Perish though we may (and perish we shall in any case), we must employ every means to stem the flood of excrement [*merde*] invading us. Let us take flight in the ideal, since we no longer have the means to dwell in marble halls and don purple gowns, have humming-bird feather divans, swansdown carpets, ebony armchairs, tortoise shell floors, solid gold candelabra, or lamps carved in emerald. And so let us blast out [*guelons*] against gloves made of shoddy, against office chairs, against mackintosh, against economical stoves, against imitation luxury, against imitation pride. Industrialism has developed to ugly and gigantic proportions. How many good people who a century ago could have lived without Beaux Arts now cannot do without mini-statues, mini-music, and mini-literature! Take a simple case—the ominous proliferation of bad drawings by lithography. . . . We are all fakes and charlatans. Pretense, affectation, humbug everywhere. Crinoline has falsified buttocks. Our century is a century of whores, and so far what is least prostituted is the prostitute. [January 29, 1854]

This all-too-familiar indictment of industrialism, mass consumption, and the "age of mechanical reproduction" begins

Madame Bovary *on Trial*

with an evocation of vanishing artificial splendor only to end paradoxically with a nostalgia for unadorned "authenticity." The hypocritical generalization of prostitution makes prostitution itself the one honest phenomenon of the age insofar as it called itself by its proper name.[1] From a perspective very much attuned to that of Flaubert and in an analysis which Flaubert immediately recognized as the only one to grasp his meaning, Baudelaire summarized the sense of context motivating Flaubert in the composition of *Madame Bovary*:

> For many years, the interest which the public is willing to devote to matters of the spirit has considerably diminished and the allotment of its available enthusiasm has steadily decreased. The last years of Louis-Philippe's reign saw the final outbursts of a spirit still willing to be stimulated by the display of imaginative powers; the new novelist, however, is confronted with a completely worn-out public or, worse even, a stupefied and greedy audience, whose only hatred is for fiction, and only love for material possessions.[2]

In this context where, since the death of Balzac, curiosity about the novel had been "dormant," the challenge facing Flaubert was great. For Baudelaire, Flaubert met it by "resolv[ing] to be vulgar . . . bewar[ing] above all of giving away [his] true feelings and of speaking in [his] own name." Rather Flaubert

---

1. In this light, the enigmatic ending of *The Sentimental Education* appears less as an evocation of lost innocence than as a rectification of names: in an age of generalized prostitution, the one proper and authentic emotion is expressed by the laughter of prostitutes at the inappropriately romantic gesture of a young man who brings them flowers. In contradistinction to other characters, the prostitutes at least recognize themselves as prostitutes. Their sincere reaction and the genuine confusion it causes in the young protagonist are perhaps the only honest experiences to be found in the novel—in this sense the best thing that happened to Frédéric and Deslauriers: *"ce que nous avons eu de meilleur,"* as they repeat in sequence. For a somewhat different view, as well as for an insightful discussion of Flaubert's works in general, see Victor Brombert, *The Novels of Flaubert* (Princeton: Princeton University Press, 1966), especially chapter 4.

2. "Madame Bovary, by Gustave Flaubert," in Paul de Man, ed., *Madame Bovary* (New York: Norton, 1965), 338. Baudelaire's article first appeared in *L'Artiste* on October 18, 1857.

took the "vague and overflexible term" of realism and filled it with "a nervous, picturesque, subtle and precise style" applied to "a banal canvas." He turned to the provinces, "the breeding ground of stupidity . . . inhabited by the most intolerant imbeciles," and he took "the tritest theme of all, worn out by repetition, by being played over and over again like a tired barrel organ"—adultery. *Madame Bovary* was born of "the impossible task, the true *gageure*, the wager which all works of art must be," for it fashioned beauty out of the most inhospitable and vulgar materials. Thus Flaubert's alchemical feat was to transform basely inartistic subject matter into a superlative work of art.[3]

That Flaubert himself found his bourgeois subject alien to the higher purposes of art is a leitmotif of his letters:

> I hate bourgeois poetry, domestic art, although I engage in it. But this is the last time. At bottom it disgusts me. This book, composed of calculations and of stylistic ruses, is not of my blood. I do not carry it in my entrails. I feel it is an entirely willed and factitious thing. This will perhaps be a *tour de force* that certain people (a very small number indeed!) will admire, and others will find in it some truth of detail and observation. But air! Air! The grand turns of phrase, the large and full periods rolling like rivers, the multiplicity of metaphors, the great bursts of style—all that I love will not be there. At best I shall emerge from it better able to write something good later on. [May 21–22, 1853]

Flaubert's self-doubt went so far as to risk falsifying the very dictum that absolute style could derive beauty from the basest of materials, for bourgeois ugliness and banality seemed so great as to defeat the illusions of formal perfection and the magic of "style":

> What drives one to despair is thinking that, even if it is successful in attaining perfection this [scene in *Madame Bovary*] can only be acceptable [*passable*] and will never be beautiful because of its very subject [or content—*à cause du fond même*]. I

3. Ibid., 338–39.

do the work of a clown; but what does a *tour de force* prove after all? No matter: "God helps those who help themselves." The cart is, however, at times quite heavy to be extricated from the mud. [July 12, 1853]

One could multiply quotations that impugn the idea that pure art was for Flaubert a simple ideology, doctrine, or credo. But for him art was nonetheless infused with a genuine pathos of belief that was contested but not simply eliminated by self-directed irony and doubt. Pure art was in this sense a surrogate for a noble religious ideal of transcendence that required a turning away from the ordinary world and a quest for the absolute. The object of belief could, however, only be entertained in a threatened way in the modern world. Secularization itself furthered the tendency of a desire for transcendence to merge unsettlingly with the possibility of transgression. And Flaubert at times defended the critically transgressive and insistently marginal status of the artist in extreme and almost self-nugatory terms.

At the present moment I believe that a thinker (and what is an artist if not a triple thinker?) should have neither religion, country, nor even any social conviction. Absolute doubt now seems to me so completely substantiated that it would be almost silly to seek to formulate it. . . . Yes, it would be a relief to vomit out all this immense contempt that fills the heart to overflowing. What good cause is there these days to arouse one's interest let alone one's enthusiasm? [April 26, 1853]

That socialism was not the good cause evoking enthusiasm was a judgment rarely qualified by Flaubert.

They have denied *suffering,* they have blasphemed three-quarters of modern poetry, the blood of Christ which is active in us. Nothing will extirpate it, nothing will dry it up. The point is not to dessicate it but to make it turn into streams. If the sentiment of human insufficiency, of the nothingness of life were to perish (which would be the consequence of their hypothesis), we would be more stupid [*bêtes*] than birds, who at least perch in their trees. [September 13, 1852]

Here, in a vitriolic reaction to the socialists which takes a markedly metaphysical turn, Flaubert moves from doubt to a pathos of belief having Christian overtones. And only a comma separates the sentiment of human insufficiency from more extreme nihilistic leanings. Flaubert saw socialism as an aggravation of the illness it purported to cure: it was the climax of vulgar materialism and indiscriminate leveling.

Have patience, when socialism is established, we will arrive at the peak of this genre [the sufferings of the artist]. In this reign of equality—and it is approaching—one will skin alive all those who are not covered with warts. What difference do Art, poetry, and style make for the masses? Give them vaudeville, treatises on work in prisons, on worker cities and the material interests *of the moment,* yet. There is a permanent conspiracy against originality,—this is what must be crammed into their brains. The more you have of color and relief, the more you offend them. From whence the prodigious success of the novels of Dumas? It's because to read him you need no initiation. The action of the novels is amusing. One is distracted while one reads them. Then, the book once closed, since no impression remains with you and all of it has passed by like clear water, *you can return to business.* Charming! [January 20, 1853]

The most modulated kind of statement to be found in Flaubert on the topic of the social responsibility of the artist and of art is represented by the following: "I am not in the least insensitive to the misery of the poor classes, etc., but in literature there are no good intentions. *Style is everything*" (January 15, 1854).

But there were numerous indications in Flaubert that "style" —like originality itself—was elusive, inadequate, difficult to define, and far from immune to doubt. In addition, Flaubert could turn doubt upon himself and see its sources in the more opaque parts of his life.

You know that I'm a man of passion and weakness. If you could only know the invisible nets of inaction which enmesh my body and all the mists which befog my mind. I sometimes feel so much weakness that I could die of weariness when I've got to do anything, and it is only by the greatest effort that I can grasp even the clearest idea. My youth drugged me with some kind of opium of boredom for the rest of my life. I hate life! That has escaped me in spite of myself—well let it stand! Yes, life, and everything which reminds me that I must endure it. [October 21, 1851]

Along with his radical doubts about modern society that shaded into a general hatred of life, Flaubert was tormented by the question of his own originality and by the possibility that even he would be contaminated by the practices of popular novelists catering to collective stupidity. Given his bourgeois subject matter, he might come to resemble Dumas, Alphonse Karr, or Paul de Kock. ("What I write at present risks being of the stamp of Paul de Kock, if I do not put it in a profoundly literary form" [September 13, 1852].) The work of the "realists" Edmond Duranty and Jules Husson Champfleury seemed mediocre to him. Champfleury, seen by many contemporaries as the greatest novelist of his time, had published *Les Bourgeois de Molinchart* just before the appearance of *Madame Bovary*. Sainte-Beuve accorded to it more unqualified praise than he saw fit to bestow on *Madame Bovary*—a fact that substantiates Proust's indictment of Sainte-Beuve as a critic who betrayed his public trust by habitually touting inferior work to the detriment of significant art. Flaubert himself had read segments of Champfleury's *Madame d'Aigrizelles* that were published in 1854, and they led him to compare Champfleury to Balzac: "As far as style is concerned, not strong, not strong [*pas fort, pas fort*]. . . . I have reread *Eugénie Grandet*. It is really beautiful. What a difference in comparison with that guy Champfleury" (August 5, 1854).

For Flaubert the poles of the contemporary novel were represented by a Paul de Kock at one extreme (that of the technically slick best seller) and by Balzac at the other. Balzac was great, but Flaubert did not want to emulate his successes. He sought different challenges in writing—challenges Balzac seemed to ignore both at his peril and as a sign of his glory. Balzac resorted to an inflation of mediocre subject matter, pandered to sensationalism, and relied upon the sure-fire techniques of the popular novelist. ("What a man Balzac would have been, had he known how to write" [December 16 or 17, 1852].) But Balzac had the verve and spontaneous power that more than excused his deficiencies. With the benefit of hindsight, one might speculate that an "anxiety of influence" prevented Flaubert from appreciating how Balzac at times achieved "experimental" effects through hyperbole supplementary to those Flaubert brought about through minimalization and irony.[4] Flaubert, however, was manifestly preoccupied less with an anxiety of influence than with an anxiety of impoverishment, exhaustion, and impotence. He had the fear of being a latecomer or epigone—the recurrent *fin-de-siècle* malaise. He saw Balzac and, especially, Hugo as the last of a vanishing breed. Indeed he could address this problem in ways one might expect more from (or even apply to) a critic such as Sartre than from Flaubert himself:

What is characteristic of great geniuses is generalization and creation. They encapsulate diverse personalities in a single type and bring new personages before the consciousness of humanity. Don't we believe in the existence of Don Quixote as in that of Caesar? Shakespeare is formidable in this respect. He was not a man but a continent; there were in him great men, entire crowds, landscapes. Writers like him don't have to worry about style; they are powerful in spite of all their faults and because of them. But as for us, the little people, our value depends on perfected execution. Hugo, in this century, will rout everybody, even though he is full of bad things: but what lung-power! I will here risk a proposition that I wouldn't dare utter anywhere else: that very great men often write very badly—and bravo for them. To discover the art of form, one should not go to them but to writers of the second order (Horace, La Bruyère). One must learn the masters by heart,

---

4. One might even observe that, in *Sarrasine*, Balzac showed uncanny reserve in not naming *l'indisable* which Roland Barthes, despite his preference for post-Flaubertian experimentalism, found no difficulty in identifying in trenchantly univocal and rather "classical" terms. Barthes reads Balzac in too "readerly," in order to rewrite him in too "writerly," a fashion. See *S/Z* (Paris: Editions du Seuil, 1970).

try to think like them, and then take leave of them forever. To learn technique, it is more profitable to go to the erudite and skillful. [September 25, 1852]

Here one seems very far from the portrait of Flaubert as the narrow-minded stylistic perfectionist who made pure art into the nihilistic sublimate of an unqualified death wish. Self-doubt converted Flaubert's option into a strategy *faute de mieux* which rested, if anything, upon an underestimation of his own talent and achievement. In many ways, it would be most accurate to say that Flaubert both intensely believed in art as a vocation and saw his own labors as the work of a clown.

At times, however, the vilification of the bourgeois age did induce faith in a saving remnant or aesthetic elite who would hold an imperilled torch aloft in a blind and inhospitable world.

What crapulous low-life these peasants are! Oh! How I believe in race! But race no longer exists! Aristocratic blood is exhausted; its last globules no doubt have coagulated in a few souls. If nothing changes (and this is possible), perhaps before a half-century has passed, Europe will languish in great shadows and those somber epochs of history where nothing shines will return. Then a few, the pure, will keep among themselves, sheltered from the wind and hidden, the imperishable little candle, the sacred fire, where all illuminations and explosions come to take flame. [March 25–26, 1853]

At most, Flaubert was able to situate his own time in a cyclical vision of history that held out a faint promise of renewal for the future. And here his own option was clearly a lesser one chosen for want of something better.

There are two kinds of literature, that which I shall call national (the better one) and then the lettered, the individual. For the realization of the first, one must have in the masses a fund of common ideas, a solidarity (which does not exist), a bond; and for the entire expansion of the other, one must have *liberty*. But what may one say and concerning what should one speak now? Things will get worse; I wish and hope for it. I prefer nothingness to evil and dust to rottenness. And then there will be renewal! Dawn will come again! We shall no longer be around. What difference does it make? [December 28, 1853]

How one might get from the second to the first condition while retaining elements of freedom and criticism was not Flaubert's concern. He contented himself with apocalyptic anticipations and rare hopes for a renaissance after his passing. His more famous and immediate wishes for redemption in the present were located in a cult of Art that often was separated by a thin line from nihilism.

> Humanity hates us. We do not serve it, and we hate it because it injures us. Let us love one another *in Art* as mystics love one another *in God*, and may all else pale before this love. . . . Lovers of the Beautiful, we are all banished ones. And what joy we feel when we encounter a compatriot in this land of exile. . . . Oh! practical men, men of action, sensible men— how I find you inept, asleep, blinkered! [August 14 and 16, 1853]

This attitude fostered an escape from politics in any ordinary sense, and it induced Flaubert's most quoted invocations to pure art.

> One must shut oneself off and pursue with lowered head one's work—like a mole. If nothing changes, there will be formed in a few years guilds [*compagonnages*] more tight-knit than all secret societies. Above and beyond the crowd, a new mysticism will grow and elevated ideas will sprout up in the shade and on the brink of precipices, like fir trees.
> But a truth seems to me to emerge from all this. It is that one has no need of the vulgar, of the numerous element of majorities, of approbation, of consecration. 1789 demolished royalty and nobility, 1848 the bourgeoisie, and 1851 the people. There is no longer anything other than a low-life and imbecilic mob. We are all plunged at the same level in a common mediocrity. Social equality has passed into our minds and hearts. One makes books for everybody, Art for everybody, science for everybody, as one builds railroads and public heating rooms. Humanity is seized by moral abasement, and I

have a grudge against it because I am part of it. [September 21–22, 1853]

In this context, one purpose of art was demoralization of the common reader. As early as September 4, 1850, Flaubert envisioned a *Dictionary of Received Ideas* whose preface "would explain how the work was intended to reestablish the public's links with tradition, order, and social norms, and [be] written in such a way that the reader couldn't tell whether or not one was putting him on [*si on se fout de lui*]." Art for the artist would function as an extreme ritual of purification from the pollution and ugliness of bourgeois or, perhaps, human reality. And it would give him an invidiously privileged access to a realm of beauty conceived as a secular surrogate or fetish for an absent sacred object. Art would negate or annihilate reality in order to permit an abstract and absolute transcendence toward pure formal beauty. Its goal would ultimately be the notorious "book about nothing":

> What seems beautiful to me, what I should like to write is a book about nothing [*un livre sur rien*], a book dependent on nothing external, which would be held together by the strength of its style, just as the earth, suspended in the void, depends on nothing external for its support; a book which would have almost no subject, or at least in which the subject would be almost invisible, if such a thing is possible. . . . From the standpoint of pure Art one might almost establish the axiom that there is no such thing as subject, style in itself being an absolute manner of seeing things. [January 16, 1852]

Thus subject or content is minimalized so that form, identified with style and beauty, may be raised to the heavens. The qualifications in Flaubert's formulation indicate that the dream is an impossible one. But the goal here is relatively clear: the reduction of content (understood as irremediably ugly and unsalvageable) and the identification of style with autonomous form. Life, moreover, is on the side of irremediably ugly content and opposed to form, style, and beauty: "Life is such a hideous thing that the only way to put up with it is to avoid it. And one avoids it by living in Art" (May 18, 1857). Or again:

"Oh! Our ivory towers! Let us climb them in our dreams, since the hobnails of our boots keep us anchored here below!" (January 29, 1854). A pure art of detached dreams might take a linguistic turn and entail the metamorphosis of art into a variant of pattern practice: "I would like to produce books that require only the writing of sentences (if I may put it that way), just as in order to live it is enough to breathe" (January 25, 1853). The objective correlative of art as a formal organism unto itself was an image from the realm of the inorganic—a material analogue of the abstract: a blank wall.

I remember having had flutterings of the heart, to have felt a violent pleasure in contemplating a wall of the Acropolis, an entirely blank wall. . . . Well! I ask myself whether a book, independently of what it says, can produce the same effect. In the precision of its assemblages, the rarity of its elements, the polish of its surface, the harmony of the whole—is there not an intrinsic virtue, a kind of divine force, something eternal like a principle? (I speak as a Platonist.) [April 13, 1876]

The Platonic substantialism guardedly referred to in a reserved aside pointed to the multiple functions of the concept of form. One of the most influential of these was of course the idea of an autotelic or self-referential art. This art seemed to require an author of sovereign impersonality whose responsibility for his work would be both total and unlocalizable.

The author in his work should be like God in the universe, present everywhere and visible nowhere. Art being a second nature, the creator of this nature should act by analogous procedures. One should feel in all the atoms, in all the aspects, a hidden and infinite impersonality. The effect for the spectator should be a sort of astonishment. [December 9, 1852]

The impersonality or impassivity of the author (narrator?) did not imply the lack of personal convictions in the man. On the contrary, an active discipline or ascesis was required to modify or suppress convictions that threatened to dominate art in unmediated ways:

As for my "lack of conviction," alas! Convictions suffocate me. I burst with repressed anger and indignation. But in the ideal that I have of Art, I believe that one ought to reveal nothing of oneself, and that the artist should no more appear in his work than God in nature. Man is nothing, the work is everything! This discipline, which can take its departure from a false viewpoint, is not easy to observe. And for me, at least, it is a sort of permanent sacrifice that I make to good taste. It would be quite agreeable for me to say what I think and to alleviate Mister Gustave Flaubert by phrases; but what is the importance of Mister Flaubert? [December 20, 1875]

It is significant that this late letter is written to Georges Sand, and Flaubert is combatting an overly direct and didactic notion of committed art. But it is noteworthy that objective art is defended in the same terms that others (such as Max Weber) would use to defend objective social science. Aspects of this letter indicate, moreover, that the practice of disciplined self-restraint could become ascetic self-denial and join up with a wish to be godlike. As Flaubert put it over twenty years earlier: "When will one write history as one ought to write a novel, without love or hatred for any character? When will one describe facts from the viewpoint of a superior joke [*une blague supérieure*], that is as the good Lord sees them from on high?" (October 8, 1852).

Here, in a magnificent feat of legerdemain, "scientific" objectivity fuses with a superior joke, and art comes to resemble both science and religion as the sovereignly impersonal author-narrator assumes the transcendentally ironic position of a hidden God. Indeed Flaubert's numerous statements of doubt, self-doubt, and despair are counterbalanced by affirmations of fanatical faith in art.

One does nothing great without fanaticism. . . . Fanaticism is faith, faith itself, ardent faith, that which creates works and is active. Religion is a variable conception, an affair of human invention, finally an idea; the other is a sentiment. . . . In Art as well, it is the fanaticism of Art that is the artistic sentiment. Poetry is only a way of perceiving external objects, a special organ which filters matter and, without changing it, transfigures it. [March 31, 1853]

At times the transcendental vision of art as surrogate religion which negated reality gave way to a more mystical and pantheistic notion of merging with the world. Here it would be the artist rather than the object that was transfigured through empathetic identification. Art might then still be seen as a refuge, but it would be a refuge at one with the world, and the sorts of works it called to mind led, as we shall see, in unexpected directions.

I am turning toward a kind of aesthetic mysticism (if those two words can go together), and I wish it were more intense. When you are given no encouragement by others, when the outside world disgusts, weakens, corrupts, and stupefies you, *decent* and *delicate* people [*gens honnêtes et délicats*] are forced to seek somewhere within themselves a more suitable place to live. If society continues on its present path, I think we shall once again see mystics, such as existed in all dark ages. Unable to spend itself, the soul will become concentrated. The time is not far off when there will be a resurgence of universal languishing, beliefs in the end of the world and the expectation of a Messiah. But lacking any theological foundation, what will be the basis of this enthusiasm that is ignorant of itself? Some will look to the flesh, others to old religions, still others to Art; and Mankind, like the Jews in the desert, will adore all sorts of idols. People like us were born too soon. In twenty-five years, the point of intersection will be superb in the hands of a master. Then prose—prose especially, the younger form—can play. Books like the *Satyricon* and *The Golden Ass* will return, but overflowing psychically as those overflowed sensually. [September 4, 1852]

Flaubert's sense of the problems created by the meeting of enthusiasm and a *manque de base théologique* seems prophetic. What is noteworthy is that art is situated among other possible responses to modern disorientation without being given any apparent privilege. At the very least, this view would indicate Flaubert's critical awareness of the partially symptomatic nature of what he at times defended as a solution in more unguarded and fanatical terms. And the works he heralds as avatars of the future—works of the declining Roman Empire with which he often compared the modern world—had a distinctive character as carnivalesque, Menippean satires.

79

Indeed, as we have seen, Flaubert at times saw pure art less as a secular surrogate for the sacred than as a compensatory *pis aller* for an epigone. And he could view form itself as a check or antidote to his mystical inclinations as well as a preservative against nervous disorder, itself somehow linked with what Freud would term the "oceanic feeling." Form in this respect would not be a sublimate of a "death instinct" but a prophylactic force for life counteracting a temptation to faint existentially in a life-denying swoon. "Without a love of form, I would perhaps have been a great mystic. Add to that my nervous attacks, which are only the involuntary declivities of ideas, of images. The psychic element then leaps across me, and consciousness disappears with the sentiment of life" (December 27, 1852).

Pure art could also move from the status of an object of faith or belief to that of an unrealizable utopia or critical fiction—even to that of an illusion. As Flaubert put it in one terse, oxymoronic sentence: "I love art and yet I do not believe at all in it" (March 20, 1847). In addition, Flaubert realized that the content or subject matter would necessarily threaten the purest of forms with contagion and expose the writer to contamination by the very bourgeois stupidity he treated in his writing. One could not entirely divorce the parodic citation or mention of cliché from its use, and the writer touching cliché would have to dirty his hands and face the threat, perhaps the temptation, of *embourgeoisement* and *bêtise*. The very practice of writing would render it impossible to lead the purely dualistic existence that Flaubert at times advocated in enjoining the writer to "live like a bourgeois and think like a demigod" (August 21, 1853).

One could adduce many quotations from letters in which Flaubert rejected the pure opposition between content and form and suggested a complex notion of style as a practice of writing that could not be identified with pure formalism or self-referentiality. Then style became something more visceral that could not entirely transcend materiality or allow an identification of the materiality of language with the imaginary. "'Poet of form!' That is the favorite term of abuse hurled by utilitarians at true artists. For my part, until someone comes along and separates the form and the substance of a given sentence, I shall continue to maintain that that distinction is meaningless. Every beautiful thought has a beautiful form, and vice versa" (September 18, 1846).

This last statement could be read as probingly dialectical or as utterly banal. What is perhaps more to the point is that "style" in its manifold and at times incompatible meanings often replaced and displaced pure formal art as Flaubert's goal. Style might mean form in some transcendent sense. But, on a more mundane and technical level, it might mean continuity of parts and surface polish. It might also be substantialized as a Platonic idea. "Sustained harmony of style" was presumably a discovery of the moderns (June 6–7, 1853). As I have already intimated, Flaubert's novelistic practice in *Madame Bovary* might more aptly be termed a dual or plural style which contested without entirely denying notions of unity and harmony in writing. And, even in the letters, the definition of style was itself elusive, perhaps "unsayable" or communicated only indirectly, yet organically felt. "What after all is style? In what does it consist? I no longer know at all what it means. But yes, but yes, nevertheless! I feel it in my stomach" (January 29–30, 1853).

What has been the purpose of the battalions of quotations I have drawn from Flaubert's letters at the risk of falling into a displaced repetition of Sénard's strategy at the trial? My goal has been to bring out the complex and often divided nature of Flaubert's "project" of pure art itself, even before one turns to the further complications introduced by another important "project" enunciated in the *Correspondance*. This strategy was necessary in view of the tendency to see "pure art" in rather restricted terms and to confine it within one-dimensional interpretations.

Before turning to the question of how the already intricate project of pure art was further complicated by at least one other project in the letters and, even more so, by the way the projects relate to the functioning of *Madame Bovary* as a text, I shall examine the interpretation of Jean-Paul Sartre. For Sartre's *L'Idiot de la famille,* despite its own convolutions, presents a line of argument that reduces the uneasy and often self-questioning heterogeneity of Flaubert's understanding of art to a rather circumscribed set of issues. Sartre is both highly selective in his use of Flaubert's letters and quite pointed in his interpretation of them. His dominant interpretation, I think, applies most cogently to the extremely lapidary articulations of the ideal of pure art in Flaubert, often ignoring or underemphasizing the relevance of qualifications or hesitations in the letters as well as the difficulties in referring "projects" to the workings of a text such as *Madame Bovary.*

In pursuing this line of inquiry, I shall try to be sensitive to the complexities of Sartre's own account that mitigate the force of certain of his theses, especially with reference to the issue of Flaubert's style. But I shall by and large confine my analysis to one stratum of Sartre's text—its thematic or "thetic" level—and only mention the tensions between it and Sartre's own practice or "style" of writing in *L'Idiot.* For my purpose here is not an intertextual reading of *Madame Bovary* and *L'Idiot.* It is rather the more limited attempt to offer a (partial) reading of *Madame Bovary* which tests critically the extent to which the theses and arguments of *L'Idiot* are informative for an interpretation of the novel and for an understanding of the relations among the novel, the trial, and Flaubert's projects.

Hence I shall approach Sartre's study through a set of specific questions. What is Sartre's view of the meaning of pure art? What is the existential basis of Flaubert's aesthetic project? What is the bond between Flaubert's life and his times? What are the more particular features characterizing the horizon of expectations of Flaubert's contemporary readership? How does Flaubert relate to the problem of commitment and, by implication, to the issue of the political significance of the way we read him? How do the general features of Sartre's argument apply to a "practical criticism" of *Madame Bovary* which Sartre, in his completed volumes, only adumbrates? What are the value and the limitations of Sartre's arguments as they apply to Flaubert's projects and to the reading of *Madame Bovary?* In addressing these questions, I shall defer treatment of what is perhaps Sartre's most interesting discussion of Flaubert's "style" to a later chapter.[5]

In Sartre's interpretation, pure art is the post-romantic

5. See Chapter 5.

ideology of Flaubert and his generation for whom romantic ideals were hopelessly compromised and bourgeois realities entirely unlivable. The musings of Musset, Lamartine, and Vigny seemed vapid and fit only for parody. A premature political attempt to realize ideals collapsed in the 1831 revolt of lycée students against school authorities in Rouen (a revolt which Flaubert, despite his extensive writing on his youth, does not even mention). The bad faith and hypocrisy of their liberal parents were revealed to the schoolboys when the older generation betrayed their anticlerical principles to line up with established authority and to preserve political ties with Royalist forces, even if it meant abandoning their children in the boys' protest against compulsory confession at school. This revolt was fresh in the schoolboys' memories when Flaubert entered the lycée in 1832. And in 1839 Flaubert himself took a leading part in another protest which centered around the quality of teaching and the intimidation of students at the lycée.

The blow dealt to political idealism by 1848 and its aftermath was even more far-reaching and complex, and it reinforced the disillusionment of the 1830s for Flaubert. In this thoroughly disabused environment, Flaubert could accept the results of the Romantic agony as foregone conclusions. His repeated plaint was that he was old before his time, and his fictional creations could be presented as existentially dessicated without having to earn their inner emptiness as the dry fruit of experience.

The term "realism" is for Sartre little more than a mask or smoke screen for aesthetic tendencies of a sort diametrically opposed to realism. The puzzle is how people at the time could identify as realistic what had such a different incentive. The animus of pure art was a systematic derealization of reality and an impossible attempt to realize the imaginary. It was no simple and anodyne doctrine of escape from an uncongenial world. It was rather a hate-filled ideology which was suicidal and genocidal to the core. If the bourgeoisie alone were the object of the artist's nihilating practice, pure art might have been a trojan horse with progressive political implications—at least from the Marxist perspective which Sartre attempts to make his own. But the object of vilification and systematic demoralization was the human being in general—the very man in man. A passive and "feminine" vindictiveness excluded all possibility of active confrontation with the sources of alienation in the real world. Proponents of pure art were in Sartre's oft repeated phrase—the leitmotif or eponym of his study—"knights of Nothingness." Their nihilistic gambit was to save or redeem themselves by annihilating reality and any hope for realistic betterment in the world through political revolution. Their use of the imagination was as an uncompromisingly satanic force for abstract negation and escape. Pure art was in this sense both the sublimate of a universal death wish and the medium of a self-centered *Erlösungspiel* or artistic drama of personal redemption. Flaubert was the most genuinely nihilistic of a post-romantic generation whom Sartre describes as "a black feodality for whom the principle of Beauty is hidden but of which Artists are imaginarily the knights of Nothingness [*chevaliers du Néant*]. The relation of Flaubert to reality is *imaginary destruction*."[6]

The specific link between art for art's sake as an aesthetic ideology and the personal history of Flaubert was a pathological condition or "neurosis" which Sartre interprets less in causal than in hermeneutic terms. Indeed his thesis becomes less controversial if one substitutes for the loaded term "neurosis" the notion of deep-seated (or "lived") existential problems, for—aside from the negative connotations apparent in Sartre's argument—he often seems to identify the two. And he will even, in the fashion of R. D. Laing, rehabilitate "neurosis" in contrast to the easy conformist compromises of the youthful *poète maudit* turned respectable bourgeois (for example, Ernest Chevalier, a childhood friend of Flaubert). But "neurosis" acquires its more negative characteristics when it is correlated with merely imaginary destruction in contrast with Marxist commitment to change in the real world.

The strategy of derealization of the real and realization of the imaginary as the work of the imagination was a "neurotic" project that became a collective norm as well as Flaubert's accepted fate (*"option subie"*). *L'art pour l'art* was a displacement and a secularization of a religious framework whereby neurosis

6. *L'Idiot de la famille*, 3 vols. (Paris: Gallimard, 1971–72). My references to *L'Idiot* are to volume and page number, and translations are my own.

filled the space left empty by the disappearance of a religious institution. Its meaningful role was to induce total dedication of the votary-artist to a quasi-monastic, secular asceticism that justified separation from, and disdain for, the "real" world. Art became a fetish as the replacement for a missing divinity, and it was existentially invested with the fallout left by the explosion of the sacred. Pure art was, in this sense, one of the residues of what Max Weber diagnosed as the Protestant Ethic. (Comparable in "fetishistic" status and equally dubious from Sartre's perspective, however, is the type of "value-neutrality" in science that Weber at times defended: pure art for Sartre is strictly analogous to "positivism" in its nature and functions.) *L'art pour l'art* was a "spirit" ostensibly hostile to the spirit of capitalism and bourgeois commercialism—but one readily accommodated to the latter in a larger political and social world where an aesthetics of pure art was impotent in transforming reality. It was also charged with more sinister and covert functions: those of expressing (and masking) the self-hatred and generalized hostility of a conquering bourgeoisie that by 1848 had little left of its formerly heroic mission.

Flaubert himself was the man for his times, as *Madame Bovary* was apparently the book answering the needs of its epoch. Flaubert in Sartre's estimation was a genuine hysteric who imitated schizophrenia. His lived experience (*vécu*) provided him with the existential depth that in subtle ways made his art an authentic response to the hidden needs of his readers, while the play-acting at madness of figures such as Leconte de Lisle destined them to a minor status. The peak event (or "identity crisis") in the life of Flaubert was his famous fainting fit at Pont L'Evêque in January of 1844. Here, in dramatic and quasi-ritualistic fashion, Flaubert fainted away from a hated "real-life" career in law and into an "imaginary" life as a writer and artist. The event had almost religious meaning as a conversion experience and as the only available answer to the word of Flaubert's own godlike father, Achille-Cléophas, who thought little of his younger son and found literature a pursuit fit only for the weak and the feminine. 1844 was also a proleptic substitute for 1848 and a herald of the Second Empire. Flaubert could be literarily ahead of his time because he was literally behind it—fixated by his crisis of 1844 and prepared by his "lived experience" to furnish what the bourgeoisie after 1848 really wanted: an ideology of antihuman hatred masquerading as realism. "Gustave in '44 already constitutes himself as the subject of the Second Empire. This is why he missed the rendez-vous of '48. Everything happens as if *his* revolution of February [1848] took place in January '44" (III, 665).

"The most profound meaning of [Flaubert's] neurosis" is what Sartre terms the game of "loser wins" (II, 1952). Flaubert was an almost intentional loser in real life in order to become a winner in the realm of art and the imaginary. His loss in life entailed sequestration, premature old age, vague illness, the habits of a crotchety old maid, and an abhorrence of practical activity. His victory was imaginary, and its significance resided in a secularization of religious values. His "neurosis" was itself meaningfully constitutive in relation to his aesthetics. The decline of orthodox religion and the unavailability of the monastery made neurosis the *via regia* of the artist in quest of ascetic discipline and a private ritual of redemption. The negation and denial of the world brought the faint promise of salvation to the one who "absented" himself from complicity in reality.

Life deranges; it risks, through its passions without force and its cares without grandeur, to turn the artist aside from his true task which is to perpetuate the shipwreck of the world through *style*. . . . Living is a distraction. . . . One day writing to Louise [Colet], [Flaubert] is astounded: how can Leconte de Lisle, an artist, waste two years in stormy and disappointing love affairs to the point of forgetting his Art? His stupor might make one laugh, but it portrays him. Why does one have to love when the unique matter of importance is to write, and style, an absolute point of view, never ceases to steal away? "Think of style," he tells the Muse, "think of it always." One would say one has a believer speaking of his God. That is the case, and it's worse still. For this uninterrupted meditation on language takes place in the throes of anguish and disgust. This Christian believes he is damned. His only chance of salvation is time. A uniform time, empty of all content, which has the savor of boredom: boredom whose each instant resembles the preceding one and which he can profitably use to invent a form adequate to his unique subject, decided upon since adolescence and never before treated. [III, 24]

This unique subject, as we shall see, is how to fashion a style indirectly communicating a neurotic experience that is literally unspeakable or unsayable (*indisable*) and that is lived in silence. Language is the impossible means of communicating this experience, and Flaubert's relation to language is both vital and deadly. The troubled, indeed anguished, relation of Flaubert to language began in infancy when he was the passive object spoken about but unable to speak. Consubstantial with Flaubert's neurosis was a profoundly passive relation to language: he never outgrew the feeling of being its spoken object rather than its active speaker. Language came to him from the outside and put words into his mouth or under his pen—words he labored on like a fanatical, masochistic, and sadistic saint but words that never became for him practical media or instruments in changing the world.

As a child of seven, Flaubert was unable to read. This fact both induced the belief of his father that Flaubert would never amount to anything and epitomized the relation Flaubert would have toward the word throughout life. He would never read. He would only reread—and in a way that revealed an inability to absorb what he read. Reading was a pretext for empty dreaming. His legendary labors to arrive at *le mot juste* were refinements of a nihilistically passive relation to language. "Life is 'a story full of sound and fury, told by an idiot.' This sentence would not pass for the last word of Shakespeare. It is the last word of Flaubert" (II, 2039).

Flaubert's "estrangement" from language has, for Sartre, "only one explanation: there is no common measure or mediation between the subjective existence of Gustave and the universe of significations: these are two perfectly heterogeneous realities of which one at times visits the other. . . . Life and words are incommensurable" (I, 26). We shall return to the elaborate implications Sartre draws from this view with respect to the crucial problem of Flaubert's style. Suffice it to say at this point that the "bad insertion into language" which Flaubert experienced may be traced to his childhood, and it created a condition the adult would take up as his own. Flaubert was forever the "signified" of language but never in the liberated position of active "signifier."

> Reduced to the contemplation of his passivity, the child cannot know that he has the structure of a sign and that the living transcendence [*dépassement*] of the lived [*vécu*] is in him, as it is in everyone, the foundation of signification. Thus language comes to him from the outside: the signifying transcendence is the operation of the other and is accomplished by a signification that determines him from the outside. . . . Words are things that the course of lived experience ferries along; he will have much difficulty in making them the living instruments of his own transcendence toward the exterior and will never completely succeed because he has been *passivized* [*passivisé*] by maternal cares. [I, 157]

The maternal cares to which Sartre refers are the product of his own elaborate speculation about how Flaubert's mother must have treated the infant Flaubert given Sartre's interpretation of the way Flaubert turned out—a speculation Sartre himself labels a fable, but a fable whose truth value is presumably redeemed by its insertion into the dialectically "totalizing" hermeneutic of existential Marxism. Flaubert's mother, we are told, handled him with painstaking, formalistic meticulousness but without genuine love. She in a sense treated the infant Flaubert in the way Sartre believes Flaubert treated the characters and objects in his stories. Flaubert's passive, objectified, reified relation to language was solidified by the manner in which his mother related to him as an infant—an imprinting which he assumed in his attitude toward his fictional world. The mother was a dutiful but unloving formalist in handling the infant: the adult would be a fanatically dutiful but genocidal formalist in handling fiction and "derealized" language.

How was Flaubert the man for his times, if not the man for all capitalistic seasons? "A work of hatred—that is, one that takes hatred as its point of view—*speaks the truth of the epoch*" (III, 325). Flaubert's work has for Sartre the predominantly symptomatic function of reinforcing capitalism and justifying alienation. But it is not simply symptomatic. It actually aggravated conditions that informed it and to which it responded. It did not so much reflect as articulate and exacerbate the most hateful and destructive animus of the times. The very understanding of Flaubert's art as realistic both bespoke a nihilistic sense of reality and concealed the nature and implications of that apprehension under a misleading label.

Thus the aesthetic of art for art's sake was itself the neurotic collective ideology of post-romanticism, and it normatively created the expectation that the artist would be neurotic. "From 1850 to the end of the century, one had to be crazy to write" (III, 41). In the eighteenth and, even more, in the seventeenth century, the author by contrast was supposed to be an "*honnête homme*" who strictly observed certain rules and was integrated into society (III, 41). In cases such as those of Rousseau or Pascal, a diagnosis of neurosis might be justified. But neurosis "was useful *indirectly*; one wrote *against one's illness,* in spite of the trouble, as did Rousseau, and not thanks to it. The essential point is that, in integrated societies, the psychoneurotic element, if it exists, is never taken as the goal of the artist and even less as the rule of his art" (III, 43). If individual neurosis exists in an "integrated" society, it is for Sartre annulled in what he calls, following Hegel, the "objective Spirit" of the time—its objectified common culture. Flaubert's time, on the other hand, demanded and expected the artist to be neurotic, for the collectivity was itself psychopathological.

At this time, the condition for creating art is to be neurotic. Not in any which way but in a precise manner which we want to define. The objective movement transforms culture on the basis of deeper transformations—but also as a function of traditions and laws proper to the cultural sector—a product of norms so rigorous and so contradictory that the contemporary movement of Art can realize itself as a determination of the objective Spirit only in the form of Art-Neurosis. This does not mean that works are neurotic but that the literary doctrines as well as the "poetic arts" are and that artists must play at neurosis or be neurotic. And since the literary fact is dual, this means as well that, for the public, reading, while it takes place, becomes a brief, provoked neurosis. [III, 43–44]

Sartre's interpretative move here is to integrate or translate a Marxist theory of alienation into its quasi-Freudian, psychological counterpart. Thus Sartre feels able to answer in the affirmative a question tentatively raised by Freud toward the end of *Civilization and Its Discontents*: "If the development of civilization has such a far-reaching similarity to the development of the individual and if it employs the same methods, may we not be justified in reaching the diagnosis that, under the influence of cultural urges, some civilizations, or some epochs of civilization —possibly the whole of mankind—have become 'neurotic'?"[7]

For Sartre an alienated culture does indeed give rise to psychological alienation or neurosis, and unlike Freud he attempts to connect an analysis of the family to a Marxist conception of the larger socioeconomic conditions operative in bringing about modification of "lived experience" in individuals. Indeed Sartre broadly extends a theory of alienation through individual life, collective ideology, and the reading experience. The work itself is presumably not neurotic but, as we shall see, its precise relation to neurosis is difficult for Sartre to define. For the intentional structure of the act of writing must participate in neurosis, and its objective correlative—the art work or text— must be an object of neurotic investments (or what Freud would term "cathexes"). Art must be seen as escaping, refusing, or denying reality, and the structure of reality itself must be definable in clear-cut, perhaps dogmatic, ways.

> The essential point [of this art] is to refuse the rigidity of oppositions—because they are the structures of reality—by derealizing them. It is ultimately a question of spontaneously imitating autistic thought. Given the inability to transcend contradictory imperatives, one makes them ceaselessly pass into one another and one transforms them into double binds [*tourniquets*]. One constructs a logic of Nothingness [*Néant*] that goes from the realization of the unreal to the derealization of reality. This makes impossibility the fundamental condition of every enterprise. One thinks on several levels, in several voices. On the surface, one attempts a *chef-d'oeuvre* because it is always possible to create one. More profoundly one undertakes it because it is impossible and in order to dream of it. . . . [The poet] founds his merit upon failure:

7. *Civilization and Its Discontents*, trans. and ed. James Strachey (New York: Norton, 1961), 91.

simultaneously aesthetics transforms itself into ethics. Grandeur consists in sacrificing oneself without reserve for causes
that are lost in advance. But merit is a requirement. What if
the reward were to be won precisely at the moment one
thought one lost? What if hard luck [*le guignon*] were only the
visible aspect of election? Depersonalization, rupture with
reality, solitude, hypostatized language, misanthropy, self-
hatred, the will to fail [*conduites d'échec*], the quest for the
impossible—these neurotic traits are only the means of writing, that is, of continuing literature in an epoch where, far
from finding one's liberty in literary autonomy, the writer is
alienated in that very autonomy, and writing places itself in
question in every written work. The possibility of creating
[*faire*] a work is no longer acquired; before the scandal of an
unfindable public and contradictory imperatives, the foundation of Art must be sought in irrationality. [III, 199–200]

In this "can't-win" situation where an impossible victory is
sought through failure, the loser can seem to win only if his
birth as artist coincides with his death as social agent.

The birth of the Artist through Art of which he is the minister requires—like religion—this precondition: social death.
Art, this Absolute, this supreme value, can only be served as a
cult by the infirm and the incapable—and no one is an artist
who has not given striking proofs of his incapacity. Behind
this conception, one of course perceives Christian ideas:
Beauty, like a divine fulguration, strikes the heart of the
humble and the dispossessed. Conversion is nothing other
than a new vision of the world grasped through the secular
failure of the convert. [III, 168]

The centuries-old background of art for art's sake is thus
Christianity. And "Flaubert writes for a Christian West." Indeed Sartre insists that "we are all Christians, even today; the
most radical disbelief is a Christian atheism, that is, it con-
serves, despite its destructive power, certain directing schemes
—for thought, very few; for the imagination, more; but especially for sensibility—whose origin is to be sought in centuries
of Christianity of which we are willy-nilly the heirs" (II, 2124).
Whatever our resistance to Christianity, the invocation of *idées-*

forces such as ascesis and redemption is a testimonial to a ghost-like heritage. "For an instant, Christians in the imaginary, we march."

But Sartre also finds more local contextual resources for Flaubert's art in his specific historical period. Especially significant were 1848 and the Second Empire. Especially after the failed revolution of 1848, a post-romantic atmosphere of disillusionment combined with an inability or an unwillingness to carry alienation beyond psychological and ideological bounds. A bar blocked constructive social and political action, and it was reinforced by guilt and hatred in the aftermath of 1848. A writer in the 1850s had to reflect and intensify a profound disgust for human nature which both excused particular bourgeois practices and passed in silence over the concrete events of '48. A work was necessary that managed to express the guilt-ridden, genocidal meaning of 1848 yet also hid it behind that veil of false universality: *la condition humaine.* Specific bourgeois principles would still be naturalized and universalized as they had been in the more progressively triumphant phase of bourgeois self-assertion, but their ideological value would pass from the positive to the negative. The writer, "in condemning *man* without recourse, would exonerate the *men* of '48, even the killers, from all particular responsibility" (III, 418–19).

Thus the writing of the 1850s—and in some sense *Madame Bovary* as the *chef-d'oeuvre* of the period—functioned as an intensified reinforcement of the ideological and psychological needs of the time. But it did so in a subtle way—not as a direct reflection of either the true or the false consciousness of the period.

When, from 1849, the knights of Nothingness publish their first works, if the cultivated public adopts them, if it makes them *its* poets and *its* novelists, the reason is not that they incite it to a coming to consciousness, nor further that they consolidate its false consciousness in presenting to it its *image* in a poem or the hero of a novel. The truth is more complex: the artist imposes himself on both the men of talent and the rich because he differs from them radically, both because they comprehend implicitly his purpose and because they arrange to misunderstand; both because they grasp the homicidal in-

tention which hides itself in its irrealization at least enough to
make it serve their end, and because a perhaps inevitable
misunderstanding defines him in their eyes as a doctrinaire of
realism. These strange and twisted links mean that no writer
has so much scorned his public and that none has more completely expressed it—not in its historical truth but in the true
pathos which founds false consciousness and ideological non-
savoir. [III, 302]

In this difficult passage, Sartre takes his distance from the
dominant thematics of such Marxist theorists as Lucien Gold-
mann and Georg Lukács. He also tries to go beyond his own
earlier understanding of bad faith that could be correlated with
a theory of false consciousness. Self-deception is still an issue as
he here formulates the problem, but it is not conceived in predominantly rationalistic or narrowly self-interested terms.
Rather Sartre's earlier notion of prereflective consciousness is
itself intensified and to some extent transformed in an interpretation of lived experience (*le vécu*) whereby an individual or
a group can see something falsely in order to mask a more
profound and "genuine" intention. In this sense, what a work
expresses is not directly an ideology or a false consciousness; it
is a pathos which is in part hidden from social agents but which
does serve their class interests—and for which they are ultimately responsible. The pathos in question here is destructive
and genocidal in intent.

Sartre will also present the Second Empire, established after
the coup d'état of Louis Napoleon in 1851, as an imaginary
realm corresponding to the "derealizing" labors of Flaubert
and his aesthetic generation. The Second Empire was a pseudo-
empire, a superstructure without an adequate infrastructure,
a hollow echo of the Empire of the first Napoleon. Indeed
Sartre's own use of Second Empire furniture as decor in his
early play *No Exit* gives some sense of the interpretation of the
period he would provide in his study of Flaubert.

In the light of his analysis, Flaubert would seem committed
to what Sartre in an interview termed "total disengagement and
the quest for a formal ideal."[8] In *L'Idiot*, pure art as a formal

8. *Situations IX* (Paris: Gallimard, 1972), 116.

ideal takes on the pathos of demoralization, derealization, and annihilation not simply of bourgeois civilization but of the human race. Flaubert is in a sense committed, but his commitment would seem to be the total antithesis of the more normative and progressive commitment advocated by Sartre in *What Is Literature?*.[9] It would even seem distant from the more subtle understanding of critical and at least partially constructive commitment traced in "A Plea for Intellectuals."[10] In our later discussion of Sartre's conception of Flaubert's "style," we shall touch upon certain reformulations of Sartre's theory of language as it bears upon the problem of commitment, but even this dimension of Sartre's interpretation takes a largely negative turn. And when Sartre explains himself in an interview in *Le Monde* concerning the meaning of commitment in Flaubert, he identifies it with a biblical passion for *personal* salvation and a project of imaginary derealization and totalization—precisely those features viewed in a predominantly negative light in *L'Idiot*.

> Total lack of commitment [*le désengagement total*] is what appears if one superficially considers everything [Flaubert] wrote. But then one notices a profound commitment on a second level that I would, in spite of everything, call political. Here we have a man who, as one knows, was a proprietor and a reactionary. But if one stops there, one does not do justice to Flaubert. To grasp him truly, one must go to the profound commitment, a commitment through which he tries to save his life. The important point is that Flaubert totally committed himself on a certain level even if the latter implied that he took blameworthy positions in every other respect. Literary commitment is in the last analysis the fact of taking up [*assumer*] the entire world, the totality. To take the universe as a whole, with man inside it, to account for it from the viewpoint of nothingness, is a profound commitment. It is not simply a

9. *Qu'est-ce que la littérature?* in *Situations II* (Paris: Gallimard, 1948), 55–330; Bernard Frechtman, trans., *What Is Literature?* (New York: Philosophical Library, 1949).

10. "Plaidoyer pour les intellectuels" in *Situations VIII* (Paris: Gallimard, 1972), 373–455; John Matthews, trans., "A Plea for Intellectuals" in *Between Existentialism and Marxism* (New York: Pantheon Books, 1974), 227–85.

literary commitment in the sense that one "commits oneself to make books." As in the case of Mallarmé, who is a grandson of Flaubert, it is a question of a veritable passion in the biblical sense.[11]

This highly equivocal statement can be read as Sartre's final reconciliation with Flaubert and an assertion of "positive" commitment in Flaubert's writings only if one is willing to indulge the myopic desire for consensus at any price which Sartre himself attacked time and again. The tone of voice has changed from the dominant tenor of *L'Idiot*. This change counts for something, but the terms of Sartre's argument remain very much the same. In *L'Idiot*, Flaubert was indeed seen as taking up the universe as a whole but only to annihilate it through imaginary "derealization" indentured to a suicidal and genocidal project of seeming self-redemption. Sartre's own overwhelmingly hyperbolic argument accounts for, I think, the most extreme and unqualified assertions of the ideal of pure art in the letters of Flaubert. It brings out their antihumanistic and even nihilistic implications, and it relates them to Flaubert's life and times in a manner that is at least suggestive. But the difficulties in Sartre's approach are many, and they are not overcome by his own hesitations in enunciating given propositions.

Sartre tends to amalgamate Flaubert's letters and his fictional texts in a primarily symptomatic or functionalist reading oriented toward a delineation of the author's life and times. The nature of the functions of literature is often treated with great subtlety, but there is less subtlety in the understanding of the relations among letters, fictional texts, and inferences concerning individual or collective life. Often Sartre has only the letters or the fiction to go on. But he is quick to extrapolate from them to the life of the author, the expectations of a readership, and the characteristics of collectivities—which he then, in circular fashion, uses to explain the writings. This procedure is facilitated in part (but not completely) by the fact that Sartre devotes the bulk of his attention to the semi-confessional juve-

---

11. *Le Monde*, May 14, 1971, p. 21.

nilia. The analysis of *Madame Bovary* was to come in a fourth volume that was never completed, and in a moment we shall raise questions about the relatively brief treatment accorded the novel in the three completed volumes. The more general point, however, is that Sartre does not pose as an explicit problem the relation of various kinds of writing to one another and to personal or collective life. By and large in *L'Idiot*, he simply employs writings in speculating, at times wildly, about the way life was or must have been.

Missing even in those speculations is the question of the relations among the symptomatic, the critical, and the features that exceed these categories of analysis. In the discussion of Flaubert's life and times, Sartre treats almost exclusively the manner in which writings or works of art were not simply symptomatic but aggravating manifestations of the most negative features of the time. (Indeed his bourgeois go beyond the stupid philistines of Flaubert's letters to incarnate the banality of evil as genocidal *bêtes*.) What is not investigated is the way the symptomatic or aggravating aspects of texts are counteracted by modes of critical disclosure that Sartre himself discussed in *What Is Literature?*. Sartre apparently does not find these features in *Madame Bovary*. In his discussion of Flaubert's readership, he does not examine the trial as an empirical instance of conventions in a key social institution that attested to existing horizons of expectation among bourgeois readers. One might, in Sartre's terms, see the trial as a defense mechanism on the part of those unwilling to recognize their own genocidal inclinations, but the view of Flaubert as scapegoat would have to account for the effects I have discussed in terms of ideological crime—effects Sartre is willing to acknowledge in cases other than that of Flaubert.

Yet, if Sartre ideologically insists on seeing man as active—even at the cost of excessively dualistic oppositions between activity and receptivity—he sees the text and often the writer as passive. How the writer mediates and modifies the obsessions or psychological investments of the author is not extensively explored as a real problem. Indeed one crucial reason for Sartre's rejection of the very notion of text is that he continues to see it in exclusively formalistic terms.

Flaubert applies himself . . . to derealizing language. Far from
utilizing it to designate a signified exterior to the Word, he
applies his art to making the thing pass into the materiality of
the word so that the sentence, sonorous and closed, cut off
from its references to the world, tending to pose itself for
itself, to become what one today calls a *text*, refers to all of
language and only to it. [III, 605]

Thus Sartre identifies the very materiality of language in
Flaubert with the project of imaginary "derealization" of the
world and the constitution of a putatively autonomous, self-
referential art. He also equates Flaubert with contemporary
theorists who see the text in neo-formalistic terms as the autotelic realm of a fully liberated "signifier." In so doing, Sartre
tends to see others as attributing to the text the position of full
liberation or freedom that he himself is often tempted to attribute to "man." But the more potent and politically relevant
understanding of the text involves a critique both of these iden-
tifications and of purely dichotomous oppositions such as those
between activity and passivity, signifier and signified. The text
is then seen not as a self-enclosed linguistic world but as a use
of language or a signifying practice related to other practices in
a multiplicity of ways. Sartre himself seems close to this other
understanding of textuality when he argues that language cannot be placed squarely either on the side of lived experience (*le
vécu*) or on that of the conceived and knowledge (*le conçu*)—
thereby implying that language undercuts his own founding
oppositions in a manner that would seem to necessitate an explicit rethinking of problems of a sort Sartre rarely undertakes:

To speak is for everyone an immediate and spontaneous,
lived experience to the extent that the spoken word [*la parole*]
is a practice [*une conduite*]; inversely, lived experience [*le vécu*]
is never pure of words [*vierge de mots*] and, often, resuscitates
worn-out designations that aim at it without being truly adequate to it. Thus verbal conduct can *in no case* be defined as
the passage from one order to another. How could this be
possible since the reality of living and speaking man is made
up at every instant by the melding of the two orders. To

97

speak is nothing other than to adopt and deepen an already speaking conduct, that is, one expresses oneself. [I, 38]

The further point would be that writing is also a practice that cannot be divorced from speech on the metaphysical grounds which Sartre will at times invoke. With reference to the issue of "neurosis," it must, however, be noted that Sartre, in his brief allusions to *Madame Bovary,* does not present this text as a pathological document or morbid case history. Thus he distinguishes it from Flaubert's ordinary life, the collective mentality (or objective Spirit) of his time, and the expectations of his readership. But why he does so is far from clear. Sartre writes that in *Madame Bovary* "horror is never present. It haunts the book without giving itself to be seen. Ceaselessly aimed at [*visée*], it escapes. Precisely for this reason, *Madame Bovary,* as a work, does not enter into the categories of pathology: it does not itself refer one either to the subject who wrote it or to his obsessions" (III, 30).

Presumably the reasons for these assertions would have come in the missing fourth volume of *L'Idiot.* I think it is plausible to argue, however, that Sartre's difficulty in providing them may have been one reason why the fourth volume itself was never completed. In the existing three volumes of *L'Idiot,* the references to *Madame Bovary* are dispersed and rarely go beyond the level of allusions, illustrations of points made on other grounds, or suggestive indications of possible interpretations. And it is difficult to see how the lines of argument laid down in the three earlier volumes could have been extrapolated to furnish a sustained, differential analysis of the novel. Sartre does not manage in *L'Idiot* to provide the dialectical comprehension of the multiple ways a text interacts with its various contexts that one might have expected on the basis of his arguments in *Search for a Method* or "A Plea for Intellectuals."[12] We shall see certain consequences of this failure in Sartre's treatment of Flaubert's notion of *l'indisable* and its relation to "style." To reiterate, Sartre's analysis of the life and times of Flaubert is

12. *Question de méthode* in *Critique de la raison dialectique* (Paris: Gallimard, 1960); Hazel E. Barnes, trans., *Search for a Method* (New York: Knopf, 1963).

most applicable to one important aspect of Flaubert's project of pure art and, to a lesser and ill-defined extent, to certain features of *Madame Bovary* as a text. In the latter respect, it would seem to inform the dimension of impersonal, "objective" narration—what Sartre terms the *"principe de survol"*—and in part the attitude of the narrator toward characters. Here elements of the inhuman distance and even hatred stressed by Sartre do appear—but not in an unqualified way.

In addition, the extent to which *Madame Bovary* invited neurotic investments on the part of its author and its readers remains a moot issue that is in part decided by the kind of reading one argues for in a critical dialogue with the novel. The paradoxical effect of Sartre's own interpretation may be to facilitate those very investments or types of reading he himself would see as politically reactionary. (Indeed it is remarkable that a certain kind of "poststructuralist" reading—which Sartre would see as antagonistic to his own theoretical position—can arrive by different routes at conclusions about Flaubert that are similar to Sartre's own.) With reference to the readers of Flaubert's own time, Sartre offers no empirical evidence for his thesis. Here his interpretation remains almost exclusively on the level of suggestive coloration. And, with reference to the author-writer, Sartre fails to investigate, or perceives in a restricted way, projects that contest "pure art" in his construction of it.

A second project discussed extensively in Flaubert's letters is what I term (following Mikhail Bakhtin) carnivalization.[13] This

13. Mikhail Bakhtin, *Problems of Dostoevsky's Poetics* (Ann Arbor, Mich.: Ardis, 1973), and *Rabelais and His World* (Cambridge, Mass.: The M. I. T. Press, 1968). See also *The Dialogic Imagination*, trans. Caryl Emerson and Michael Holquist (Austin: University of Texas Press, 1980). The role of carnivalization in Flaubert has recently been stressed by Arthur Mitzman who provides much useful contextual information concerning Flaubert's life and times. "Roads, Vulgarity, Rebellion, and Pure Art: The Inner Space in Flaubert and French Culture," *Journal of Modern History* 51 (1979), 504–24. Mitzman sees pure art as a "sublimation" of the carnivalesque. But he thereby obscures the tensions between the two projects, and he furnishes little analysis of their relation to the functioning of Flaubert's novels. One may note, however, that pure art is perceived by Mitzman as a "protest of withdrawal" in a sense that attributes a critical function to the very turn toward formalism and the rejection of existing society. From Sartre's perspective (which Mitzman does not discuss), this putative act of aesthetic resistance is of course tantamount to escape and aggravation of nega-

project has an uneasy, indeed agonistic, relation to that of pure art, although the two may at times establish unexpected connections with one another. But the carnivalesque cannot simply be subordinated to the quest for pure art in Sartre's sense of a derealization of the real and a flight into the imaginary. Nor can it be reduced to double binds that postulate bourgeois stupidity only to convert it through impotent laughter into merely demoralizing buffoonery. For this possibility is only the extremely negative end of a spectrum of carnivalesque effects that, while specific in nature, have a significant critical function and a crucial part to play in any larger project of sociocultural transformation. Indeed one way in which the project of carnivalization entered Flaubert's novels was through a many-sided contestation of the ideal of pure art itself. And a more prominent and lively role for carnivalizing forces may be seen not merely as a means but as part of the end of social action in its broadest sense.

Evidence for a carnivalesque project can be adduced from Flaubert's letters and from their bearing upon Flaubert's biography. The first known essay in prose that Flaubert wrote was an *éloge* of Corneille followed by an *éloge* of constipation.[14] Jean Bruneau, in his study of the early works of Flaubert, has stressed the role of relatively unmediated carnivalesque elements.[15] Yuk in *Smarh* was, for example, an ambivalent god of laughter. And of himself Flaubert wrote: "Whatever one may say, at

---

tive forces in society and culture. Mitzman also makes the suggestive remark that "one may view *Madame Bovary* as an extended metaphoric charivari against bourgeois marriage" (521). My own general view is that the ideal of pure art can itself be seen as a "sublimation" of the carnivalesque largely in the paradoxical sense that something may turn into its opposite. The artist turned his back on society in quasi-ritualistic impudence. But he also sought an ideal of purity or transcendence and engaged in a quest for the absolute. The carnivalesque contests this very ideal through what Bakhtin calls "jolly relativity," and it is necessarily a mode of interaction and "impurity." But the carnivalesque itself did appear in a more "sublimated" or muted form in Flaubert—notably on stylistic levels where carnivalization is related to the entire problem of the role of irony and shifts in narrative perspective.

14. See Geneviève Bollème, *Extraits de la correspondance ou préface à la vie d'écrivain* (Paris: Editions du Seuil, 1963), 22.

15. *Les Débuts littéraires de Gustave Flaubert* (Paris: Armand Colin, 1962), 150–60. Bruneau's study should be read as a companion piece to, and a check upon, Sartre's interpretation in *L'Idiot de la famille.*

bottom I am a showman [or mountebank—*saltimbanque*]. In my childhood and youth, I had a boundless love of the stage. I would perhaps have been a great actor if heaven had made me been born poor" (August 6 or 7, 1876). The analogue of Yuk in the life of the young Flaubert and the outlet for his theatrical sense was *Le Garçon,* a ribald and self-critical personification of the spirit of laughter. In *Le Garçon,* laughter, irony, and parody were combined with unsettling effect. *Le Garçon* was a fictive creature invented by Flaubert and his friends for theatrical representations they would perform in the billiard room of the Flaubert residence, the *Hôtel Dieu. Le Garçon* would assume the role of bourgeois, but he would carry that role to satirically hyperbolic extremes that would explode it convulsively from within. As Jean Bruneau puts it: "[*Le Garçon*] represents simultaneously the bourgeois at the time of Louis Philippe [*le bourgeois louis-philippard*] and the *farceur* who makes fun of the bourgeois. In and through him, Flaubert and his friends could satisfy both their idealistic aspirations and their pointed sense of satire and farce."[16] *Le Garçon* was a kind of roundhouse, Rabelaisian Robert Macaire from whom the performer, as a part of his role, would take a (self-)critical distance. In the words of Flaubert's niece, Caroline, the *Garçon* "was a sort of modern Gargantua, of Homeric exploits, in the skin of a travelling salesman. The *Garçon* had a peculiar, noisy laugh which was a sort of rallying cry among initiates."[17] While the *Garçon* was not a purely nihilistic figure, he did have a sinister and even quasi-nihilistic side which lends partial support to Sartre's interpretation of his role.[18] His laughter could be hysterically shrill, and his excavation of the bourgeois could go beyond the limits of this social role to undermining faith in man. It might not be too far-fetched to see one analogue of *Le Garçon* in that carnival figure out of season, that image of death in *Madame Bovary,* the Blind Man. Yet, as Flaubert recognized, there was a perverted remnant of the *Garçon* in Homais, the deadly adversary of the Blind Man: "The ridiculous char-

16. *Flaubert Correspondance* (Paris: Gallimard, 1973), 852.
17. Quoted by Albert Thibaudet, *Gustave Flaubert* [1922] (Paris: Gallimard, 1935), 20.
18. *L'Idiot de la famille* II, *passim.*

acter in my novel is a Voltairian, a materialist philosopher (like the *Garçon!*)" [December 31, 1856]. The linkage between the *Garçon* and Homais in this letter is somewhat suspect, however, since the letter is written to convince a Bonapartist editor (Edmond Pagnerre) of Flaubert's innocence of the charges levelled at him during the trial. Still the *Garçon* does live in Homais in the restricted but often uproarious form of unself-conscious self-parody. More generally, the *Garçon* might be described as a "double inscription" or dual rendition of bourgeois stupidity in the largest sense—one both trading in the object of scorn and subjecting it to grotesque ridicule.

Another interesting fact from Flaubert's youth is his attendance at Legrain's marionette theater at the fair of Rouen—and one of his greatest pleasures as an adult was when Legrain publicly recognized him in the audience. Flaubert first saw the story of Saint Anthony in Legrain's marionette version of it. The more outlandish forms of the carnivalesque, transformed into a proliferating pageantry of beliefs, heresies, and temptations, may have been one element that shocked his friends, Maxime Du Camp and Louis Bouilhet, in the first and most unbridled version of *The Temptation of Saint Anthony*—a characteristic that did not entirely disappear from its more disciplined versions. And *Bouvard and Pécuchet* has aspects of marionette theater in the bizarre and sometimes slapstick spectacle of minimally characterized, stock figures who are differentiated by a plethora of fragile and disorienting surface distinctions. Bouvard and Pécuchet seem like a doubling of *Le Garçon* in a modernized form of puppet or shadow theater.

Flaubert's early letters are often written with a burlesque and scatalogical sense of excess that caused the expurgation of certain of them. His later letters do not abandon this mode altogether, but they do moderate it somewhat. A letter to Louis Bouilhet, written during the composition of *Madame Bovary,* is especially compelling in its use of a Rabelaisian style and orthography. It is dated the day after Christmas, 1852, and signed Flaubertus Bourgeoisphobus.

Par affinité d'esperits animaulx et secrète coniunction d'humeurs absconses, ie me suys treuvé estre ceste septmaine hal-

lebrené de mesme fascherie, a la teste aussy, au dedans, voyre;
pour ce que toutes sortes grouillantes de papulles, acmyes,
phurunques et carbons (allégories innombrables et méta-
phores incongrues, ie veux dire) tousiours poussayent emmy
mes phrases, contaminant par leur luxuriance intempestive, la
nice contexture d'icelles; ou mieux, comme il advint à Lucius
Cornelius Sylla, dictateur romain, des poulx et vermine qui
issoyent de son derme a si grand foyson que quant et quant
qu'il en escharbouylloit, plus en venoyt, et estoyt proprement
comme ung pourceau et verrat leperoseux, tousiours engen-
drant corruption de soy-meme, et si en mourut finalement.

Through an affinity of animal spirits and a secret conjunction
of hidden humors, this week I found myself to be exhausted
by the same annoyances in the head and, indeed, internally as
well; so that all sorts of swarming papulas, acnes, furuncles
and carbuncles (I mean innumerable allegories and incongruous metaphors) grew up among my sentences, contaminat-
ing by their unseasonable luxuriance the latter's nice contexture; or better, as it befell Lucius Cornelius Sylla, the Roman
dictator, by the effect of lice and vermin which issued from
his skin in such a great plenty that, as soon as he squashed
them, more would come, and he was like a proper porker and
a leprous boar, always engendering corruption from himself,
and in the end died of it. [This translation is intended only to
give some sense of the meaning of the passage. It does not
render Flaubert's astounding ability to capture Rabelais style
and word-play.]

Mikhail Bakhtin, in his study of Rabelais, does not discuss the
role of carnivalesque elements in Flaubert's novels or in more
modern writers in general. He does indicate that modern literature is perhaps the privileged repository of modern carnivalesque tendencies which have nonetheless been reduced in force
and form when compared with Renaissance manifestations, in
part because of the separation of the modern carnivalesque
from prominent public institutions such as carnival itself. Bakhtin's study of Dostoevsky nonetheless reveals the possibly re-
vitalizing role of carnivalesque features in modern literature,
and his work has helped to sensitize scholars to expressions of
the carnivalesque in more out-of-the-way or relatively sub-

merged aspects of modern culture.[19] Bakhtin himself provides a note on the early letters of Flaubert which is worth quoting:

> An important role is usually played by the unpublicized spheres during the juvenile period of an author's development, when they prepare his creative originality (which is always related to a certain destruction of the prevailing world picture and to its revision at least in part). See, for instance, the role of these spheres of speech during the youth of Flaubert. In general, the letters of Flaubert and of his friends (during all periods of his life) offer rich material for the study of phenomena discussed here (familiar forms of speech, indecencies, friendly abuse, and aimless comic forms). See especially the letters of Poittevin to Flaubert and of Flaubert to Feydeau.[20]

Actually the appeals to the carnivalesque in Flaubert's letters go beyond the references indicated by Bakhtin, and they at times provide some insight into his novelistic practice. In excusing to Louise Colet his tendency to speak more of Shakespeare than of their relationship, Flaubert unguardedly declares: "I have tasted more than others the pleasures of the family, and as much as a man of my age the joys of the senses, more than many those of love; well none of these has given me bliss [*jouissance*] approaching that afforded me by a few illustrious dead whom I read, and whose works I contemplate" (October 3, 1846).

Those whose works he was reading and rereading during the composition of *Madame Bovary* included—aside from Shakespeare—Cervantes, Rabelais, Voltaire (notably *Candide*), Petronius, and Apuleius. We have seen how, in a letter of September 4, 1852, he looked forward to the rebirth of books such as the *Satyricon* and *The Golden Ass*, Menippean satires informed by a carnivalesque spirit. And he defended the "lung power" of Hugo as a force that would give his work lasting value. He also

---

19. See, for example, Victor Turner, "Frame, Flow and Reflection: Ritual and Drama as Public Liminality" in *Performance in Postmodern Culture*, ed. Michel Benamou and Charles Caramello (Madison, Wis.: Coda Press, 1977), 33–55.
20. Mikhail Bakhtin, *Rabelais and His World*, 422 n.

tells us what he appreciates in Cervantes—not pure art as the "derealization" of the real but the interaction between the real and the imaginary: "What is prodigious in *Don Quixote* is the absence of art and that perpetual fusion of illusion and reality that make it such a comic and poetic book" (November 22, 1852). And he sounds a call for the renewal of the "robust outrages" of Rabelais:

> I am furiously rereading Rabelais, and I feel as if I am reading him for the first time. He is the great fountain of French letters. Our strongest writers draw from him by the cupfull. We must return to his spirit—to robust outrages. Literature, like society, needs a curry-comb to fell the pests that devour it. In the midst of all the weaknesses of morality and spirit—since we all waver like exhausted people and there is in the atmosphere of our hearts a thick fog that prevents us from discerning straight lines—let us love the true with the enthusiasm one has for the fantastic and, in the measure that others lower themselves, we shall rise. [November 22, 1852]

The elitist tinge of this declaration is tempered by the feeling that all men share in a common lot. And while the dream was for Flaubert always the pinnacle of true art, the reading and rereading of the classics were not mere pretexts for day-dreaming in the sense of absenting oneself from reality. They were ways of keeping in touch with those works of quality and robust power Flaubert felt he could never equal but whose example would provide him with worthy objects of emulation in the face of temptations toward mediocrity. The directions in which Flaubert's artistic practice took this idea were quite different from those espoused by Matthew Arnold, but it is nonetheless important to note the similarity of concern motivating two exponents of "high culture" who are often seen as worlds apart. "Modernism" in Flaubert came bound up with a deep respect for the classics, a conviction that they alone merited intimate study, and a belief that modern art would have to seek different paths in part because it could not equal them. Their time had passed, and the difficulty was to take leave of them in the attempt to find a way in modern times to produce significant art.

Leave-taking did not, however, imply the irrelevance of, or a total rupture with, the past. To some extent, the past might furnish an idea of what was ˙missing but necessary in the present. In referring to figures of the past who might answer to needs of the present, Flaubert looked not for a Christ but for an Aristophanes of art:

> Ah! What's missing in modern society is not a Christ, nor a Washington, nor a Socrates, nor even a Voltaire; it's an Aristophanes. But he would be stoned by the public. And then what's the use of all that, always to reason and to blab. Let us paint, paint without making up theories, without concerning ourselves with the composition of colors or with the dimension of our canvases, or with the duration of our works. [December 16 or 17, 1852]

Yet, of course, Flaubert did attempt to theorize in his letters, and his theorizing at times departed from the ideal of pure art. Flaubert was, however, aware of the muted or toned-down nature of the carnivalesque elements in his own work, and this recognition blended with the feeling that he could not attain the heights of past masters. "My readings of Rabelais mix with my social bile and there forms a need for flow [*flux*] to which I can give no outlet and which even bothers me, for my Bovary is tied with a cord—laced, corseted, and strung to the point of strangulation" (January 29–30, 1853).

It is significant that the need for "flow" is seen as coming from a mixture of "social bile" and the reading of Rabelais, thereby intimating the socially critical potential of the carnivalesque in modern life. In a letter five years earlier, Flaubert put the point in a more personal way:

> For me the sad grotesque has an unheard-of charm. It corresponds to the intimate needs of my buffoonishly bitter nature. It does not make me laugh but dream at length [*rêver longuement*]. I take hold of it wherever it is to be found, and I, like everyone, carry it in me: that's why I love to analyze myself. It's a form of study that amuses me. What prevents me from taking myself seriously, although I have a rather grave spirit, is that I find myself very ridiculous—not with that relative ridiculousness which is the theatrical comic but with that ri-

diculousness intrinsic to human life itself and that springs from the simplest action or from the most ordinary gesture. For example, never do I shave without laughing, so stupid [*bête*] does it seem to me. All that is very difficult to explain and must be felt. [August 21–22, 1846]

The notorious comment about shaving might be interpreted in Sartrean fashion as evidence of Flaubert's tendency to detach actions from goals that give them purposive meaning and thereby to dehumanize them. But this interpretation, while not altogether off the mark, is extremely limited. It is important that Flaubert's comment comes in the context of the muted carnivalesque where ordinary human activities become intrinsically ridiculous or sadly grotesque when they are seen differently or experienced as laughably stupid in a noninvidious comic spirit. This spirit need not be understood solely as evidence of neurosis, pathological passivity, or "pithiatism." It is to some significant extent a specific variant of the comic having distinctive affinities with automatic gestures that become strange once they are deautomatized—a view put forth by Henri Bergson and the Russian formalists (among others). As Albert Thibaudet writes in this regard:

> Life appears comic to Flaubert only because he sees it immediately under the aspect of automatism. Shaving is stupid and comic only because it is a daily, mechanical action. But he knows it, while everything that is exactly foreseeable in the human individual becomes comic to the extent that he who says or does it is ignorant of the fact that it is foreseen. *The Dictionary of Received Ideas,* elaborated by Flaubert with so much joy, is the dictionary of clichés that a bourgeois would necessarily put forth in given situations. *Madame Bovary* like *Don Quixote* consists in incorporating this automatism of life in a work of art. Emma Bovary or Homais, Don Quixote or Sancho, are just that: the grotesque or the sad ridiculousness which makes one dream, which makes one think.[21]

The "aesthetic" perception of a simple act like that of shaving brings together an ordinary or "symptomatic" activity and

21. *Gustave Flaubert,* 80.

one that may take on uncanny dimensions that are grotesque enough to induce dream. It is this peculiar intersection of the ordinary and the disconcerting that is especially troublesome in the art of Flaubert, for it points to the possibilities and limits of criticism and to the manner in which the pure opposition between practical action and receptivity does not cover all significant problems. This certainly does not emasculate criticism, but it does pose a barrier to a view that would found itself on unproblematic oppositions and the apocalyptic hope for total transformation of the given. For, on the most banal level of daily demands, the act of letting one's beard grow might appear as sadly grotesque as that of shaving it off, particularly in certain contexts.

It may be remarked that in one of his fullest plans for the preface to his *Dictionary of Received Ideas,* Flaubert described it in strikingly carnivalesque terms:

Have you noticed that I'm becoming a moralist? Is it a sign of old age? But I am certainly turning toward high comedy. Sometimes I have an itch to lash out at my fellow humans, and some day I will, ten years from now, in a long novel with wide range. Meanwhile an old idea has come back to me—that of my *Dictionary of Received Ideas* (do you know what it is?). The preface, especially, greatly excites me, and in the way I conceive it (it would be a book in itself) no law could touch me although I would attack everything. It would be the historical glorification of everything generally approved. I would demonstrate that majorities have always been right, minorities always wrong. I would immolate the great men on the altars of fools, deliver the martyrs to the executioners—and that in a style pushed to the extreme, with all possible fireworks. For example, I would show that in literature, mediocrity, being within the reach of everyone, is alone legitimate, and that consequently every kind of originality must be denounced as dangerous, ridiculous, etc. I would declare that this apologia for human vulgarity in all its aspects—and it would be raucous and ironic from beginning to end, full of quotations, proofs (which would prove the opposite), frightening texts (easily found)—was aimed at doing away, once and for all, with all eccentricities, whatever they might be. That would lead to the modern democratic idea of equality, using Fourier's remark that "great men won't be needed"; and it is for this purpose, I would say, that the book is written. It would include, in alphabetical order and covering all possible subjects, "everything one should say if one is to be considered a decent and likeable member of society". . . .

I think that as a whole it would deliver a strong punch. There would not be a single word invented by me in the book. If properly done, anyone who read it would never dare open his mouth again, for fear of spontaneously uttering one of its pronouncements. Furthermore, certain items could be gone into in quite splendid detail, for example, MAN, WOMAN, FRIEND, POLITICS, MORES, JUDGE. And a concisely written list of types could be included, to show not only what one could *say*, but what one should *seem to be*. [December 16 or 17, 1851]

The *Dictionary of Received Ideas* that Flaubert finally produced is a heteroclite amalgam of definitions not all of which are wrong or totally inept but all of which are—or are suited for conventional acceptance as—commonplaces. The *Dictionary* was to be supplemented by a *sottisier* in which Flaubert gathered quotations he hoped to make familiar from writers who were taken as authorities in various fields. The *sottisier* was dedicated not to the truly great, although even they might be caught napping, but to those accepted as great at a given time—the *demi-nantis* of the spirit who serve as guides to a larger public. Their pronouncements had the stupid or self-cancelling dormitive virtues characteristic of the authors consulted by Bouvard and Pécuchet in their mock-heroic quest for absolute knowledge and *phronesis* (practical wisdom). The *Dictionary* and the *sottisier* may have been intended as the compendium of raw materials that Bouvard and Pécuchet, after the failure of their attempt to live the messages conveyed in them, were to end their days copying—in a return to their origins or a grotesque creation myth that is an apparent reflection on the activity of their "creator." Indeed both the *Dictionary* and the *sottisier* raise the question of the relations among cliché, stupidity, the carnivalesque, and art in Flaubert himself.

The problem of cliché and its relation to stupidity represents one area in which the projects of pure art and carnivalization intersect in a manner having significant implications for Flaubert's actual practice in writing. The cliché or *idée reçue* is a social definition of reality that may attain the status of a secularized ritual object. Communication in the form of an exchange of clichés is a mainstay of collective life essential to civility and perhaps to social solidarity. Indeed the cliché is a limiting case of the problem of language use in general, for it raises the question of the relation between the given or the traditional and its critical reworking. And it may evoke more uncanny situations wherein the rapport between tradition and criticism becomes difficult to decipher.

When clichés are hollow or devoid of meaning, conversation that trades in them epitomizes the banality and stupidity of everyday life. Yet when the cliché is a sacred formula, its use may be rare and awe-inspiring; it is reserved for the supremely special moments in the rhythm of social life. The totemic emblem as described by Emile Durkheim might be seen as a hallowed cliché in this sense:

> That an emblem is useful as a rallying-center for any sort of group is superfluous to point out. By expressing the social unity in a material form, it makes this more obvious to all, and for that very reason the use of emblematic symbols must have spread quickly once thought of. But more than that, this idea should spontaneously arise out of the conditions of common life; for the emblem is not merely a convenient process for clarifying the sentiment society has of itself; it also serves to create this sentiment; it is one of its constituent elements.
>
> In fact, if left to themselves, individual consciousnesses are closed to each other; they can communicate only by means of signs which express their internal states. If the communication established between them is to become a real communion, that is to say, a fusion of all particular sentiments into one common sentiment, the signs expressing them must themselves be fused into one simple and unique resultant. It is the appearance of this that informs individuals that they are in harmony and makes them conscious of their moral unity. It is by uttering the same cry, pronouncing the same word, or

performing the same gesture in regard to the same object that they become and feel themselves to be in unison.[22]

When a society is faced with a *manque de base théologique,* the hallowed becomes hollow, and cliché is converted into the code words or common currency of mass communication. Then the question is whether cliché itself provides some oblique mode of access to the sacred, perhaps through the narrow gate of stupidity. Insofar as language is crystallized into secular set pieces, the writer must come to terms with it. The obvious but potentially staggering problem is how to do so. In Flaubert, the cliché emblematizes the more general problem of writing as a mode of "double inscription" involving variable forms of proximity and distance in relation to the given. Proximity required the use of the given, perhaps empathy with it. Distance could be achieved through mention of the given, notably in ironic and parodic registers. Through complex modulations of proximity and distance that remain to be investigated, Flaubert could process or recycle the clichés of ordinary discourse and of literary writing.

The type of cliché from which Flaubert as narrator and as writer tried to take maximal distance was that of ordinary bourgeois stupidity. When this sort of cliché is employed in "objective" narration in *Madame Bovary,* it is often (but not invariably) italicized. The italic functions as an apparent alienation-effect to show that the narrator is not simply using the word or expression in his own voice but rather citing from another source. (As Stephen Ullmann remarks: "Italics play here the same role on the written page as intonation would in the spoken language, and we have . . . noted the close connection between intonation and the free indirect style.")[23] When the cliché appears in the mouth of a character, it may be set in a direct quotation for which the narrator as objective reporter has even less responsibility. It is noteworthy that Homais is never presented "from the inside" but only through objective

22. *The Elementary Forms of the Religious Life* [1912] (New York: Free Press of Glencoe, 1965), 262.
23. *Style in the French Novel* (New York: Barnes & Noble, 1964), 109.

description, quotation of dialogue, and rare free indirect style where the ironic effects are rather blatant. In an earlier version of the novel, Flaubert considered concluding with an "insider's" portrait of Homais, but he tellingly decided to exclude it. In the version he published, the narrator's relation to Homais approaches the extreme of total ironic distance.

Yet distance can never be "total" enough, and there is always some taint of complicity or contamination when the narrator transmits the words or reactions of another—notably in the form of free indirect style. And it is always possible—given the strength of stupidity itself—that irony or parody will be misread and simply taken straight. Even Homais could conceivably be taken seriously as a model in life. Indeed, while Homais is never treated empathetically, there are signs that the relation of the narrator to him involves elements of self-parody and self-directed irony. Homais is, after all, more intelligent in his technocratic and pompous way than those around him. He is, moreover, the only writer in the novel. After the *First Sentimental Education,* Flaubert never directly presented an alter ego in the person of a writer as character in quest of pure art, perhaps because that fragile ideal would, in its fully exposed incarnation, be excessively open to the test of irony. But insofar as *Madame Bovary* is in some indirect and residual manner a *Kunstlerroman,* it is in part because of Homais. Indeed the partially self-parodic and ironic analogues of pure art in the novel are multiple. And Homais' technical, inflated use of language divorced from the utilitarian or pragmatic needs of everyday life itself bears some analogy to the role of language in pure art.

In fact, one quixotic path to pure art or the book about nothing would be the book composed entirely of clichés cut off from referents in reality and ironically distanced from the "voice" or views of the author. Here irony would be at its nihilistic and transcendental extreme in giving the author (narrator?) the position of a hidden God playing a cosmic joke on characters and readers alike. He would simply gather from social life or from books bouquets of petrified stupidity and report them with detached impassivity, thus giving the reader no clue as to how to react to them. This dream did entice Flaubert, and he approached it at times in a work such as

Bouvard and Pécuchet. But even in that limiting experiment, the two *cloportes* acquire absurdly endearing qualities, and their achievement of the ability to recognize stupidity while no longer tolerating it is but one indication of their complicity with their "creator."

Thus maximal distance through ironic and parodic effects is sought in relation to the clichés of bourgeois stupidity, even though the quest—in some sense identical with the quest for pure art itself—is an impossible one. And one must recall that bourgeois stupidity covers a great deal of territory in Flaubert, including the discourses of political power, conventional religion, family life, and seduction. (It is almost like an oil slick that coats everything in its path.) Narrative distance is also marked but perhaps less extreme with reference to the clichés of romantic love. Indeed two analogues of the quest for pure art as an impossible absolute are Emma Bovary's quest for romantic bliss and Charles's idolatry of Emma. Emma's quest is hopelessly compromised (but perhaps not totally annihilated) by the vulgarity of the objects that are imbued with her imaginings. But Charles's devotion to Emma, especially after he discovers the love letters from Léon and Rodolphe which divorce his ideal of Emma as fully as possible from reality, is a "purer" form of dedication bearing the closest of resemblances to Flaubert's own paradoxical dream. To say this, however, is also to imply that the dream of purity or the quest for an absolute is always threatened by ironic deflation. The nature of that irony in its relation to pathos and empathy is the variable issue.

For irony in Flaubert is not always of a nihilistic or transcendentally distanced variety—and it can in any case only approximate that extreme. As Flaubert himself put it: "Irony takes nothing from the pathetic; on the contrary it increases it" (October 9, 1852). Contemporary views of irony which, it is true, owe a great deal to Flaubert, at times stress its negative and equivocally self-serving sides. But in Flaubert there are essential modulations of irony bound up with pathos and empathy, and they serve to cast an uncommon light on certain forms of stupidity.

Flaubert's most hostile and negative irony is clearly directed against complacent bourgeois stupidity, although even here the author-narrator-writer is not free of all complicity in the object of scorn. The bourgeois not only traded in cliché; he believed he was actually saying something meaningful in "communicating" or communing in the hollow ritual of exchanging received ideas. The *Comices agricoles* or agricultural fair scene in *Madame Bovary* is a telling instance of Flaubert's treatment of clichés that are the mainstay of stereotypical modes of discourse. The clichés of romantic love (Emma's), of manipulative seduction (Rodolphe's), and of flatulently seductive political rhetoric (the speakers' at the fair) are not only cited; they are actively set against one another in a self-destructive crossfire or potlatch through which the language of cliché is reduced through static interference to noise and ultimately to empty silence.

There are, however, other modes of stupidity and cliché in Flaubert, and they have a different kind of relation to irony, for irony does manage to increase their pathos. And silence or inarticulateness itself may take on more positive qualities in the process. Stupidity here exists both below and above the commonplace plateau of bourgeois complacency—and there is an important sense in which the two manifestations of marginality meet in Flaubert's art. Indeed, in a rather subtle fashion, the very understanding of great art in Flaubert aligns it with the position of the oppressed or victimized.

Beneath ordinary bourgeois stupidity is the plight of the inarticulate victim or, more generally, the person at a loss for words who may be pathetic or ridiculous but who is also awe-inspiring and worthy of respect. Here the irony of the narrator is not absent; but it has a function not identifiable with subjective transcendence or infinitely narcissistic play. Rather irony heightens pathos as very mixed feelings are evoked.

To some extent, Charles Bovary and Catherine Leroux in *Madame Bovary* may be seen in this light. But perhaps the most striking example is to be found in *Un Coeur simple*. This story is based on a skillful inversion of the normal expectations concerning the way irony functions. Normally, the first sense or reading is supposed to be literal or straight and the second, ironic. In the standard formulation of the nature of ironic statement, one says one thing and means another. In *Un Coeur simple*, the first or obvious meaning is ironic. For irony is blatantly on the surface in the story of Félicité, the old servant who, after multiple disappointments, has her dead parrot stuffed and fetishistically worships it, identifying the dilapidated bird with the paraclete and in some sense sacralizing the death of language as the parrot-talk of cliché. Yet the arresting turn in the story is its ability to supplement inexpungeable irony with genuine pathos and feeling. Félicité emerges as a truly moving figure who leaves the reader with feelings he or she would prefer to leave mixed. Indeed Flaubert himself went so far as to assert that his "récit d'une vie obscure" was "in no way ironic as you may suppose, but on the contrary very serious and very sad" (June 19, 1876).[24]

The penultimate scene in *A Sentimental Education* involves, I think, similar processes. As Frédéric returns to meet an aging Madame Arnoux, his clichéd words of love are a memorial to the past that seem entirely divorced from their contemporary setting or real "referents." They are like secular ritual objects having no practical meaning—verbal blazons unhitched from reality.[25] Yet this impression is not the only one conveyed in the passage. The entire meeting is permeated by the suspicion that Madame Arnoux, the "fetishized" object of Frédéric's fixation, has finally come to offer herself to him and thus to fall from the pedestal of purity that elevated her above a society of gen-

24. Philip Spencer writes: "It is as though Flaubert, after his personal trials, had transcended the harsh conception of *Bouvard and Pécuchet* and granted that a humble life of sacrifice and duty, however innocent of critical intelligence, possessed an intrinsic beauty and therefore an intrinsic meaning. To describe the accident that befell Félicité on the Honfleur road, Flaubert harked back, as Gérard-Gailly has shown, to the first incident of his illness outside Bourg-Achard [the fit at Pont l'Evêque]. The procedure is important, for it involves a parallel between Flaubert and Félicité, if not some degree of identification, and implies that if he could discover a pathetic but significant beauty in the life of the old servant, he also accepted the significance of his own suffering. It is a hint rather than an indication—a hint that Flaubert was not confining value to art but extending it to life, which for so long had seemed a "foolish joke." The accident outside Bourg-Achard and the years of tormented sensitivity from which there was no escape might after all have an unsuspected worth; and Flaubert was hovering on the brink of that exacting and courageous belief." *Flaubert* (London: Faber & Faber, 1951), 222–23.

25. This interpretation is cogently developed by Jonathan Culler, *Flaubert: The Uses of Uncertainty* (Ithaca: Cornell University Press, 1974), 224–28. Culler's interpretation of cliché, irony, and stupidity in Flaubert may in general be compared and contrasted with the one I put forth.

eralized prostitution and profanation. Yet Frédéric's own motives for shying away from physical intimacy are equivocal: he
wants to preserve his ideal if only in memory; the encounter
broaches both incest and imprudence; and the proferred object
is now old and ugly. (Frédéric lights a cigarette to avoid what
Rodolphe in *Madame Bovary* negates as he, a cigar between his
teeth, mends with a knife the broken bridle of a horse.) The
glimmer of light that reveals Madame Arnoux's gray hair is an
intrusion of "reality" into the scene which Frédéric receives as
if it were a blow in the chest. But the fact that these threats of
"rude awakening" do not entirely destroy the poignancy of
their meeting indicates that the mingling of memory, sentiment, reality, and cliché engages an interchange of irony and
pathos that may gain in force from its very lack of "purity"—
including the purity of negative transcendence.

There are scenes in *Madame Bovary* that approach these high
points of pathos and irony—one of them being the final encounter between Charles and Rodolphe. These scenes in general approach the nodal point at which art is not entirely exhausted by the categories of the symptomatic and the critical—
the point at which it evokes possibilities that would have a place
in any social setting—but a place whose broader significance
would certainly vary with the quality of that larger setting. At
this point art itself broaches a "higher" form of stupidity and
even a secular analogue of the sacred. This is the stupidity of
the masterpiece that is ultimately—or perhaps recurrently—
beyond interpretation in the way it approaches the inarticulateness or silence of both nature and the speechless victim. But it
may do this in a manner that does not simply revoke the power
of criticism and that may even relate it to the more comprehensive possibilities of carnivalization—possibilities which touch
upon fundamental forms of ambivalence that cannot be identified with ordinary equivocation or perceived in a spirit of invidious distinction, for they always bear upon the "self" as well
as upon the "other." Indeed the very quest for *le mot juste* in
Flaubert is itself a search for a higher-order cliché—one that
goes beyond conventional cliché in finding that sacred and perhaps mythological turn of phrase that seems just right or irre-
placeable. But the comprehensive function of art as a "higher"

stupidity was formulated in more general and powerful terms by Flaubert himself—terms, of course, that do not entirely transcend cliché:

> What seems to me the highest thing in art (and the most difficult) is not to evoke laughter or tears, or lust or anger, but to work as nature does: that is to say, to induce reverie [*faire rêver*]. And the most beautiful works have in fact this quality. They are of severe aspect and incomprehensible. As for their technique, they are immobile like cliffs, stormy like the ocean, full of foliage, greenery and murmurs like woods, sad like the desert, blue like the sky. Homer, Rabelais, Michelangelo, Shakespeare, Goethe seem to me *inexorable*. Such works are unfathomable, infinite, multifarious. Through little gaps one glimpses precipices; there is a darkness below, dizziness. [August 23, 1853]

5

Dual Style

> Anybody will tell you: "Flaubert is the author of *Madame Bo-vary*." What is then the relation between a man and his works?
> . . . We shall see that it is double: *Madame Bovary* is defeat and victory; the man who portrays himself in the defeat is not the same as the one who is required in the victory; we must understand what that means.
>
> Jean-Paul Sartre, *L'Idiot de la famille*

Flaubert's actual practice in a novel such as *Madame Bovary* may be approached in terms of a notion of dual style or double inscription. On one level, he seems to conform to ordinary social and literary conventions or departs from the expectations they create only in ways that may plausibly be perceived as standard deviations. On other levels, however, conventional norms and expectations are tested and contested in more subversive fashion, at times with a force sufficient to bring about a radical reworking of problems and possibilities. On these other levels, it might be more appropriate to speak of a multiple mode of writing or a plural style, for the effects of the novel are many and varied. One has a complex interaction of critical and more uncanny—or generalized carnivalesque—processes, notably in the form of shifting narrative perspectives. Here duality or multiplicity reemerges through modulations of proximity and distance, empathy and irony, in the relation of the narrator to characters and other objects of narration. And the question arises of the connections among effects that reinforce, criticize, and disorient conventions—as well as between these effects and Flaubert's more explicit "authorial" projects of pure art and muted carnivalization.

Madame Bovary is, as I have already intimated, in a somewhat distinctive position among Flaubert's "mature" works. For it is on the very threshold of experimental literature. In it the conventional level of social and literary expectation continues to have a very strong hold and to be operative in a form that cannot be reduced to the level of mere appearance. Its realism is more than *trompe-l'oeil,* and its world is very close to the recognizable social world of its own time (and, in certain ways, of our own time). It directly transplants elements and situations from a documentary repertoire, and it simulates the documentary—or the ways of conventional reality—in other respects. It may stylize realistic elements in given directions, but the judgment of the extent to which it does so carries with it an ineradicable subjective aspect that would be difficult to control through ordinary procedures of verification or falsification. In any case, its world resembles the ordinary social world of provincial nineteenth-century France to an extent that makes both recognition and discomfort possible. And, in larger respects, what it reveals about that world has a resonance in the problems experienced in later "postindustrial" contexts.

Similarly, there are enough elements of the traditional novel present to make a conventional reading plausible. Flaubert himself was quite aware of this problem and most often saw it in terms of the way he would be contaminated by—or the novel fall short of beauty or pure art because of—its bourgeois subject matter. (For example: "This bourgeois subject brutalizes me. I feel the effects of my Homais" [June 2, 1853].) Flaubert was visibly anxious about becoming stupid in the conventional sense because of the matter he narrated, and he feared resembling those novelists who consorted with similar subjects. Yet at least one blatant differentiating factor in *Madame Bovary* would seem to be the absence of an authoritative center of moral and cognitive judgment to serve as a reliable guide for the reader. The argument of the defense at the trial, however, is enough to show that this figure may be constructed from various bits of circumstantial evidence and projected into the novel. Flaubert's own striving for harmony and for a unity of style that would conceal more disconcerting movements in narration is effective enough to make those movements pass unnoticed on a more "naive" level of reading. And the very impersonal effect of stylistic unity may itself invite personification that presents a narrator or an author as the unifying force bringing off the harmonizing impression of flowing continuity in narration. Thus Flaubert himself seems to invite an "argument from design" in interpreting the novel. Conversely, with the prosecuting attorney, one may find a simple absence of such a narrator in order to condemn the novel's deviation from the norm. How *Madame Bovary* elicits conventionalizing (or "recuperative") readings and places them in radical jeopardy will be discussed at greater length in the chapters that follow. Both the conventional relation to ordinary literary and social expectations (conformity and deviance) and the more radical questioning of these expectations are essential for the workings of the novel.

In addition, the radical questioning of convention is itself complex in nature. There is a level on which *Madame Bovary* engages in a form of criticism that can be called ideological or political crime. Its disclosive force places in fundamental question the norms, categories, and oppositions of a social and political world, and it at least indirectly raises the issue of the need for basic transformation. The untenability of the opposition between marriage and adultery or between the sacred and the profane attests to a perception of sociocultural and political crisis that is shocking in its magnitude. Emma's behavior goes beyond conventional deviance in its threatening tendency to reveal the hollow core of the two pillars of bourgeois order: the family and property. The world in which Emma is driven to suicide and Charles is totally excavated while Homais receives the Legion of Honor does stand condemned. The very discrepancy between what norms should viably do and what they fail to do or allow to be done is an ideological and ethical scandal.

But there are also levels of the novel on which more disorienting or "unsayable" effects—especially modulations of narrative perspective or "voice" that can be jarringly vertiginous—complicate the problem of criticism and render its objects and, even more, viable alternatives to those objects rather difficult to determine. But complication cannot be identified with cancellation or simple avoidance and denial. Indeed it broaches the question of the actual and desirable roles of more uncanny effects in society and culture, including any program for major transformation. These large and even unwieldy issues help give *Madame Bovary* its liminal position in the history of the novel—a position that makes it an object of ever renewed fascination and a source of interminable commentary.

Sartre also sees in Flaubert a dual style or mode of writing which he relates to an entire series of problems. Sartre raises the question of "style" with reference to the interaction between signifying and nonsignifying dimensions of language use in Flaubert. The signifying use of language involves propositional functions, reference, and disclosure of aspects of the world in a manner linked to practice that can change the given. Its manifestation in literature would seem to be a critical realism in which art functions as a "critical mirror" of the times. The nonsignifying is a matter of indirect communication of what cannot be directly said but only shown in the way language is used. The signifying gives us "what" literature says and the nonsignifying, "how" it says it—its *"manière de dire."* The nonsignifying also bears on the question of the materiality of language, and Sartre further relates it to what Flaubert termed *l'indisable* (the unsayable). For Sartre, the relation between the signifying and the nonsignifying is further connected with the fact that Flaubert did not refer to himself as a novelist or even as a poet but wanted to attain the rigor of poetry in prose that remained prose. "'I am a writer,' he said. What should one understand by that?"[1]

An initial understanding of the fact that Flaubert referred to himself as a writer might be that the problems engaging him could not be entirely confined to a given genre such as the novel or even to fiction in contradistinction to nonfiction. These problems had to do with the use of language and its relation to the world on a very fundamental level—problems Sartre approaches in terms of the signifying and nonsignifying dimensions of language use. In "A Plea for Intellectuals," Sartre formulates in pointed fashion the reasons why Flaubert might be seen as positioned at the very crossroads of modern

1. *L'Idiot de la famille* (3 vols.) (Paris: Gallimard, 1971–72), III, 665. Further references are to volume and page number, and translations are my own.

literary problems, and his formulation in certain respects remains operative in *L'Idiot de la famille*:

> The *word* the writer uses has a much denser *materiality* than, for example, the mathematical symbol that effaces itself before the signified. One might say that it wants simultaneously to point vaguely toward the signified and to impose itself as a *presence*, drawing attention to its own density. This is why it has been possible for people to say that to name is simultaneously to present the signified and to kill it, to swallow it in the verbal mass. The word of ordinary language is simultaneously *too rich* (it overflows by far the concept by its traditional age [*son ancienneté traditionnelle*], by the ensemble of violences and ceremonies which constitutes its "memory," its "living past") and *too poor* (it is defined in relation to the ensemble of language as a fixed determination of the latter and not as a supple possibility of expressing the new). In the exact sciences, when the new arises, a word to name it is simultaneously invented by some and rapidly adopted by all. . . . [The writer] prefers to utilize a "current" word and to charge it with a new meaning which is superadded to the old: in general, one might say that the writer has vowed to utilize the *whole* of ordinary language and nothing but it, with all the misinformative characteristics that limit its range. If the writer adopts ordinary language, it is thus not only insofar as language can transmit knowledge. To write is simultaneously to possess language . . . and not to possess it to the extent that language is *other* than the writer and *other* than men. . . . Roland Barthes distinguished between *écrivants* [literal writers] and *écrivains* [literary writers]. The literal writer uses languages to transmit information. The literary writer is the custodian of ordinary language, but he goes beyond it and his material is language as nonsignifying or as misinformation. He is an artisan who produces a certain verbal object by working on the materiality of words; he takes significations as means and the nonsignifying as end. . . . If *writing* consists in communicating, the literary object appears as communication *beyond language* through the nonsignifying silence which is enclosed by words although it is produced by them.[2]

2. "Plaidoyer pour les intellectuels," *Situations VIII* (Paris: Gallimard, 1972), 433–37.

It is significant that Sartre in "A Plea for Intellectuals" applies this analysis to "the contemporary writer, the *poet* who has declared himself to be a *prose writer* and lives in the post-World War II world."[3] But it informs his analysis of Flaubert and, aside from giving a fuller idea of Sartre's understanding of Flaubert's contemporaneity, it is, in *L'Idiot de la famille,* specified to apply to the hermit of Croisset. Indeed the near identity in Sartre's analyses of Flaubert and of contemporary structuralists and poststructuralists provides some sense of what is at stake for Sartre as he comes to terms with Flaubert—a confrontation in which an "anxiety of influence" merges with an anxiety of anticipation. For Sartre's interchange with Flaubert tends to coincide with his debate with contemporary theorists to influence the course of future theory and practice.

In the case of Flaubert as in that of more contemporary theorists, Sartre is often so agitated over the possibly harmful effects of subordinating the signifying to the nonsignifying aspects of language that he devotes relatively little attention to more reciprocal modes of interaction between the two. He does at times see Flaubert as "aiming always at two goals: the coherence of an oriented discourse and the irrealization of this discourse through formal beauty, never losing sight of one or the other under the pain of falling into incoherence or pure information" (II, 1620). Yet as Sartre analyzes the interaction of the signifying and the nonsignifying in Flaubert, the relationship tends to become one-directional and to be explained in terms of the theory of the imagination that Sartre enunciated as early as *L'Imaginaire.*[4] The signifying in Flaubert is simply a means to the nonsignifying, and his realism is mere appearance that veils the activity of the pure imagination (III, 20). The goal of Flaubert's writing is pure art as the nihilating and nihilistic force that derealizes reality and language itself in favor of an impossible quest for imaginary totalization. This imaginary totalization is further identified by Sartre as Flaubert's lived experience which is neurotically passive and can be communicated only indirectly through "style." Paradoxically, Sartre is able to

3. Ibid., 432.
4. (Paris: Gallimard, 1940); Bernard Frechtman, trans., *The Psychology of the Imagination* (New York: Washington Square Press, 1966).

name the unsayable and to fixate the uncanny effects of Flaubert's writing: *l'indisable* is Flaubert's neurotic experience as a passive object of language which the adult writer takes from the child and converts into a "passivized" project or *option subie*. Thus Sartre's analysis of Flaubert's "style" ultimately joins up with the interpretation we have discussed in the last chapter, and it thereby tends to circumvent the knotty problem of the relations among the symptomatic, the critical, and the more radically disorienting features of Flaubert's writing.

Sartre's own theory of the imagination, which he sees as covering Flaubert's writing practice, itself presents the relation between the imagination and reality in dichotomous and one-dimensional terms: the imaginary nihilates the real in the impossible desire for "totalization" in the form of absence or unreality. I have already suggested that this "theory" applies at best to the most extreme and unqualified side of the quest for pure art. Indeed it is less a general theory of the imagination than a hyperbolically unilinear expression of imaginary desire which verges on hysterical withdrawal and paranoid schizophrenia. In any event, it neglects the productive and reproductive interaction between the imagination and reality as well as the possible problematization of the boundary between the imaginary and the real—what Flaubert found in Cervantes and what Freud discussed as the "uncanny." In Sartre's theory, one has an arrested dialectic of the real and the imaginary and little room for a readjustment of the boundaries between the two. There is only the passage from the one to the other in an impossible quest for total purity or transcendence that is tantamount to total absence. Given this "theory," it is not surprising that Sartre's account tends to stress the life of the author and to employ the writings as symptomatic evidence of authorial experience most often construed as "neurotic": "The Flaubertian revolution comes from the fact that this writer, mistrusting language from childhood, begins, in contrast to the classics, to pose the principle of the non-communicability of lived experience [*le vécu*]" (II, 1986). Whether Sartre's speculation applies to the author or not, it tends to lose sight of the writer and of the text in the use of language that can harbor the project of imaginary "derealization" only as one tendency—

more precisely as an impossible quest for a transcendental absolute—in a complex and internally contestatory field of forces. The problem here is not whether one has an either/or choice between existential man masterfully speaking language and structural man passively being spoken by language. It is rather that of the actual and desirable relations between active and receptive roles in the relation of speaker or writer to language. As Sartre himself intimates, writing or speaking as uses of language are not constitutive of pure theory in contrast to pure practice—a vision that easily lends itself to a hypostatized and simplistic opposition between the study and the streets. The comprehensive question is that of the ways in which the use of language as a material and a signifying practice is articulated with reference to related activities. This question is the larger frame for discourse analysis.

Here a further feature of Sartre's approach may be noted. Even on the level of larger units of discourse analysis, Sartre's treatment of narration in Flaubert focuses almost exclusively on impersonal or impassive narration in which Sartre finds a *"principe de survol"* coinciding with the desire for imaginary transcendence. He does not treat the larger narrative context in which impersonal narration takes place. It is quite remarkable that Sartre says nothing about Flaubert's so-called "free indirect style" which for other commentators was Flaubert's most pronounced stylistic contribution to the history of the novel.

Flaubert's use of the "free indirect style" is a telling instance of the intricate fashion in which Sartre's conception of Flaubert as an antihuman ideologist and stylist of pure art is qualified, indeed contested, by a significant set of factors that Sartre does relatively little to elucidate. Perhaps the most insistent of these factors is the way art always harbors some "complicity" with traditional or situational "givens," may effect a critical disclosure or imaginative reworking of them, and possibly engages in dizzying movements of radical ambivalence that, while not simply denying the importance of tradition and its critique, do stimulate those dreamlike overtures that Flaubert saw as the exploding stars or black holes of the aesthetic process.

6

Narrative Practice and Free Indirect Style

> Style. 1. An instrument used by the ancients in writing on waxed tables. 2. Anything resembling the ancient style in shape or use; as: *a* A pen. *b* A graver. *c* An etching needle. *d.* A phonograph needle. *e* The pin, or gnomon, of a dial. *f Surg.* A stylet; probe. 3. Mode of expressing thought in language; esp., such use of language as exhibits the spirit and personality of an artist; characteristic mode of expression; as, a *terse* style.
>
> Stylite. One of a class of ascetics who lived on tops of pillars.
> *Webster's New Collegiate Dictionary*

In this chapter we shall turn from general features of Flaubert's "dual style" to specific problems in his mode of narration. Flaubert's narrative practice in *Madame Bovary* combines extended passages of "objective" or "impassive" description, very brief interludes of quoted dialogue or interior monologue, and significant use of so-called "free indirect style." The rhythm of his narration, as well as the interplay between unifying and disseminating forces in it, is a function of the way these narrative procedures are woven together. When shifts in narrative procedure are drastic enough, the text threatens to become unstitched as more uncanny or unsettlingly carnivalesque forces come into play. Perhaps the most puzzling dimension of Flaubert's narrative practice is the so-called "free indirect style" whose significance we have already encountered.

Free indirect style has the peculiarity of being very easy to recognize but rather difficult to analyze. Commentators will invariably agree on the selection of passages in which it is present, but they will vary significantly in their explanations of it. The free indirect style should not be isolated from Flaubert's narrative practice in general; it should be seen in the larger context of shifting narrative perspectives that typifies his approach to narration. For free indirect style applies *within* a passage the modulation of perspectives or "voice" that the combination of objective narration, quoted dialogue, interior monologue, and free indirect style itself effects among passages in the comprehensive narrative movement. And the issue of narrative perspective itself relates to the even more general problem of the nature and implications of the interaction between unifying and disseminating forces in the novel as a whole. Indeed the question of "style" and of narrative practice cannot be separated from the larger sociocultural and political issues we have already raised. One of the preoccupations at Flaubert's trial, it may be recalled, was whether there was a unified and reliable center of judgment in the novel, as well as the consequences of its presence or absence.

The trial of course did not investigate the problem of the so-called free indirect style. And Flaubert himself does not use the term *style indirect libre*. In fact he says relatively little in his letters that bears directly on the concept. By contrast, he expatiates on the in's and out's of impersonal or impassive narration, and at times he discusses the seemingly opposed possibility of losing himself entirely in what he is writing. It should not be surprising that the extremes of total, transcendental objectivity and of mystical immanence meet. Indeed for Flaubert the height of impersonality eliminated the particular forms of subjectivity, as did complete merger of the narrating self with the object of narration. "You are disseminated in all. Your personages live and instead of an eternal declamatory personality, which cannot even be clearly constituted given the lack of precise details through the travesties which disguise it, one will see human crowds in your works" (March 27, 1852).

The problem, however, is whether the distribution of the narrative self is in practice more complex than is indicated in the unmediated extremes of impassive transcendence and mystical pantheism. A number of commentators have underemphasized the complexities of narration in Flaubert and stressed instead the role of the narrator as impersonal or hidden God, present everywhere and visible nowhere—although they have also noted the presence of more mystical or pantheistic ideas in the letters. Anthony Thorlby's formulation agrees in many respects with that of Sartre. He argues that the ideal of impersonal narration sacrificed "the values of personality to an impersonal ideal of the truth, an ideal which virtually denied the value of existence altogether, while maintaining the validity of a kind of absolute knowledge."[1] This view corresponds to Sartre's analysis of the quest for pure art through the principle of *"survol"* whereby the narrator-author, in a stable ironic position, is a transcendental ego having a nihilating relation to characters and to deceptively realistic details. The superior joke played by this narrator would be on the puppetlike characters and on demoralized readers, for the narrator would be securely *hors jeu*. The narrator would keep his hidden hands clean (or, in the more equivocal phrase of James Joyce, be off

1. *Gustave Flaubert and the Art of Realism* (London: Bowes & Bowes, 1956), 138. For many recent commentators, the "absolute knowledge" sought by Flaubert merged with his quest for pure art. The resultant knowledge was a mode of absolute negativity, the realism purely linguistic, and the conception of language self-referential. Along this interpretive path commentaries related to non-Sartrean perspectives can converge with the conclusions of Sartre's *Idiot* or assimilate aspects of it in a seemingly unproblematic way. This tendency at times appears in Jonathan Culler's *Flaubert: The Uses of Uncertainty* (Ithaca: Cornell University Press, 1974). It also surfaces in Naomi Schor's "Pour Une Thématique Restreinte: Ecriture, parole et différence dans Madame Bovary," *Littérature* (May, 1976), 30–42. For Schor, the various structural oppositions employed and undermined in *Madame Bovary* are "as if transcended [*dépassées*] by Flaubert's radical distrust of language in general" (p. 43). Leo Bersani, in *Balzac to Beckett* (New York: Oxford University Press, 1970), presents *Madame Bovary* as the realization of Flaubert's quest for pure art as purely autotelic language: "Flaubert's novels are most interestingly about . . . the arbitrary, insignificant, inexpressive nature of language. . . . Fundamentally, language refers to nothing beyond its own impersonal (and discouraging) virtuosity" (p. 144). The problem of language is of course at issue in *Madame Bovary* in ways these studies often illuminate brilliantly. And their specific discussions of Flaubert's writing frequently place in question an overly facile dichotomy between the "positive" and "negative" dimensions of language use, thereby intimating that the process of self-contestation in Flaubert's novels may be a direct or indirect force for renewal. The tendency to converge with Sartre's conclusions, however, threatens to obviate the need for a more complex investigation of the manner in which this process engages broader sociocultural issues.

somewhere paring his fingernails). The pantheistic tendencies expressed in Flaubert's letters might from this perspective be put down to the "double binds" that were brought about by pathological passivity or "pithiatism." The narrator would never be present in his own human voice but would oscillate between a securely ironic impersonality and a mystical or pantheistic swooning.

This view is too restricted to enable an understanding of the modulations of perspective or voice in Flaubert's narrative practice, including the workings of the "free indirect style." Given the difficulty in elucidating the latter, my own procedure will be to discuss three of the most important attempts in English to provide a theoretical account of it and then to comment critically upon them. The seminal works of Stephen Ullmann, Dorrit Cohn, and Roy Pascal[2] are especially instructive in that they tend to summarize existing scholarship on the relevant issues.

Many of Ullmann's suggestions are taken up and developed by Cohn and Pascal. Ullmann notes that, in free indirect style, the narrator does not simply report in a neutral or impersonal way that something occurred. Nor does he directly express his own subjective views or quote the words of characters. As Ullmann concisely puts it:

1. The very existence of the construction makes for variety in style. The author can choose between three different forms of

2. Stephen Ullmann, *Style in the French Novel* (New York: Barnes & Noble, 1964); Dorrit Cohn, *Transparent Minds: Narrative Modes for Presenting Consciousness in Fiction* (Princeton: Princeton University Press, 1978); Roy Pascal, *The Dual Voice: Free Indirect Speech and Its Functioning in the Nineteenth-Century European Novel* (Manchester: Manchester University Press, 1977). See also Marguerite Lips, *Le Style indirect libre* (Paris: Payot, 1926); Albert Thibaudet, *Gustave Flaubert* [1922] (Paris: Gallimard, 1935), 221–85; and especially V. N. Vološinov, *Marxism and the Philosophy of Language* [1930], trans. Ladislav Matejka and I. R. Titunik (New York: Seminar Press, 1973). Vološinov furnishes a penetrating study of the entire problem of "reported speech." He also offers an analysis and critique of the contrasting approaches to the study of language of Saussure and Karl Vossler. E. Lorck and E. Lerch were members of the Vosslerian school which was especially important in Germany in contrast to the role of the Saussurian school in the French-language context. For a discussion of the moot issue of the precise nature of the undoubtedly close relation of Vološinov to M. M. Bakhtin, see Tzvetan Todorov, *Mikhaïl Bakhtine: le principe dialogique* (Paris: Editions du Seuil, 1981).

reported speech [direct, indirect, and free indirect] and can alternate them in a number of ways.

2. Free indirect style combines the advantages of the two orthodox methods. The author is not committed to an exact reproduction of words or thoughts; yet he is able to dispense with explicit subordination [involved in phrases such as "he said that" or "he felt that"] and to retain the emotive and expressive features and the very inflexions of the spoken language.

3. Free indirect style is reported speech masquerading as narrative. It means a break in continuity and a certain shock to the reader. It is essentially an oblique construction and provides a discreet but effective vehicle for irony and ambiguity and for the description of reveries, dreams, and hallucinatory states.[3]

Ullmann remarks that the use of free indirect style was quite uncommon in the Enlightenment during which more clear-cut and analytic methods of language use were preferred. (La Fontaine, whom Flaubert greatly admired, was one noteworthy exception.) But Ullmann also notes that free indirect style is to be found in the very first French literary text on record, "The Sequence of Saint Eulalia." Departing from Ullmann's own commentary, one may perhaps add that it is both fitting and ironic that free indirect style is employed in a text with a religious subject and that the tale involves a loss of virginity or a primary form of transgression. Indeed the proper name Eulalia evokes the common noun eulalia, hence speaking in tongues and echo effects. Flaubert was always concerned with the problems of purity and transgression, and, in his relation to canonized uses of language, he put into practice a strategy of citation with effects of irony and empathy that are epitomized in the free indirect style. Flaubert's relation to cliché and to conventionalized social or literary discourse brought into play an elaborate use of echo effects with modulations of complicity and distance in the relation between the narrative self and the narrated object. The writer necessarily spoke in the tongues of given social and literary discourse, but the crucial issue was the

3. Ullmann, *Style in the French Novel,* 116.

nature of the variations he played upon them.[4] With respect to the problem of purity and transgression, one may quote from a letter written just prior to the composition of *Madame Bovary* where Flaubert enunciates three subjects:

> As for subjects, I have three, perhaps they are all the same, a thought that galls me considerably. *One*: *Une Nuit de Don Juan*, which I thought of in quarantine at Rhodes. *Two*: *Anubis*, the story of the woman who wants to be laid by the god. This is the loftiest of the three, but full of atrocious difficulties. *Three*: my Flemish novel about the young girl who dies a virgin and mystic after living with her father and mother in a small provincial town, at the end of a garden full of cabbages and fruit trees beside a stream the size of the Robec. What torments me is the kinship of idea of these three projects. In the first, insatiable love in the two forms: earthly love and mystical love. In the second, the same story, only there is fornication in it, and the earthly love is less exalted because more precise. In the third they are combined in the same person, and the one leads to the other; only my heroine dies of religious masturbation after indulging in digital masturbation. Alas! It seems to me that when one is as good as this at dissecting children yet to be born, one doesn't harden up enough to create them. My clear-cut metaphysics fills me with terrors. [November 14, 1850]

The third story was indeed "hardened up" and transformed into *Madame Bovary*. The second bears some resemblance to *Salammbô*. And Francis Steegmuller notes of the first: "Flaubert's outline for *Une Nuit de Don Juan* exists. It consists chiefly of two dialogues: between the Don and Leparello, about the Don's way of life; and between the Don and a nun with whom he spends the night in her convent, about earthly and mystical love."[5] The interest of these projects is to suggest that the issue

4. On the general problem of quotation in the novel, see Hermann Meyer, *The Poetics of Quotation in the European Novel* [1961], trans. Theodore and Yette Ziolkowski (Princeton: Princeton University Press, 1968); and Gerhard R. Kaiser, *Proust-Musil-Joyce: Zum Verhältnis von Literatur und Gesellschaft am Paradigma des Zitats* (Frankfurt a. M.: Athenaum, 1972).

5. *The Letters of Gustave Flaubert 1830–1857* (Cambridge: Harvard University Press, 1980), 131.

of narration engages problems of language use and metaphysical pathos that characterize not only limited sketches but Flaubert's entire lifework.

Flaubert's novelistic world is one wherein the clear and present danger is the systematic profanation of ideals culminating
in the addled nature of ideals themselves. This constant state of
trivialized transgression threatens to make all actions and
words either hypocritical or parodic. It deprives transgression
itself of its possible fascination, for there is no real temptation
when everything is profaned. What this world lacked is an engaging tension between commitment and transgression—the
social and personal rhythm that sets up a viable interplay
among the affirmation of norms, the allure of forbidden desire,
and the evanescent effulgence of liminal invitations or non-
fixated events of "transcendence." Indeed the ideal of pure art
was itself a fleeting image of transcendence that Flaubert was
tempted to convert into a fetish. Yet it had to be transgressed—
and nowhere more insistently and subtly than in the modulations of the "free indirect style." For the latter was in some
sense a mode of "impurity" in the complex relation of narrator
and narrated, yet one that held out some promise of recreating
a relational network more worthy of affirmation.

Dorrit Cohn centers her ambitious study around the problem
of the representation of consciousness in fiction. There are
difficulties with the terms in which Cohn articulates the problem as well as with the general idea that the very uniqueness of
fictional uses of language lies in the representation of consciousness.[6] But we shall touch upon these difficulties only as
they bear upon specific points in the analysis of the "free indirect style."

Cohn distinguishes among three modes of narration. "Psychonarration" is a consciousness-centered variant of objective
narration in which one has the author's discourse about the
mind of a character. "Quoted monologue" is Cohn's term for
the more standard notion of stream of consciousness wherein
the "mental discourse" of the character is directly rendered.
"Narrated monologue" is Cohn's suggested term to encompass

6. Cohn, *Transparent Minds*, 7.

free indirect style. Cohn's account of narrated monologue is close to Ullmann's idea of "reported speech masquerading as narrative." As Cohn puts it: "Linguistically it is the most complex of the three techniques: like psychonarration it maintains the third-person reference and [past] tense of narration, but like the quoted monologue, it reproduces verbatim the character's own mental language."[7] Thus:

> It may be most succinctly defined as the technique for rendering a character's thought in his own idiom while maintaining the third-person reference and the basic tense of narration. This definition implies that a simple transposition of grammatical person [from third to first] and tense [from past to present] will "translate" a narrated into an interior monologue. Such translation can actually be applied as a kind of litmus test to confirm the validity of a reader's apprehension that a narrative sentence belongs to a character's, rather than to a narrator's, mental domain.[8]

Cohn will also argue that the relation of the narrator to the character's "mental language," "thought," or "mental domain" will involve variable forms of irony and empathy.

Concerning Flaubert, Cohn writes:

> The decisive turning point for the narrated monologue came, of course, with Flaubert. Perceptive students of his style agree that his systematic employment of the *style indirect libre* is his most influential formal achievement. . . . Flaubert himself, when he comments on his impersonal narrative method, employs phrases that come close to pinpointing the narrated monologue itself, especially in the following passage to Georges Sand [December 15–16, 1866]: "I expressed myself badly when I told you that 'one should not write with one's personality on stage.' I believe that great Art is scientific and impersonal. One should, by an effort of the spirit, *transport oneself into the characters, not draw them to oneself.* That, at any rate, is the method." [Cohn's emphasis] Translating this kinetic image into linguistic terms would yield an exact de-

7. Ibid., 14.
8. Ibid., 100–101.

scription of the narrated monologue—as would the theological image Flaubert used elsewhere, when he referred to the *"faculté panthéiste."*[9]

Cohn notes that the possibility of an "insensible shading of narrated monologue into psychonarration is very frequent in figural [character-oriented] narrative situations." But she still tends to see this shading as a borderline phenomenon and asserts that it does not in any case typify Flaubert's novels where "the lines between the techniques are clearly marked."[10] To illustrate this point, Cohn quotes the following passage from *Madame Bovary* where the italics are inserted by Cohn to designate narrated monologue:

> Then she tried to calm down; she remembered the letter. *It had to be finished, but she didn't dare. Besides, where? How? She would be seen.*
> —No, she thought, here I'll be alright.[11]

Cohn notes that free indirect style (or "narrated monologue") generates the problem of the relation between the narrator and the narrated—notably the character's "mental language," "thought," or "mental domain." But the vacillation in the characterizations of what it is in the character that is rendered by the narrator indicates the problem in Cohn's analysis itself. The term "narrated monologue" may of course be introduced to denote the case wherein a narrator narrates in the third person the "thoughts" of a character in that character's own language or idiom. But the term then fails to cover Flaubert's practice in *style indirect libre.* In Flaubert it may be the case that the language is such that the character himself might employ it (with appropriate changes in person and tense). In other cases, however, this is either not clearly, or clearly not, the case. The very term "monologue" obscures what would seem distinctive about free indirect style: the creation of a *dialogical* relation of a complex sort between narrator and character. The narrator is both

9. Ibid., 113–14.
10. Ibid., 136.
11. Quoted, ibid., 134–35.

inside and outside the character's "mind" in a manner involving variations of irony and empathy. The use of the character's own words or types of discourse would have ironic effect only in cases where the nature of that discourse can be counted upon to "self-destruct," as in the case of Homais' pomposity or at times of Emma's romantic clichés. But the ironic effect of what Walter Benjamin saw as phosphorescent, self-exploding quotation may backfire, for it may pass unperceived by the reader. The more general point is that the language used in free indirect style has differential relations to the language typical of characters, and these differential relations are bound up with modulations of irony and empathy. Cohn notes the role of the latter but provides a definition or "litmus" of the "narrated monologue" that fails to account for them. A basic consideration would seem to be that the free indirect style is in some sense a threshold or highly ambivalent phenomenon involving various degrees of liminality in the relation of the narrator and the narrated. The intricate dialogical possibilities in this relation are obscured or obliterated when stress is placed on monologue or on the report of a character's thought or speech. (It is of course "dialogization" that Bakhtin relates to highly carnivalized uses of language.) The quote from Flaubert's letter to Georges Sand itself seems to vacillate between objective impersonality and subjective identification in attempting to describe a mode of narration whose very criterion would seem to be the ability to undercut or problematize the opposition between the objective and the subjective (or the ironic-impersonal and the empathetic-pantheistic). It is this very ability that may have uncanny effects related to an indeterminacy of narrative voice and to a possible rendition or "representation" of more unconscious and "primary" processes in language use. Indeed what Cohn would like to confine to a borderline case and to exclude from Flaubert's practice altogether would seem to be typical of the very marginal or liminal possibilities of *style indirect libre* itself. For this "style" involves a dialogue between narrator and character that assumes changing positions on the threshold between "self" and "other."

Roy Pascal's study is more limited in scope than Dorrit Cohn's, but it is in many ways more directly related to certain of the issues I have tried to raise. The studies of Pascal and Cohn were published within a year of one another, and it is useful to compare them on certain key points. Pascal's work helps to situate certain of Cohn's tendencies while it joins up with them in a number of respects. Most remarkable is a discrepancy between the theoretical observations of Pascal and the directions taken in his particular discussion (or "practical criticism") of Flaubert. Given the interest of a number of his theoretical and historical comments, however, it is worthwhile to quote Pascal at length. Indeed what is striking in his study is his apparent critical self-doubt about the very terminology used to designate the nature and workings of "free indirect style." (Cohn's selection of another term might also be seen as a sign of dissatisfaction with traditional terminology and attendant analyses.)

Pascal observes that the *style indirect libre* was first named and analyzed in 1912 by the linguist Charles Bally, a former pupil of Ferdinand de Saussure. And Bally himself initiated the attempt to relate grammatical criteria to broader discursive considerations.

> Since this . . . form has the pronouns and tenses of simple indirect speech, Bally considered its name should indicate this relationship. Further, since in distinction from simple indirect speech, it has no linking conjunctions ("that," "whether," etc.), and may often lack the introductory verb, *verbum dicendi* or *credendi* ("he said," "he thought," etc.), Bally associated the term "free" with "indirect." He noted, however, that the form has some of the distinctive features of direct speech, and gives the feeling of direct speech. While simple indirect speech tends to obliterate the characteristic personal idiom of the reported speaker, [*style indirect libre*] preserves some of its elements—the sentence form, questions and exclamations, intonation, and the personal vocabulary—just as it preserves the subjective perspective of the character. . . . Bally acknowledged that [*style indirect libre*] cannot be defined solely in grammatical terms. On grammatical grounds it often cannot be distinguished from normal authorial report, and as a result pointers like "he thought" may be required to make it clear that a statement emanates from the character and not from

the author. Frequently the reader cannot, in fact, be sure whether the statement belongs to one or the other.[12]

The last consideration in the above quote broaches the problem of a possible indeterminacy of voice in the *style indirect libre* or the way in which a use of language may play in two registers —those of the character and the narrator—with the possible modulations of irony and empathy this entails. Pascal himself stresses this possibility in his title—*Dual Voice*—and helps to situate Cohn's emphasis upon identification of narrator with character (or the narration of a character's monologue) as one end of a spectrum or sliding scale of possibilities. At least, Pascal does this in theoretical terms, although even on this level there are hesitations or equivocations in his account. For example, he disagrees with Bally's view that free indirect style is a literary in contrast with a normal or ordinary use of language, and he cites as evidence for its ordinary usage the fact that writers such as Jane Austen, who apparently do not draw from a literary heritage in their employment of it, nonetheless make such fluent and effortless use of the form. Yet he does agree with Bally's extremely rationalistic derivation of free indirect style from indirect speech by "the simple elimination of the wearisome repetition of verbal introductions like 'he said,' 'he thought,' and of repeated conjunctions—'he said that . . . , that . . . , and that . . .' etc."[13] This inference would make free indirect style derivative on purely speculative grounds which are, I think, related to the metaphysical desire (also evident in Cohn) to subordinate sharply more liminal or ambivalent forms to clear and distinct, analytically separable ones.

Pascal argues that Bally's analysis and terminology have lasting value, and he contrasts them with what he sees as the more dubious Germanic legacy of reflection on the issue. Etienne Lorck coined the term *"Erlebte Rede"* in his book (1921) of that title, and he was critical of Bally for not seeking the "spirit" behind grammar. Like another German scholar of the time—Eugen Lerch—Lorck made the direct evocation of char-

---

12. Pascal, *Dual Voice*, 9–10.
13. Ibid., 10.

acter the distinctive feature of "experienced speech." For Lorck, the style "arose in a state of intense imagination, when the writer so identifies himself with the creatures of his imagination that he 'inwardly experiences' what they experience."[14] (Thus one may further situate Dorrit Cohn's approach in the Germanic tradition, although in Cohn the focus shifts from writer or author to narrator, and the greatest possible diminution of distance between narrator and character is seen in terms of identification rather than of full identity, thereby allowing in some way for irony. One may also note that Sartre's readiness to read texts symptomatically or confessionally as authorial expressions owes much to the tradition of *Lebensphilosophie* as practiced, for example, in the work of Wilhelm Dilthey and, at times, in the early Heidegger.)

The chief reason Lorck invented the term *"erlebte Rede"* was to stress the irrational and rapturous in contrast to the informational function of language. It was thus related to philosophies of "life" and immediate "experience." Pascal demurs from a discussion of Lorck's philosophy of language and takes issue with him on "stylistic" grounds.

> In his theory, as in his analysis of texts, Lorck fails to recognize the narratorial function of the *"style indirect libre."* Almost all critics and linguists, among them Stephen Ullmann and Norman Page, have recognized that it fuses the narratorial and the subjective modes. Lorck uses a similar phrase, but in fact ignores everything apart from the subjective function, the direct evocation of the character, the contrast to simple indirect speech and to normal narratorial description. But [*style indirect libre*] always embodies a narratorial element, clearly proclaimed in the first place through the verbal tense and the pronomial forms. The narratorial presence is communicated in three main ways: through the vocabulary and idiom, through the composition of the sentences and the larger passages, and through the context.[15]

In Cohn the narrator tended to become a cipher for the character's impressions. Pascal sets up the duality of the rela-

14. Ibid., 22.
15. Ibid., 25.

tion between character and narrator—a duality that is neither a dualism nor an identity. "Always the language is mixed, implying an interpreting intermediary; often of course it bears a strong implicit narratorial comment, notably of irony."[16] Pascal's own strictures should be kept in mind when we come to his discussion of Flaubert, for then Pascal himself tends to gravitate back in the direction of restricting the role of the narrator to a largely passive function. Before reaching this point, we may quote Pascal's definition of free indirect speech (the term he prefers) as well as certain remarks he makes concerning the relation between it and history or historiography.

Free indirect speech is a stylistic device based upon the form of simple indirect (reported) speech, i.e. using the tenses and person proper to the latter. It injects into this rather colourless form the vivacity of direct speech, evoking the personal tone, the gesture, and often the idiom of the speaker or thinker reported. In its simplest form it is found in the mimicry of odd expressions characteristic of a person, but in more complex, extensive forms is used for the dialogue and the articulate soliloquy, short or long, as also for pre-verbal levels of nervous and mental responses and non-verbal registrations of sense-impressions, ranging from the most evident and readily expressed observations to the most obscure movements of the psyche.[17]

Pascal cautions against a conventional idea of a history of free indirect speech, and the terms of his argument suggest an understanding of its role over time in terms of a process of repetition with varying degrees of dominance or submergence in relation to other forms:

To conceive of a history of [free indirect speech] invites a misunderstanding. For, although the form crops up here and there since the Middle Ages, there is until modern times, after Flaubert, no continuous tradition of its use and transmission as a literary technique; until Flaubert no writer seems to have

16. Ibid., 26.
17. Ibid., 136–37.

used it with a clear consciousness of its stylistic identity and meaning. So that, although one can observe its appearance in this or that author since the Renaissance, one cannot draw a graph of a tradition or of an evolution from crude beginnings to artistic accomplishment. Indeed, when it first appears as a prominent and continuous feature in a novel, in Goethe and Jane Austen, it is already used with the greatest skill and propriety. This fact alone seems to suggest that, with such slight literary antecedents, there must be some linguistic habit in common usage on which these authors were drawing.[18]

These apposite remarks would seem to exclude not the possibility of a history of the form but rather of a certain preconceived idea of history itself as a continuous, developmental, teleologically oriented unfolding of a principle. Yet Pascal will relate the prevalence of free indirect speech to the relative importance in modern fiction of "the depiction of states of mind, temperament, moods, rather than external actions."[19] This concordance with Cohn's emphasis upon the "artist's journey to the interior" may, however, be too simple an explanation to account for the prevalence of free indirect style which involves varying degrees of proximity and distance between (narrative) self and (narrated) other as well as the problem of variable positions of the narrating subject itself, not to mention its relation to the authorial or biographical self. Indeed I would offer the speculation that the larger cultural context that induces or facilitates the widespread use of free indirect style at least in the form it takes in Flaubert is one wherein the writer is fairly definite about what he rejects in the larger society (for example, "bourgeois stupidity") but relatively uncertain and clearly undogmatic about viable alternatives. In this sense, the free indirect style might be seen (in an extension of Bakhtin's analysis) as a complex, exploratory, and often muted form of satire with carnivalesque features. It involves a dialogue not only between self and objectified other but one within the self—a dialogue entailing a high degree of uncertainty and doubt. It is a procedure that is effective and potentially disorienting in

18. Ibid., 34.
19. Ibid., 34.

sounding out accepted conventions, clichés, and modes of discourse, and the degree of undecidability it puts into play may go to extremes. Indeed its more exorbitant forms reinforce the rapid or drastic oscillations of Flaubert's general narrative practice to create a dismemberment or distribution of the narrative self that is extremely difficult to track. This limit marks the point of intersection between critical and uncannily disquieting forces in more hyperbolic movements of a carnivalized "style." And it raises in a particularly insistent way the question of the interaction among symptomatic, critical, and transformative effects in the relation between writing and culture.

It is interesting that Pascal cautions against the use of free indirect style in historiography and literary criticism, although he sees some use of it as inevitable. It is not (as in Cohn) the representation of consciousness in general but rather free indirect speech that should be primarily confined to fiction. (Cohn's view would place psychology, psychobiography, and an important variant of the history of ideas in peculiarly untenable positions.)

> Free indirect speech postulates a relationship between narrator and character, a knowledge of the inner processes of another person that can never exist in real life, and that inevitably introduces a fictional element if it is used in historical writing. . . . I think historians feel the same resistance about the use of free indirect speech, and are well advised to prefer the actual words of their historical characters or a narrative form that clearly demarcates the sphere of the narrator from that of the character.[20]

One may conclude from these remarks that the historian should largely restrict himself to direct quotation, and, when he departs from its complement in objective narration, he should make clear the nature of inferences about "inner" states and the positions of self and other in any dialogue with the past. Pascal is warranted in emphasizing the need for special controls in the use of mixed modes involving an ambivalent interplay of

20. Ibid., 136.

proximity and distance, empathy and irony, in historical or "nonfictional" uses of language. At the very least, the nature of fictions and of their use in framing hypotheses or in orienting research should, one might argue, be subject to checks. Yet the idea that the historian is an author who narrates in his own objective voice or clearly and distinctly quotes and documents the "voices" of others begs a number of questions. To what extent does all writing in more or less distinctive ways involve a difference between author and narrator with the possibility that the narrator will take certain liberties with language or have them taken (perhaps unawares) with him? To what extent are there differential norms regulating the relation of author and narrator in different areas or "genres" of writing and to what extent are they subject to variation or question over time? How do "modern" contextual constraints bear upon the writing of history or criticism? When the historian, for example, does not speak in his own voice or is even uncertain as to the nature of that "voice," does he simply cease writing history? ("C'est beau, peut-être, mais ce n'est pas de l'histoire," a voice says. Whose voice? Certainly not the voice of the historian but a higher-order, "metahistorical" voice that defines what is to count as history.) Should one attempt to recast the relations among genres or areas of discourse in terms of norms regulating author-narrator relations: fiction at one end—that of disquieting play—and history at another—that of reassuring veracity—with other discursive modes such as philosophy falling somewhere in between or perhaps rising masterfully above? Does this neo-Aristotelian enterprise founder—or at least leave open certain questions that both situate and are situated by it? How do, and how should, distinctions of degree relate to oppositions of kind? What does one do with intractably realistic aspects of fiction or fictive dimensions of historical narration? With these questions one of course enters the babel-like scene of contemporary controversy about the nature of discourse.

What is significant in the recent past is the subversion of the norms that Pascal seems to take for granted. In Sartre's own *Idiot de la famille*, something approaching a generalized free indirect method of inquiry often makes it difficult to distinguish between fact and fiction in the account which Sartre himself terms a "true novel." The free indirect method is essential to "fictionalized" modes of reporting in general, for example, in the work of Norman Mailer. And, from a different direction, recent literary criticism that seeks to undermine the category of the author, question the status of the "signature," and stress the anonymity of language use in a critical discourse that "creatively" rewrites or emulates its object seems, when taken to the limit, to generalize a free indirect style in a rather discomforting way. One may note that, in his specific commentary on Flaubert, Pascal himself seems to draw back from the more disconcerting uses of free indirect speech in fiction itself.

Of Flaubert, Pascal asserts:

> His avowed aim was to get away from the obtrusive narrator of the novel, the author who directs our attention, explains events and people to us, and proffers moral judgments. This was more than a revolt against the obtrusive personal author of the Thackeray type; it was also, in a sense, aimed at the impersonal narrator, the pure story-teller. Flaubert wanted to hide the very function of story-telling, as it were, to allow the story to tell and interpret itself, as far as this was possible; hence the narrator should, as he puts it, "transport himself into his characters." This free indirect speech is not an occasional device, nor something employed for a specific situation or person; it is a major instrument for achieving the Flaubertian type of novel. Flaubert's realism did not imply the sort of objectivity that belongs to natural science, an objectivity founded on communicable skill and authoritative control over the (imaginary) object; on the contrary, it meant an imaginative self-submergence in the object, participation in the imagined character's experience, in communication of the intuitive experience.[21]

In this stress upon self-effacing objectivity and figural empathy as criteria of Flaubert's style, Pascal seems to fall back on the "Germanic" tradition he criticizes and to join with Cohn's emphases (even quoting from the same letter of Flau-

---

21. Ibid., 98.

bert). The role of the narrator is subordinated, and identification with characters is stressed. Indeed Pascal's discussion of Flaubert is often close to that of Percy Lubbock in *The Craft of Fiction*. The "essence of the free indirect form" becomes for Pascal "the reproduction of the inner processes of the character."[22] And criticisms are addressed to Flaubert when he departs from a norm of figural or character-oriented narration that Pascal himself places in theoretical question.

Pascal locates two major difficulties in Flaubert. "The first difficulty arises from the interweaving of [free indirect speech] and narratorial description. Once [free indirect speech] has become of frequent incidence in a novel, once we have become used to descriptions that are projections from the viewpoint of a character, we tend to expect it everywhere, and may find it confusing if the objective, narratorial mode is used instead. This is especially likely when few and unobtrusive indicators accompany [free indirect speech] passages."[23] Thus, in discussing the visit of Emma and Léon to the wet-nurse, Pascal is disturbed by the detailed description of many items in the room which reflects "authorial interest" and "Flaubert's inclination towards realism in the more usual sense, a Balzacian concern for the social genre scene." This change of focus presumably "thwarts his most characteristic artistic purpose, the construction of the mental world of his characters."[24]

The second putative difficulty stems from "uncertainties" that "occasionally involve a further problem . . . inherent in the use of free indirect speech. It is a question of the language, the style, in which such passages are given. We have already seen what opportunities [free indirect speech] offers for reproducing the gestures and intonation of a character, the vivacity of his peculiar personal expression, perhaps his slang, in contrast to narratorial description and simple indirect speech. . . . Flaubert . . . does not allow his characters a highly personalized idiom, but usually, when giving in indirect style the words or articulate thoughts of his characters, provides enough of a characteristic tang to enable us easily to identify their source. . . .

22. Ibid., 107–8.
23. Ibid., 103.
24. Ibid., 104.

But the personalization and differentiation is much less easily achieved when an author gives, through free indirect speech, the less formed, less articulated mental processes of a character, at a stage when they have not taken a recognizable shape."[25]

In certain passages, Pascal even finds what he terms "narratorial usurpation" where the use of language clearly goes beyond the capacities of a character and may ironically inflate desires and dreams to an uncomfortably excessive extent. For Pascal, usurpation transgresses the permissible limits of ironic-empathetic narratorial inflexion to steal the scene from the character's own consciousness. It "seems to arise from Flaubert's obsession with style in the abstract, with '*le mot juste*' and with structure and rhythm of sentence and paragraph, in the sense that, on occasions, when he is seeking to convey through [free indirect speech] the character's own perspective, his feeling of 'rightness' is determined not so much by the specific situation of the character as by the contemplating narrator, or perhaps here we should say by the author. For Hugo Friedrich understands the unremitting search for '*le mot juste*,' this obsessive artistry, as Flaubert's means to counterbalance the world for which he felt such bitter distaste, to 'exorcise' the hateful, inane world he evokes in his novels." For Pascal, this "usurpation" in passages which "purport to reproduce the attitude and vision of characters" constitutes "not only confusion but a threat to a very delicate nerve of the work, since it may impute to a character—Emma Bovary, for instance—an aesthetic compensation she is far from seeking or feeling."[26]

Both these supposed difficulties are not anomalies but rather constitutive elements of Flaubert's narrative practice of which the free indirect style is emblematic. The shift from the perception or idiom of a character to that of the narrator or even the author is typical of Flaubert's approach to narration. The modulation of (empathetic) proximity and (ironic) distance within free indirect speech passages is writ large in the tropisms that take one from free indirect speech to objective narration, quoted monologue, or interior monologue. And at times the

25. Ibid.
26. Ibid., 110–11.

tense relation between narrator or author and character may convert more or less internalized dialogue into a struggle for the possession of language or the right to describe a character, object, or impression. These at times wrenching shifts are indeed unsettling—as they proved to be both for the prosecutor at the trial and for literary critics ever since. But the reason is not purely formal or "stylistic" in any narrow sense. The question may be a question of style, but it is stylistic in a very broad sense that engages deeply disturbing social, political, and cultural issues. To see the question in terms of presumably formal difficulties that one imputes to Flaubert's narrative practice is both inaccurate in accounting for that practice and perhaps diversionary with respect to the larger issues.

Pascal quotes an especially perplexing passage from the famous *Comices agricoles* scene:

> Her profile was so calm that it could not be deciphered. It stood out clear in the light of the oval of her bonnet which was tied with pale ribbons like blades of reeds. Her eyes gazed straight ahead through her curving lashes and, although wide open, seemed a little hampered by the cheek-bones, because of the blood that gently pulsated beneath her delicate skin. . . . Her head inclined towards one shoulder, and you could see between her lips the pearly tips of her white teeth.
>
> Is she playing a game with me? Rodolphe wondered.[27]

Pascal comments: "The wondering question of Rodolphe, so unemphatically linked to the description, makes it clear (if there was any uncertainty) that we have been absorbing *his* impression of Emma."[28]

Yet there emphatically is uncertainty about whose impressions *and* language we have been absorbing—and this uncertainty increases the shock effect of Rodolphe's concluding question. Certain of the perceptions in this passage are too delicate and refined for a man of Rodolphe's taste and sensibility, and the phrase introduced by "because" could be attributed to him only by an implausible stretch of the imagination. Indeed the

27. Quoted, ibid., 102.
28. Ibid., 103.

entire sentence concerning Emma's protean eyes would not seem to make definite sense from any one or any combination of perspectives. It is unclear why wide-open eyes would seem "hampered" by cheek-bones because of blood pulsating beneath delicate skin. The word Pascal translates as "hampered" is "*bridé*." De Man (97) translates it as "slanted," thus giving an exotic twist to the passage. One might suggest the superiority of the more literal translation—"bridled." The image of a horse being pulled up by the bridle adds to the evocativeness and allusive range of the sentence. It anticipates the horse ride when Emma and Rodolphe will "make love" for the first time and after which Rodolphe will repair the bridle of a horse with a knife (a knife that intimates his proximity to both Charles and Léon who also carry knives—and the fact that Charles does is a sign of his resemblance to a "peasant" for Emma). One might say that Emma's eyes although wide open seem "bridled" by the cheekbones because the bridling action causes the blood to flow and to appear to frame or compress the eyes. But this would be a highly debatable interpretation, as would even more far-fetched ones it might call out. In any case, the suggestive discursive indefiniteness of this grammatically precise sentence is typical of Flaubert as writer and narrator rather than of Rodolphe as character.

The relation of Flaubert's narrative practice to his projects is at least dual. On the one hand, the role of "objective" narration and of shifting perspectives that seem to return to impassivity in their own way might be related to the ideal of pure art. The modulations of perspective or voice, which may at times be abrupt or extreme, create such a multiplicity of points of view that they seem to cancel out or erase one another. Multiplication of positions of the narrating subject and of relations to the narrated object would seem through profusion or excess to engender the effect of white noise and to return the text to silence. This effect is in one sense that of language writing or speaking itself but not emanating from a secure or fixed source and not communicating a precise message or evaluative position with respect to characters and events. The limit of this mutual cancellation of narrative perspectives would come in the pure exchange of clichés or of entirely conventionalized modes of discourse for which no one—author, writer, narrator, or character—would bear responsibility. Pure art would be the book about nothing in the sense of a book of pure cliché presented in a mutually self-cancelling or bewilderingly indeterminate multiplicity of perspectives. The effect would be like that of a self-destructive, negative dialectic of banalized proverbs that contradict one another to provide no guidance whatsoever. The position of the narrator would be one of stable ironic transcendence placing him in a secular position analogous to that of a hidden God—but one with little to distinguish him from his satanic adversary. (Here the *Comices agricoles* scene might be taken as paradigmatic.)

Yet this limit of pure art, while it may be approximated, is never reached. It is countered by more carnivalesque tendencies. But the role of the carnivalesque is itself multiple in Flaubert. I shall simply mention in summary fashion three positions of the carnivalesque in *Madame Bovary* and return to them in later chapters.

First, the carnivalesque is represented in the narrated world of the novel as distorted, avoided, repressed, or suppressed— and this very status exacerbates the ugliness and deadly repetitiveness of everyday routine. There are, as we shall see, numerous instances of the distortion or repression of the carnivalesque in the world represented in the novel and, if anything, one should be surprised by their very ubiquitousness. But, second, the ideal of pure art is itself carnivalized in *Madame Bovary*, specifically through the variable empathetic-ironic handling of its analogues—Emma's romantic quest for absolute love, Charles' idolatry of Emma, Binet's perfectionist grinding of gratuitous objects, Homais' striving for a positivistic language of full mastery over the "other." Third, the very multiplication of narrative positions and of relations to objects of narration itself retains a resonance and an insistence that counteracts effects of mutual cancellation. It rehabilitates the carnivalesque on the level of narrative practice or "style" itself. Thus, while the carnivalesque is repressed in the narrated world of the novel (for example, in the lives of characters), it is to some extent reactivated in the mode of narration. The various perspectives and voices in the novel remain active to provide a myriad of more or less subtle perspectives and evaluations vis-à-vis characters and events. The effect here is a carnivalization of narrative voice and a dissemination of the narrator—at times the author—in the text. Often this creates the possibility of delicate judgments and value-shadings that are both tied to situations and indicative of flexible normative principles. At other times, the result is a hyperbolic proliferation of points of view and dialogical relations that seem to wreak havoc with any semblance of stable judgment. This narrative practice can be seen as a self-questioning mode of satire that arises in the context of perceived cultural crisis: the problem confronted by the reader is that of the degrees and ways in which it is both poison and antidote in relation to the larger sociocultural complex it confronts. Flaubert's world is in this sense an uneasy and discomforting world that requires a line-by-line reading of novels and of life, and it is still in many fundamental ways the world in which we continue to live for good and ill.

7

Selected Passages

> Today, if in a circle of novelists and critics, one begins a
> discussion about the art of the novel, the example of *Madame
> Bovary* will soon be introduced and will recur invincibly in
> support of all theories and will nourish a good part of the
> discussion.
>
> Albert Thibaudet, *Gustave Flaubert*

> Flaubert, creator of the "modern novel," is at the crossroads
> of all the literary problems of today.
>
> Jean-Paul Sartre, *L'Idiot de la famille*

How do Flaubert's "dual style" and use of shifting narrative
perspectives operate in practice? The most drastic, yet easily
unnoticed, shift in perspective in *Madame Bovary* is the change
from the first-person plural with which the story begins to the
third-person narration that is instated after the initial scenes. It
sets the tone for more subtle modulations that are to follow and
that constitute what might be called the nonlinear subplot of
the novel. The narration becomes third-person after a paradoxical statement that serves as a circuitbreaker or an alienation effect: "It would now be impossible for any of us to remember any thing about him" (6). Not only does this sentence
follow lengthy descriptions of the young Charles Bovary's
family life that could not plausibly be known to the "we" narrator who seems to be one of his classmates. It raises the rhetorical question of who else could remember anything about the
fictional Charles if not the narrator who is telling the story.

There is an intriguing parallelism between characterization
and story line in the novel which begins with Charles, turns to
Emma, and ends with Charles. This structure invites gratu-

itously circular "explanations" that attempt to make sense of the beginning and ending focus upon Charles by appealing to his importance in the story. But one reason for his importance in the story is precisely the fact that it begins and ends with him. This point signals the less obvious parallelism between Charles and Emma, for the husband is in many respects the reduced model of the wife. Charles daydreams at his little window, has miniature reveries of escape, sees the cafe (rather than the ball at Vaubyessard) as the scene of a magical society, and is depressed by his environment. In beginning and ending with Charles, the story does not entirely depart from Emma, and in turning to Emma, it displaces but does not obliterate the focus on Charles. There is indeed a shift, but it would not seem to be as extreme as that from first to third person on the level of narration.

Let us look more closely at the initial scenes narrated in the first person. The novel's beginning sentence reads: "We were in class when the headmaster came in, followed by a new boy, not wearing the school uniform, and a school servant carrying a large desk." (Note the marked contrast to the last sentence of the novel: "He [Homais] has just been given the cross of the Legion of Honor.") On his first day in class, Charles Bovary is the butt of a kind of charivari or *chahutage* that quickly goes off key and turns into an odious scene centering on Charles's grotesque cap. The narrator seems to adopt the point of view of the boys on the benches in ridiculing, indeed scapegoating, Charles. A point that complicates this complicity, however, is that in the semi-autobiographical text, *Mémoires d'un fou*, Flaubert applies to himself the story of a class that turns viciously on a dreamy outsider.[1]

Charles's cap is one of those over- or underdetermined symbols in Flaubert that seem to signify both too much and too

---

1. "I was in *collège* beginning at the age of ten, and I soon contracted a profound aversion for human beings. This society of children is as cruel for its victims as that other little society, that of men. . . . I can still see myself, seated on the benches of the class, absorbed in my dreams of the future, thinking of whatever the imagination of a child can dream of the most sublime, while the teacher ridiculed my Latin verses, and my comrades looked at me as they chuckled sneeringly." *Mémoires d'un fou* in *Oeuvres 10* (Paris: Conard, 1910), 490.

little for adequate interpretation—a heteroclite monument in the text that simultaneously stimulates a quest for meaning and signals its limits. It is also the mark of the victim that seems to turn on whoever would master its disparate features or integrate them into an organic image or fully unified sense.

> It was one of those head-gears of composite order, in which we can find traces of the bear- and the coonskin, the shako, the bowler, and the cotton nightcap, one of those poor things, in fine, whose dumb ugliness has depths of expression, like an imbecile's face. Ovoid and stiffened with whalebone, it began with three circular strips; then came in succession lozenges of velvet and rabbit fur separated by a red band; after that a sort of bag that ended in a cardboard polygon covered with complicated braiding, from which hung, at the end of a long thin cord, small twisted gold threads in the manner of a tassel. The cap was new; its peak shone. [2]

This cap would seem to exist in a context where there is little or nothing to monumentalize—a world in which the Paris Opera is on the way to becoming early modern Woolworth. It might also evoke the fool's or jester's cap at the point when this carnival figure has been reduced to the status of dunce or inarticulate victim. Paul de Man notes: "The description of this amazing headgear is based on a drawing that appeared in the satirical paper *Charivari* of June 21, 1853. The relationship between *Charivari* and 'Charbovari' a few lines further may or may not be a mere coincidence" (2 n.). What would seem significant is that, while a picture may have suggested the verbal description of the hat, it is difficult to reverse the process of translation between media and to conjure up a picture from the verbal description. The passage back is somehow blocked, and the object seems to take on an almost purely verbal existence. Indeed what is jarring is the dissonance between the serial amalgamation of elements and characteristics in the aimless initial catalogue and the crisp denotativeness of the last sentence in the description. The subsequent scene introducing "Charbovari" has an equally chilling effect for one's understanding of language.

"Rise," repeated the master, and tell me your name.

The new boy articulated in a stammering voice an unintelligible name.

"Again!"

The same sputtering of syllables was heard, drowned by the titters of the class.

"Louder!" cried the master. "Louder!"

The new boy then took a supreme resolution, opened an inordinately large mouth, and shouted at the top of his voice as if calling someone, the word "Charbovari."

A hubbub broke out, rose in *crescendo* with bursts of shrill voices (they yelled, barked, stamped, repeated "Charbovari! Charbovari!"), then died away into single notes, growing quieter only with great difficulty, and now and again suddenly recommencing along the line of a seat from where rose here and there, like a damp cracker going off, a stifled laugh.

However, amid a rain of penalties, order was gradually re-established in the class; and the master having succeeded in catching the name of "Charles Bovary," having had it dictated to him, spelt out, and re-read, at once ordered the poor devil to go and sit down on the punishment form at the foot of the master's desk. He got up, but before going hesitated.

"What are you looking for?" asked the master.

"My c-c-c-cap," said the new boy, casting troubled looks round him.

"Five hundred verses for all the class!" shouted in a furious voice, stopped, like the *Quos ego* [a reference to the scene in Vergil's *Aeneid* where Neptune calms the winds], a fresh outburst. "Silence!" continued the master indignantly, wiping his brow with his handkerchief, which he had just taken from his cap. As to you, Bovary, you will conjugate '*ridiculus sum*' twenty times. Then, in a gentler tone, "Come, you'll find your cap again; it hasn't been stolen." [2–3]

This scene is precariously positioned on the border between vaudeville and horror, and language itself seems to be on trial in it. It "represents" words and gestures as falling into a compulsive pattern of repetition that furiously gets out of control only to be stopped by a depersonalized, authoritarian command bringing "repressive sanctions"—a command softened only by an inappropriately kind word. If theft is an issue, it is not the literal theft of the cap that is at stake. Charles opens his mouth in fishlike incompetence, out of touch with language and self, calling out his name as if it belonged to another—as if he were calling for help in trying to find his "presence of mind." The proper name itself seems not to designate a personal identity but to be close to a cliché at which a "character" inarticulately grasps. Through no seeming fault of his own, Charles is victimized, ridiculed, and punished more severely than the others. The master (like the narrator) is a strange accomplice of this class of jeering boys whom he would control, but he is also an accomplice of Charles whom he comes to resemble. For he too is being overwhelmed by events, and he has a cap—almost a magic cap—from which, in in his confusion, he pulls out a handkerchief. One is tempted to suggest that one has in this scene an allegory of the emergence of articulate speech (in the "primary" form of the proper name) from some more inarticulate, drivelike substratum—or, perhaps, not a substratum but rather an ever-present lateral murmuring in the wings—a nonsignifying musicality bordering on mere noise into which the name, recurrently, threatens to collapse. And the question of language is bound up with the questions of power, discipline, invidious distinction, and scapegoating.

The way this scene is written would seem to intensify the disorienting power of victimization, to re-stage it critically, and to leave the reader with a heightened, raging sense of wanting to say or to do more in coming to terms with the problems it raises. A new boy appears in class, and a demoralizing, slapstick scene is played out. The class finds its identity as a brutish pack of hecklers that can be quelled only by repression. The differences among members of the class are submerged both in their prior familiarity with the practice controlling what-to-do-with-hats-upon-entering-the-classroom and in the "spontaneous" reaction to the outsider who does not know the rules of the game and seems too stupid to learn them. The subarticulate collective effervescence of the class is brought within bounds by the command of a harried master who may be exceeded by events and who certainly loses his impassivity.

The narrator too is in jeopardy, for the scene he narrates may be getting out of hand, and his complicities are even more complicated than those of the schoolmaster. The narrator like the master tries to compose the scene. But he is also on the benches with the boys at least through the "magic" of memory. He pulls from his cap a day in class as told from the perspective of the boys. But in his narration things emerge from perspectives other than that of the benches. There is a force of sympathy with Charles, for example, that is stronger than the schoolmaster's. For one of the others to whom Charles calls may be the narrator himself. And if one recalls that Flaubert in his *Mémoires d'un fou* placed his narrative self in a position like that of Charles, the sense of the proximity of the narrator to Charles is intensified by an intertextual reference. Charles himself is presented in highly ambivalent terms—an innocent victim, a hapless carnival figure, and a hopeless fool who cannot be entirely free of responsibility for his fate. He is also the outsider, the marginal man, the disconcerting supplement of stupidity *and* of novelty in the class who is reduced to the familiar through scapegoating. If the class has an individualist, it is Charles who comes to assume this "heroic" position in a grotesque manner that is as unearned or unmerited as is his victimization. But Charles is nonetheless presented in the liminal position of "holy fool" that will attach itself to him in other ways in the course of the novel—notably in his idolatrously "mimetic" relation to Emma and in his ultimate role as "analogon" of the pure artist steadfastly clinging to an ideal totally contradicted by reality.

This initial scene offers us a familiar secular ritual of the French classroom, but it is a ritual that in the represented world of the novel would seem to be predominantly negative in nature. It is not a rite of passage for Charles who never comes into his own as "one of the boys." And its carnivalesque potential for the class and the schoolmaster turns bitter and ugly. Yet the text itself is not confined to this level of representation, for it brings out all this and more in ways that compel the reader to confront both what it discloses and the very manner of its disclosure. For in its way of staging the problems it re-presents, it casts them in a light that is both critical and disturbing—a light that colors differently the images of fool, member of a class, schoolmaster, and teller of tales.

A second brief passage is especially intriguing. It concerns Charles's first meeting with Emma. And it is in clear contradiction to the views of critics who see the consciousness of characters as the primary vessel of narration or who would subordinate the "free indirect style" to a narrative report of characters' perspectives.

> Charles was surprised at the whiteness of her nails. They were shiny, delicate at the tips, more polished than the ivory of Dieppe, and almond-shaped. Yet her hand was not beautiful, perhaps not white enough, and a little hard at the knuckles; besides, it was too long, with no soft inflections in the outlines. Her real beauty was in her eyes. Although brown, they seemed black because of the lashes, and her look came at you frankly, with a candid boldness. [11]

This supremely serene passage is in certain ways astounding. It seems to begin with Charles's perception of Emma. Yet it includes allusions, such as the one to the ivory of Dieppe, that seem to be beyond Charles's sensibilities. Then critical comments are made about Emma's hands that also appear to be criticisms of Charles's own limited perspicacity. The narrator intervenes or intrudes more actively to direct attention to details that contradict Charles's perception and that take the privilege of describing Emma away from him. Indeed the narrator (almost like an impatient schoolmaster) seems to say in *sub rosa* fashion: "Forget about her hands, you oaf! Look at her eyes. That's where her true beauty lies."

The narrator might almost be said to contest the possession of Emma with Charles as well as with Emma's other men. He struggles with them for the right to describe her, to dress and undress her with words—a right that in the case of a fictional figure is tantamount to full possession. In a sense the narrator becomes one of Emma's men, fascinated by her (as was the prosecutor at the trial), just as she becomes his creation. And it is an open question whether he can control her—whether his "voice" or "point of view" is more dynamic and powerful than hers.

The shift of attention from Emma's hands to her eyes is so

delicate that it might pass unperceived—and these eyes have a protean quality that makes them as labile as the mode of narration itself. The image of Emma in general is a magnificent figure for the interplay between determinacy and indeterminacy in the text. We know a few (at times variable—her eyes change color in the course of narration) things about her face and her body. And we know what she could not be (an overweight or an emaciated blonde, for example). But we do not know precisely what she does look like, and we are tempted to say that, presented with any picture of her, we would exclaim: "That's not quite it." This figure of Emma that always leaves something for the imagination to fill in is in this sense emblematic (with variations in stress) both of her "world" and of the narrative "voice" (or "voices") attempting to come to terms with her.

A third passage is especially remarkable for its pronounced shifts or mutations in narrative perspective. I shall divide it into numbered segments to facilitate discussion of it.

[1] "Oh," she went on, "I love you! I love you so that I could not live without you, do you see? There are times when I long to see you again, when I am torn by all the anger of love. I ask myself, where is he? Perhaps he is talking to other women. They smile upon him; he approaches. Oh no; no one else pleases you. There are some more beautiful, but I love you best. I know how to love best. I am your servant, your concubine! You are my king, my idol! You are good, you are beautiful, you are clever, you are strong!"

[2] He had so often heard these things said that they did not strike him as original. Emma was like all his mistresses; and the charm of novelty, gradually falling away like a garment, laid bare the eternal monotony of passion, that always has the same shape and the same language. [3] He was unable to see, this man so full of experience [*pratique*], the variety of feelings hidden within the same expressions [*la dissemblance des sentiments sous la parité des expressions*]. [4] Since libertine or venal lips had murmured similar phrases, he only faintly believed in the candor of Emma's; he thought one should beware of exaggerated declarations which only serve to cloak a tepid love; [5] as though the abundance of one's soul did not some-

times overflow with empty metaphors, since no one has been able to give the exact measure of his needs, his concepts, or his sorrows. [6] The human tongue is like a cracked cauldron [*un chaudron fêlé*] on which we beat tunes to set a bear dancing when we would make the stars weep with our melodies. [137–38]

This passage could of course be broken down further, but let us be satisfied with our crude divisions. The first segment of the passage gives us Emma's words to Rodolphe in the form of a quoted monologue. It is one of the very longest in direct quotes to be found in the entire novel. The narrator withdraws as a "voice" and allows Emma to speak in her own words. Hers is the voice of incantation which through illusionistic verbal magic creates its imaginary object of discourse. It is Rodolphe, the quintessential hollow phallus, who is the real "referent" of these words, and Emma displaces him utterly, transforming him into a reincarnation of the vicomte at Vaubyessard who was himself a token of the elusive imaginary lover. Rodolphe thus assumes the Platonic position of imitation of an imitation in a world where the highest reality is identical to the purely imaginary: Emma's world. She is of course in love with an idea of love that is itself ungraspable and whose real embodiments must be inadequate instances of the absolute.

With 2 we have a process of sobering up, as the narrator provides an objective report of Rodolphe's disabused reaction. The first sentence is impersonal and businesslike: Rodolphe is not impressed, and the prose is not impressive. But with the second sentence of 2, the narrator in "free indirect" manner begins to fade back in, and it is unclear who is putting forth these general reflections about "the charms of novelty, falling away like a garment" to lay bare "the eternal monotony of passion, that always has the same shape and the same language." And here it might seem that the charm of novelty is the illusion—the clothing—and that the eternal monotony of passion is the reality—at least in Rodolphe's world which the narrator's perspective in this respect often seems to approximate. For the world presented by the narrator tends to be one of hollow repetition wherein projects or dreams of escape inevitably collapse into failed hopes and *"le train-train de la vie ordinaire."* Yet in this instance the shape and the language of this deromanticized world are given a parity in relation to one another and to the levelled-off world itself—under the category of "the same."

With segment 3, the narrator intrudes to emit a seemingly harsh judgment on Rodolphe as seen "from the outside." Ironic distance between narrator and character appear to be at a maximum. Yet Rodolphe is criticized for not seeing, despite or because of his "experience," the variety or dissimilarity [*dissemblance*] of feelings or sentiments under the sameness or parity [*parité*] of expressions. Feeling, if not passion, is presented by the narrator in terms of difference or dissimilarity, while expressions are given the reductive function of compressing feelings to the same level. This "romantic" narrative gesture in defense of the variety of feeling and the inadequacy of language to express it presents feeling as reality and now construes language as a form of deadening metaphor that betrays it. Yet the word used to denote feeling in its variety—*dissemblance*—also connotes dissemblance, thereby blurring the lines and introducing the possibility that feeling may harbor its own illusions. In addition, a problem is created by the question of whether the narratorial intrusion really applies to its seeming referent—Emma. Is she not ruled by the same passion or desire for the imaginary that is differentiated only on the level of its "expressions" which may readily be substituted for one another? Is there, in other words, a sense in which Rodolphe's reaction is right?

With 4, the difficulties in the passage intensify. The grounds for a harsh narratorial judgment about Rodolphe become shaky without implying a justification of Rodolphe. Does the narrator—or the reader—believe more than faintly in the candor of Emma's phrases? Has not the narrator himself seen and induced the reader to see Emma largely or at least partly as Rodolphe here sees her? Are not her incantatory and illusionistic declarations exaggerated ways of cloaking a tepid love or at least of pumping up an uncertain sentiment to grandiose proportions? Does she have a full soul which words cannot adequately express or an empty soul that fills itself with self-deceptive romantic clichés? And where can one situate the narrator in these respects? Is his seeming defense of Emma a way of justifying himself on dubiously projective grounds?

Segment 5 offers an extended analogy or "as if" construction. Language appears more directly as "empty metaphors," and the reality whose "exact measure" it cannot take is displaced from "passion" and "feeling" to the rather heterogeneous series of "needs, concepts, and sorrows." Given the linguistic forms in which it is expressed, the very nature of the "reality" to which language is compared becomes more uncertain. The distinction among real, imaginary, and linguistic orders begins to waver. The reference to the "abundance of one's soul" seems difficult to classify or to localize in terms of a referent. Who in the novel is the vehicle of this abundance? Yet the very force of this image of overflowing plenitude is mitigated by a "sometimes" of indeterminate status: Is it that the abundance can at times—however inexactly—express itself other than in empty metaphors or that its only other choice is silence, with the doubt that silence may always evoke? In any event, the implication here would seem to be that an excess on the side of the "other" of language (passion, feeling, need, concept, sorrow) and a lack in language are supplemented by the possibility of a lack on the side of the signified or the referent and an excess in language, at least in the form of a flood of empty metaphors. This reversibility is reinforced by a later passage about language: "Speech is like a rolling machine that always stretches the sentiment it expresses" (169).

The lapidary, epigrammatic quality of segment 6, with its poignant contrast between Romantic agony and behavioristic bathos, seems to emblematize the entire problem of language and its use. The comparison of the human tongue or language to a cracked cauldron itself cracks or doubles the medium of articulation and communication. For "*la langue*" is both tongue and language, material organ and symbolic order. The possibilities and limits of language are evoked in a condensed statement whose formal and expressive power seems to belie the pathos of its message. Indeed with the knotty aphoristic beauty of these final words, we are close to the narrator or to Flaubert in some more comprehensive sense. For in this rare direct statement about the nature of language, we could be reading from the letters at one of their most intense moments when author, narrator, and writer are in intimate dialogue with one another.

The famous fiacre scene was expurgated by the *Revue de Paris* and is one of the few passages in *Madame Bovary* to elicit extended commentary from Sartre in *L'Idiot de la famille* (II, 1275ff).

"Oh Léon! Truly. . . I don't know. . . if I should. . ." She simpered. Then, in a serious tone:

"It's very improper, you know, it isn't done."

"Everybody does it in Paris!" replied the clerk.

This, like a decisive argument, entirely convinced her. She had made up her mind.

But no cab arrived. Léon shuddered at the thought that she might return into the church. At last the cab appeared.

"At least you should go out by the northern gates," cried the verger, who was left alone on the threshold, "and look at the Resurrection, the Last Judgment, Paradise, King David, and the damned burning in the flames of Hell!"

"Where to, sir?" asked the coachman.

"Anywhere!" said Leon, pushing Emma into the cab.

And the lumbering machine set out.

It went down the Rue Grand-Pont, crossed the Place des Arts, the Quai Napoleon, the Pont Neuf, and stopped short before the statue of Pierre Corneille.

"Go on," cried a voice that came from within.

The cab went on again, and as soon as it reached the Carrefour Lafayette, set off down-hill, and entered the railroad station at a gallop.

"No, straight on!" cried the same voice.

The cab came out by the gate, and soon having reached the Mall, trotted quietly beneath the elm trees. The coachman wiped his brow, put his leather hat between his knees, and drove his carriage beyond the side alley by the meadow to the margin of the waters.

It went along by the river, along the towing-path paved with sharp pebbles, and for a long while in the direction of Oyssel, beyond the islands.

But suddenly it turned sideways across Quatremares, Sotteville, La Grande-Chaussée, the Rue d'Elbeuf, and made its third halt in front of the Jardin des Plantes.

"Get on, will you?" cried the voice more furiously.

And at once resuming its course, it passed by Saint Sever, by the Quai des Curandiers, the Quai aux Meules, once more over the bridge, by the Place du Champ de Mars, and behind the hospital gardens, where old men in black coats were walking in the sun along the ivy-covered terraces. It went up the Boulevard Bouvreuil, along the Boulevard Cauchoise, then the whole of Mont-Riboudet to the Deville hills.

It came back; and then, without any fixed plan or direction, wandered about at random. The cab was seen at Saint-Pol, at Lescure, at Mont Gargan, at La Rougue-Marc and Place du Gaillardbois; in the Rue Maladrerie, Rue Dinanderie, before Saint-Romain, Saint-Vivien, Saint-Maclou, Saint-Nicaise—in front of the Customs, at the Basse-Vielle-Tour, the "Trois Pipes," and the Cimetière monumental. From time to time the coachman on his seat cast despairing glances at the passing cafés. He could not understand what furious locomotive urge prevented these people from ever coming to a stop. Time and again he would try, but exclamations of anger would at once burst forth behind him. Then he would whip his two sweating nags, but he no longer bothered dodging bumps in the road; the cab would hook on to things on all sides but he couldn't have cared less, demoralised as he was, almost weeping with thirst, fatigue and despair.

Near the harbor, among the trucks and the barrels, and along the street corners and the sidewalks, bourgeois stared in wonder at this thing unheard of in the provinces: a cab with all blinds drawn that reappeared incessantly, more tightly sealed than a tomb and tossed around like a ship on the waves.

One time, around noon, in the open country, just as the sun beat most fiercely against the old plated lanterns, a bare hand appeared under the yellow canvass curtain, and threw out some scraps of paper that scattered in the wind, alighting further off like white butterflies on a field of red clover all in bloom.

Then, at about six o'clock the carriage stopped in a back street of the Beauvoisine Quarter, and a woman got out, walking with her veil down and without looking back. [176–77]

This selection begins with scenes of heavy-handed but extremely funny irony. The irony is dramatic in that it stems from the nature and situation of the characters—Emma's simpering uncertainty, her perennial sense of bourgeois propriety, her rapid willingness to be taken in by an "argument" or one-liner that combines an appeal to her provinciality with an invocation of what is proper in the city of her dreams; Léon's impatience that for once makes him the more active or aggressive of the pair, his subjection to circumstances that might return him to a passive role in the church, and his impetuosity once a cab arrives; and the final appearance of the verger who climaxes his ludicrous postponement of the couple's encounter with the final series of appropriately incongruous, missed sights of the cathedral. The irony is of course also narratorial, as Flaubert arranges the scene and drops references, notably the one to Léon as the clerk. The very heavy-handedness of the irony in these initial exchanges contrasts markedly with the recounting of the ride in the cab itself. For the quality of "irony" undergoes an abrupt and decisive transformation. The broad humor is gone, and a more damnable and cuttingly critical tone takes it place.

Now the narrator seems once more at a maximal distance from events and characters, and the text almost seems to write itself. The problem of language is again staged but in an insistently indirect way. Indeed one is tempted to read the passage as an extended allegory of the fate of language in a mystifyingly uncertain world. The coach itself is like language. It houses a copulating couple whose unison is hidden from view in a manner that can hardly be called altogether discreet. The seemingly aimless multiplication of place names that pinpoint the haphazard ride serves as an effective but frustrating mechanism of displacement in relation to what is happening inside the cab. Indeed, violence is on the verge of breaking out in this passage, and its verbal equivalents at times erupt from the coach in impersonal commands that seem to lead nowhere. Sexual frenzy parallels linguistic frenzy in the closest proximity to anomic abandon. The positions of the coach in relation to the larger reality of the town increase with an excessive prolixity that prevent one from finding coordinates that map out a followable course. Madly proliferating place names that should orient an itinerary serve only to disorient. The coachman is like a disconnected Platonic driver on the brink of total perplexity and manic despair. He is not altogether sure—perhaps he does not want to know—what the couple within is doing. And he has little idea of where they want to go. He is driven by his horses, and his carriage becomes the tottering plaything of the paths it follows. The bourgeois in the street, who gaze in astonishment at the unaccustomed sight, are like "naive" readers looking at a moving object from the outside and trying to find their bearings.

Emma and Léon are depersonalized in an extreme way. They do not engage in their usual duet of affectedly naive romantic clichés. Dramatic illusion is trenchantly rejected (not simply botched, as Sartre implies), as are the ordinary techniques of narration related to it. The drama shifts from characters to language and its wayward drift in the world. And in this passage one is at the limits of defamiliarization. A voice not identified as Léon's shouts pointless orders from within the cab. A hand not identified as Emma's throws white fragments of a letter from the window, and they perversely recall both Rodolphe's letter and the fluttering black fragments of Emma's own wedding bouquet as they fly up the chimney. The torn fragments are those of the farewell letter of Emma to Léon that she could not deliver because she did not know the location of the addressee. (Color symbolism—yellow curtain, white butterflies, red clover—becomes as unmotivated as the movement of the cab.) And finally a woman with lowered veil hurries from the coach. The coach itself is like a funeral wagon or a mortuary ship of fools.

One does have something approaching puppet theater in this passage—but the position, even the existence, of the puppet master is in doubt. For the control of the narrator seems both assured by his transcendent irony and assailed by the movement of his linguistic vehicle. He is so far removed from the scene of the action that language does not seem to need him any more. The very term "irony" seems paradoxical in naming the position of the narrator, for, once the cab gets under way, there is nothing in the passage that offers a hook on which to hang some contrasting perspective. The invidious distinction that Sartre seems to assume in asserting that the narrator treats the characters as "puppets" rather than as human beings appears to lack a sufficient basis or ground on which to establish itself.

This passage could be read as a symptomatic expression of linguistic disorder, as a strangely satirical critique of sociolinguistic and sexual relations—call them para-bourgeois—in modern society, and as a limiting exploration of the fate of symbolism in an anomic context. Yet it marks one extreme position—that of narratorial externality—in a larger field of variable positions of the narrative subject. And it depends for its shocking effect upon its specific function in that larger field of narrative practice.

Near the end of the novel is the final encounter between Charles and Rodolphe.

One day when he had gone to the market at Argueil to sell his horse—his last resource—he met Rodolphe.

They both turned pale when they caught sight of one another. Rodolphe, who had only sent his card for the funeral, first stammered some apologies, then grew bolder, and even invited Charles (it was the month of August and very hot) to share a bottle of beer with him at the terrace of a café.

Leaning his elbows on the table, he chewed his cigar as he talked, and Charles was lost in reverie at the sight of the face she had loved. He seemed to find back something of her there. It was quite a shock to him. He would have liked to have been this man.

The other went on talking of agriculture, cattle and fertilizers, filling with banalities all the gaps where an allusion might slip in. Charles was not listening to him; Rodolphe noticed it, and he could follow the sequence of memories that crossed his face. This face gradually reddened; Charles nostrils fluttered, his lips quivered. For a moment, Charles stared at him in somber fury and Rodolphe, startled and terrified, stopped talking. But soon the same look of mournful weariness returned to his face.

"I can't blame you for it," he said.

Rodolphe remained silent. And Charles, his head in his hands, went on in a broken voice, with the resigned accent of infinite grief:

"No, I can't blame you any longer."
He even made a phrase, the only one he'd ever made.
"Fate willed it this way."
Rodolphe who had been the agent of this fate, thought him very meek for a man in his situation, comic even and slightly despicable. [255]

Within a few lines of this scene, Charles dies—of "nothing"—and the novel itself draws to a close. This final encounter between Charles and Rodolphe leaves the reader with a queasy feeling—"comic even and slightly despicable." For the scene has the makings of comedy or of farce, but they do not quite come off. The mood fails to elevate, just as Emma's wake itself did not serve to return mourners to life but either left them indifferent or, in the case of Charles, hollowed out. The final encounter with Rodolphe threatens to be overdetermined by eerie echo effects. Charles is at the market to sell a horse which may be the one he bought for Emma's rides with Rodolphe. Rodolphe invites Charles to the café—a place where Charles as a young man had his dreams of the future. Charles is lost in Emma-like reverie at the sight of Rodolphe's face. By the same token he enters further into Emma's narcissistic orbit, for what he beholds is the object upon which Emma projected her own imaginings. Rodolphe has a cigar between his teeth as he did after making love to Emma. The entire scene also recalls the *Comices agricoles* with its mingling of talk of agriculture and of seduction. There seems to be a momentary build-up to a confrontation between the two men. Rodolphe at first stammers like Charles. For the first time, he seems visibly frightened by the weak husband, in contrast to his flippant rejoinder when Emma alluded to the threat posed by Charles's discovery of the affair. But the hint of apocalypse quickly dissipates, and the scene turns into one of mildewed but disorienting recognition and even reconciliation. Charles's hot flash of aggressiveness momentarily gives way to the impossible desire to have been the man in whom he now seems to retrieve a part of the idolized other. Thus Charles both repeats a crucial facet of Emma's desire (hysterical identification with the aggressor) and desires to become the other who was the hollow receptacle of

Emma's own impossible desire. Indeed he literally repeats that he cannot blame Rodolphe, and in his first effort at phrase-making—his invocation of fate—he also repeats what Rodolphe invoked both in seducing Emma and in leaving her. Yet the reader can hardly side with Rodolphe and his reaction. For at least Charles has earned the right to a cliché. Who would be-grudge him the support or consolation of a commonplace that, given his inarticulateness, is for him something of an achievement?

What is especially difficult to determine in this passage is the position of the narrator himself. There is not the transcendent "objectivity" and extreme irony one might detect in the fiacre scene. The potential for vaudeville in the encounter between the cuckold and the seducer is suggested, but it is decidedly played down in the aftermath of death and desolation. If there is a glimmer of empathy, however, it goes toward Charles in spite of the fact that Rodolphe's final judgment is not entirely inaccurate. Yet the dominant tone seems to be one of insistent silence, precisely at the point where the reader would like some narrative response to orient his own reactions. The narrator is almost like an analyst or anatomist who refuses to become a guidance counselor and an easy friend. What remains is a question about the world in which encounters such as this can take place—a question whose very nature (universal, particular, re-current; psychological, social, political—and in what combina-tion?) this passage, which itself functions as an "instant replay" of Emma's "fate," obdurately leaves up to the reader to define.

The few selections I have discussed were intended as in-stances of the problem of shifting narrative perspectives which was a source of difficulty at the trial and has continued to be troublesome for later criticism. I have stressed the point that Flaubert's narrative practice follows conventional expectations to a point, critically sounds them out, and at times enters into an uncanny play that cannot be entirely decided in terms of the opposition between what is symptomatic and what is critical of the given. Yet certain things are quite definitely criticized: the security and fixity of a center of judgment, including the fully autonomous or "monadic" bourgeois individual as well as the religious believer; the tenability of the founding oppositions and contextualized norms that were taken as unproblematic at the trial; and the viability of various discourses that are meant to articulate social and cultural reality and to provide guidance for the subject in attempting to tell the story of his or her own life. In *Madame Bovary*, one has a multiplication of positions of the narrating subject that cover a large spectrum of relations to objects of narration, and the shifts of perspective range from the drastically abrupt to the imperceptibly subtle. A line-by-line reading of the novel would have to chart the modulations of narrative "voice" in an analysis that might prove interminable. For Flaubert decenters the subject of narration and brings about its multiple insertions vis-à-vis the narrated objects, at times with intense effects of undecidability or hyperbolic "stylistic" carnivalization. But the narrative does not simply disintegrate into a series of "part-objects" or totally disjoined scenes, for the work of narration relates conventional schemata, critical reworking of the given, and effects of mutual cancellation as well as of mutual contestation, while it poses to the reader the problem of how to respond to the network of relations it deploys.

8

Aspects of the Novel

Do not speak to me about modern times, with respect to the grandiose. There is not enough there to satisfy the imagination of a feuilletonist of the lowest order.

Flaubert, June 7, 1844

It's equally fatal for the mind to have a system and to have none. It will simply have to decide to combine the two.

Friedrich Schlegel, *Athenaeum Fragments* (1798)

Approaching more general aspects of the novel, I shall enlarge the focus on narrative perspective to include other dimensions of Flaubert's novelistic practice, for his "dual style" affected other standard components of the novel: themes, plot, characterization, and setting or context. While my treatment of these issues may in certain respects be anticipated given the preceding discussion, it is nonetheless useful to render more explicit the manner in which *Madame Bovary* recast the traditional novel.

In the analysis of cliché, irony, and stupidity, I intimated that *Madame Bovary* lends itself to thematic unification up to a point but also provokes a questioning of the very thematic lines or leads it holds out to the reader. The trial centered its readings upon the themes of the family and religion. Associated with them was the theme of the novel itself in influencing behavior in "real" life. The prosecution and the defense were in agreement on the ability of fiction to trigger "mimetic" effects in ordinary life, for good or ill. They both assumed that readers would read *Madame Bovary* as Emma herself read novels, and, in attributing great importance to this theme, they joined literary critics who present Emma's own quixotic attempt to live what she reads as the unifying explanation which the novel seems to furnish in accounting for her life.

It might, however, be argued that within the novel itself the explanation of Emma's "fate" through the reading of novels has only a limited validity. It is in no sense a total or univocal explanation of her life. That Emma attempts to lead her life as if she were living a novel and that her actual reading of "romantic" novels as a girl helped to shape her conception of life are blatantly apparent postulations of the novel itself. But they are mediated, qualified, and dislocated by other considerations in a complex of relations that is not entirely coherent. There is, for example, a tension between Emma's more transcendent aspirations toward an absolute and her earthbound, indeed vulgar, desires: both are in some sense "romantic," but they cohabit uneasily. Nor is there any simple coincidence between Emma's romantic excesses and her financial imprudence. Love and money are two forms of impropriety in her life, and they combine to help undermine the status of the bourgeois family. But they do so from different directions that intersect only at certain points (gifts for her lovers or expenditures for the planned escape with Rodolphe). What they share is an extremely transgressive relation to conventional norms of bourgeois respectability, but the mode of transgression is not unitary: there is little romance in Emma's financial problems. A similar relation holds between erotic dreams and conventional religious inclinations in Emma, for they merge in mawkish amalgams that attest to the implausibility of their combination. Indeed Emma, in paradoxical contrast to her idealizing romanticization of secular love, takes too literally the image of a celestial lover and the belief that material practices are the path to true religious faith.

In all these senses, *Madame Bovary* is not simply a "tragedy of dreams" that places responsibility for Emma's "fate" on her reading of romantic novels which create "mimetic" desire in her. One telling defect of this interpretation is that it does not inquire into the way in which it is both invited and critically situated by the novel itself. The fact that Emma's mother-in-law offers the reading of romantic novels as the cause of Emma's "problems" is enough to give one pause and to cast a shadow of doubt upon the explanation. The shadow is lengthened by the additional fact that Charles and Rodolphe are the bearers of the belated Greek message that "fate" determined the course of events. Indeed a general problem in offering any given interpretation of a Flaubert novel is to see whether and how that interpretation is already put forth and positioned in the novel itself, for example, which of the characters one sounds like in offering it. One may then find that the trojan horse in which one takes refuge has a rather uncomfortable fit.

On a related level of composition, symbols and images also raise problems in providing agencies of unification or coherent organization that tend to break down or become questionable. We have already mentioned Charles's hat—a symbol that manifestly seems to stand for him yet is both too full and too empty for adequate interpretation. The image of the window serves as another remarkable instance of the possibilities and limits of unified thematic interpretation. Jean Rousset begins his famous discussion of *Madame Bovary* as the "book about nothing" (in which the art of narrative transition is nonetheless crucial) only to have his analysis veer in the direction of making the novel a book about windows.[1] This Alice-in-Wonderland metamorphosis from a formalistic reading of the novel as the realization of pure art to a thematic and image-centered reading may be emblematic of the duality of the novel itself in exploring the interplay of opposites without being reducible to them. The window in *Madame Bovary* does partially lend itself to thematic analysis as an image inducing phenomenological reverie that is more subtle and extensive than Emma's own. The closed window is often related to claustration and self-enclosure, while the open window is the scene of dreams in the provinces—dreams that provide at least imaginary communication with an outside world. Yet there are instances in the novel that block the comprehensive coverage of this interpretation. For in the use

1. *Forme et signification* (Paris: Librairie José Corti, 1962), 109–33. Included in Paul de Man, ed., *Madame Bovary* (New York: Norton, 1965), 439–57.

of the window with its quivering hook as the father's signal to announce Emma's acceptance of the proposal of marriage to the inarticulate Charles, as well as in the "absurdist" gesticulations of Emma and Binet as perceived by the two old busybodies, it is the open window that functions as a barrier to communication and a bar to dreams.

All this is not to say that thematic organization is beside the point. But the text puts into practice a complex interplay between thematic determinacy and indeterminacy, proffering certain consistent lines of interpretation to the reader while simultaneously indicating their shortcomings or possible dead-ends. Jonathan Culler has written extensively about the uses of uncertainty in Flaubert.[2] It is important to recognize that it is a question of *uses* of uncertainty and not simply a provision of "a *theory* of the indeterminacy of experience."[3] The reader may of course attempt to formulate this theory. The novel furnishes certain elements for it and tests the limits of their validity, thereby raising the question of the tenability of such theories in its world and, by implication, in other possible worlds. Here one sees again how *Madame Bovary* is a novel situated on the threshold between traditional novels and experimental texts. The latter will often leave the furnishing of conventional interpretations or expectations up to the reader rather than inscribe them within the text itself. *The Sentimental Education* and *Bouvard and Pécuchet* move further in this direction. But *Madame Bovary* is positioned between tradition and its often disorienting critique, and for this reason is accessible to large numbers of readers (or misreaders) and even seems to invite misreading or at least reading on only a relatively "naive" level. This active use of "deviations" that are unremarkable enough to pass unnoticed, yet insistent enough to disconcert once they are noticed or even subconsciously sensed, may also be observed on the levels of plot and characterization.

When one attempts to provide a linear plot summary of

2. Jonathan Culler, *Flaubert: The Uses of Uncertainty* (Ithaca: Cornell University Press, 1974).

3. The idea that Flaubert provides such a theory is put forth by Gerald Graff, *Literature against Itself* (Chicago: University of Chicago Press, 1979), 160.

Madame Bovary, one invariably begins to echo either the prosecution or the defense at the trial. Rather than repeat the
story of adultery in the provinces, I shall try to indicate how
modifications in narrative perspective provide a nonlinear
subplot—one in which the use of language engages the problem of sense-making and its limits. And I shall relate this
story to the role of temporality in the novel.

Chronology in the ordinary sense is not very well defined
in *Madame Bovary* (in contrast to a novel such as *The Sentimental Education* where the implausible length of Rosanette's pregnancy or the gap between 1851 and 1867 are marked by
their contrast to the precise dating of other events). For the
world represented in *Madame Bovary* is that of everyday life in
the provinces where *plus ça change, plus c'est la même chose*. The
events of the novel can be roughly dated as taking place in
the late 1830s and the 1840s, and drawing to a close somewhere around 1848. (Why 1848 is not mentioned may be
formulated as a problem, and one may suggest that Emma's
suicide takes its place.) But dating is possible on the basis of
inferences from a few passing allusions, for example, Homais'
reference to floods in Lyon and the government's reaction to
insurrection in Poland. The novel is definitely not a chronicle
of its time in any topical or circumstantially detailed way. It
rather brings out the nature of life in a provincial context
that is characterized by what recent social historians call *la
longue durée*.

But the proverbial cliché about change and sameness does
not fully account for the treatment of time in the novel. On
an other than chronological level, the novel treats at least
three forms of temporality that are woven together in a fourth
dimension of time—that of nonlinear narrative itself. These
three temporalities are those of the project, of hollow or
deadly repetitiveness, and of reverie.

The time of the project is closest to that of linear plot in the
ordinary neo-Aristotelian sense. Plot is itself the comprehensive structure modelled on the project and including specific
projects as subplots. Here one's attention is drawn mostly to
the story of Emma. Indeed she is distinctive in the novel in
that she is the one character who does have some semblance

of dynamic projects or goals. (Her closest counterpart in this respect is, paradoxically, Homais who has a sustained will to succeed.) Emma at least wants to escape the constraints of her tedious milieu and will go to any lengths to get what she wants. She creates her men in her image and uses them as crosses on which to nail her dreams. She is in the "active" position, clearly with Léon who is described as her mistress, also with Charles who behaves after their wedding night as the virgin of the day before, and even with Rodolphe who, superficially in control, is a stock figure given substance by Emma's imagination and overwhelmed by her demands.

Emma's projects transcend her environment only in the most evanescent of fashions—just as she is a tragic heroine only in the most equivocal of senses. Indeed another fault in the interpretation of her fate as a "tragedy of dreams" is that tragedy requires substantial oppositions while her dreams and imaginings are as friable as her realities. Her world in general is too messy and low-life for "tragic seriousness" but too pathetic and, in one attenuated sense (that of a displaced metaphysical quest for the absolute), elevated for full absurdity. She is in the zone between the tragic (including Erich Auerbach's modern realistic sense) and the absurd, for her tragic potential is dubious, and the absurdist possibilities in her position have yet to emerge clearly.

Thus Emma has projects—at least projects of escape—but they flare up only to collapse into the repetitive pattern that permeates the world from which she would escape. She moves in a vicious cycle of boredom and hysteria: a situation she cannot stand, a man she cannot tolerate (or who can no longer tolerate her), provoke dreams of another scene, another man. But these dreams deflate after a time only to rise again— repetition as death in life, repetition also as the path frayed to suicide. Emma is of course in love with her own idea of a lover and in this sense in love with herself. The other is never on the level of her projections, imaginings, and dreams. The dreams are emptied of content or compromised in sordid reality, and they retain some semblance of force only on a metaphysical level where desire cannot but meet with frustration in the mundane round of daily life.

This time of empty, deadly repetition is the dominant mode of existence represented in the novel. Things in it may follow one another, but sequence does not add up to progress or even to a promise of renewal. Cliché is the sociolinguistic definition of this social reality, and all life seems consumed by it. Here, for example, is what is written of the days of Emma's life:

> So now they would keep following one another, always the same, immovable and bringing nothing new. Other lives, however flat, had at least the chance of some event. One adventure sometimes brought with it infinite consequences and the scene changed. But nothing happened to her; God had willed it so! The future was a dark corridor, with its door at the end shut tight. [45]

The one escape from hollow repetition into a seemingly atemporal realm is provided by extremely fleeting moments of reverie. And Emma is the mistress of reverie. With Charles and the narrator, she is the one "person" allowed these transient experiences of time out of time, especially at her window where she stands framed by her desires of escape. The narrator is closest to Emma at these moments. Yet the longest passage of "pantheistic" reverie is reserved for a narratorial description of nature which displaces the reader's attention from the first sexual encounter between Rodolphe and Emma and is itself rudely interrupted by the depiction of Rodolphe after the event. Dreamlike moments of relief, besides being immediately dislocated, are frustratingly brief: they are not developed with the flow of metaphor that might give them more duration and a greater chance to alleviate daily routine. Indeed Flaubert's practice in revision might anachronistically be termed decidedly anti-Proustian, for he pared down the more protracted figures of oblivion or metaphoric embrace until they no longer even seemed to provide havens of bliss in the lives of his characters or the movement of events. That he was capable of writing those passages is revealed in the Leleu-Pommier edition of variants. That he was aware of their allure is evident in his letters.

It is a delicious thing to write, whether well or badly—to be no longer yourself but to circulate in the entire creation of which one speaks. Today, for example, man and woman together, lover and mistress at the same time, I rode on horseback in a forest, on an autumn afternoon, and I was the horses, the leaves, the wind, the words they spoke to one another, and the red sun that made them half-shut their eyes drenched with love. Is this pride or pity? Is it a silly overflow of exaggerated self-satisfaction? Or a vague and noble religious sentiment? But when I turn over these experiences of bliss, after having undergone them, I am tempted to offer a prayer of thanks to the good Lord, if only I knew he could hear me. Let him be praised for not having me be born a cotton merchant, a vaudevillian, a wit, etc.! Let me sing to Apollo as in the first days, and breathe deeply the cold air of Parnassus; let us strike our guitars and our cymbals, and whirl like dervishes in the eternal clash [*brouhaha*] of Forms and Ideas. [December 23, 1853]

But that the indulgence of these flights would be at best a minor part of Flaubert's novelistic practice is a matter of record. His whirling dervishes would take other forms. In *Madame Bovary*, reverie is and remains fleeting—a hinted iridescence in the collapse of projects and the course of empty repetitiveness. Indeed the world represented in the novel seems to be one of almost unrelieved frustration of hope, punctuated by ineffectual reverie (and by the equally evanescent appearance of characters one is tempted to describe as "positive": the adolescent Justin, the old servant Catherine Leroux, and the good doctor Larivière). Insofar as the reader inserts himself into this world through identification, it is plausible to argue that demoralization is the result.

Yet Flaubert's narrative practice does not simply conform to the three modalities of temporality represented in the novel. It binds and unbinds them, as the narrator weaves in and out of the story told. For the time of narration is itself punctuated by the variations of proximity and distance and the inflexions of irony and empathy that we have already discussed at length. And, on this level, the issue of temporality is related to the imbrication of reinforcing, critical, and transformative tendencies in the interaction between what is "represented" in the novel and its mode of "representation" or narration. But here, perhaps more clearly than elsewhere, one has in the foreground the problem of the possibilities and limits of language in coming to terms with things. Insofar as the mode of narration sensitizes the reader to this problem, it does not demoralize him. It confronts him with a range of issues which its own periodicity in the use of language may help to resolve or at least to pose in more articulate ways.

/ It may be observed that, in discussing plot and temporality, I have also been discussing characterization. This is unavoidable given the mutually implicated parallelism of the two. On a linear level, the story begins with Charles, moves to Emma, and ends with Charles. On a nonlinear level, it involves characters in the temporal movements I have just evoked. Rather than trace this process in detail, I shall attempt to take the discussion of characterization in somewhat different directions.

The relation of narrator to characters at times goes beyond the boundaries of empathy and irony to less sublimated forms of love and hate, and nowhere is this ambivalence more pronounced than in relation to Emma. The narrator-character relationship is even further complicated by the relation of the author to the narrator. "Madame Bovary, c'est moi" is one of Flaubert's most quoted pronouncements. Yet the enigma lies in the nature of the "moi." For Flaubert also said repeatedly that the novel was so difficult for him to write because he put nothing of himself in it and because the characters were so antipathetic to him.

The one thing that is clear in this oscillation between identification and denial is the intensity of Flaubert's investment in the novel. The readiest way to resolve the ambivalence of that investment would be in terms of the dialectic between romantic illusion and novelistic truth. Emma is a deluded romantic infected by mimetic desire that is caused by her participatory reading of novels. She tries to lead her own life as if it were a romantic novel. Flaubert, recognizing that this illusion has no

4. For this analysis, as well as for a discussion of "mimetic desire," see René Girard, *Mensonge romantique et vérité romanesque* (Paris: Grasset, 1961).

future, lucidly reveals its true status and writes fiction ironically and critically serving the interest of a higher truth.) That the relationship between "Flaubert" and his "creation" cannot be so simple is bound up with the suspicion that the mutual implication of author, narrator, and characters is more intricate and even bewildering than this scenario allows. Let us raise a few questions that will resurface in the course of our discussion. Does "Flaubert" face problems comparable to those of Emma (as well as of other characters), and can we be altogether sure about whose response is most justifiable or "authentic"? Can we be entirely reassured that "Flaubert" masters the hysteresis unleashed by this "hysterical" woman who fascinates him to the point of identification and denial? These questions may in certain respects be taken as variations of a question raised by the prosecutor at the trial (who is in a position to condemn Emma?), but the point of our inquiry is rather different, for it may generate residual doubts about directions taken by our own analysis. I shall not pretend to eliminate these doubts, but I shall attempt to situate them to the extent that I find it possible.

Emma was the central figure in the novel for both the prosecution and the defense at the trial. She is also the character in whom metaphysical desire for an absolute—desire which ennobles and sets one apart—is endangered, even hopelessly contaminated, by banal and pathetic attempts at evasion that are symptomatic of the milieu they would transcend. She has velleities of purity and a thirst for something better: she makes demands on her environment. Yet she is a narcissistic creature of her romantic dreams and longings with little or no concern for the needs or the existence of others. She oscillates between boredom and hysteria, recognizes only what comes in cliché, and unites the "pleasure principle" with a deadly pattern of repetition. "Incapable . . . of understanding what she did not experience or of believing anything that did not take on a conventional form," Emma "rejected as useless whatever did not contribute to the immediate satisfaction of her heart's desire—being of a temperament more sentimental than artistic, looking for emotions, not landscapes" (31, 26).

The narrator who can analyze her ironically and critically is also fascinated with her—as are the other men who come into contact with her. When narratorial fascination reaches the limit of identification, it approaches the emulation of Emma that marks Charles at the end of the novel. The sense that the narrator in relating to Emma is also relating to himself—and beyond his fictive role to the authorial or biographical Flaubert —makes his ambivalence all the more difficult to pin down. Emma is manifestly, as the prosecutor at the trial (who himself courted becoming "involved" with her) observed, the most forceful creature in the book—more forceful perhaps than the author-narrator who gives birth to her. Men cannot handle her; she cannot handle herself. And "Flaubert" threatens to be overwhelmed by her less sophisticated, less sublimated, and in certain respects more powerful desires and demands. She insistently wants something out of life and is willing to take major risks to get it. If one can speak of her "problem," it is in no sense a simple problem, and it is perplexingly bound up with the "problems" of her world.

Indeed the figure of Emma represents a crucial breakdown in the circuits of sexual, socioeconomic, and linguistic exchange and reproduction. Given the interference of these circuits with one another, she also signals a more general short-circuiting in society and culture at large.

Sexually, Emma's position is not fixed: it is far from stable in any regard. She is a woman who refuses to play the traditional woman's role. And, despite her own weaknesses, she is the most active and "masculine" figure in the novel, dominating not only other characters but threatening to dominate the author-narrator as well. For Baudelaire, Flaubert poured his own masculine blood into Emma's veins, while for Sartre, in a kind of reverse transfusion, Emma is Flaubert feminized. This chiasmic criss-crossing of perspectives—each turn of which is equally plausible or equally exorbitant—indicates that Emma's masculinity is not a question of ordinary role reversal and that her relation to Flaubert is implicated in a tangled web of involvements. Indeed Baudelaire saw Emma's hysteria in terms that broached the problem of androgeny:

The Academy of Medicine has not as yet been able to explain the mysterious condition of hysteria. In woman, it acts like a stifling ball rising in the body (I mention only the main symptom), while in nervous men it can be the cause of many forms of impotence as well as of a limitless ability at excess. Why could this physiological mystery not serve as the central subject, the true core, of a literary work?[5]

The image of a ball rising in the body might suggest that of a cat that chokes "hysterically" on a fur ball caused by licking the self, and it metaphorically links hysteria and narcissism. The relation between impotence—for example, that felt by the epigone—and excess points to the interplay between lack and limitlessness that preoccupied Flaubert in the world he represented and in his own narrative practice.

Emma herself is in character neither for the traditional man nor for the traditional woman, for her desires both exceed and fall short of the expectations of both. She does at times affect masculine dress and behavior, but she does not simply want to be a man in the traditional sense. Nor does she want to have this kind of man, assuming that he exists in her world. The man of whom she dreams transcends ordinary incarnations of "manhood" to the point of becoming vaguely utopian.

Nor will Emma assume the role of traditional housewife. Her activity in the family departs from the conventional code in an extravagant way. She performs her duties with obsessive finesse, or she abandons them with peremptory negligence. In both cases, she really seems to be elsewhere. She does wish that her child were a boy, and she loses interest in the poor creature who has the misfortune to be born a girl. "George" might have had the chances denied to Emma and provided her with a vicarious sense of fulfillment—at least as long as "George" remained as imaginary as Emma's other longed-for men. The girl child is an absence in the novel, almost a literal figure of castration. Emma takes leave of the role of *"mère de famille"* before the standard Oedipal triangle has a chance to get started, for the child is a blank in her life. In this sense, even her pregnancy was hysterical, and its product, which is not an object of

5. *"Madame Bovary,* by Gustave Flaubert" in Paul de Man, ed., *Madame Bovary,* 341.

imaginary investments or narcissistic identification, loses all interest for her.

Equally significant for the rupture of the generational cycle is the fact that Emma's mother is dead as the story opens, and she does not seem to play a significant part in Emma's life. Far from identifying with her mother, Emma escapes motherhood and behaves in a way that establishes an association between the position of her mother and that of her child: both are absences. Indeed the first explicit reference to Emma's mother in the novel comes from the mouth of her father, and it is an analogy between the woman and Charles's first wife. The analogy is situationally ironic, for it is intended to console Charles after the passing of the unlamented Héloïse—herself a widow he had married under false pretenses. The second and last reference to Emma's mother recalls that Emma cried much the first few days when her mother died, and she sent her father a letter "full of sad reflections on life" and requesting that she be buried in her mother's grave (27). This reference is followed by her father's anticlimactic reaction (the "old man" thinks she is ill and comes to see her) and by Emma's own self-satisfaction in attaining "at a first attempt the rare ideal of delicate lives, never attained by mediocre hearts"—an ideal immediately linked to "Lamartine, . . . harps on lakes, . . . all the songs of dying swans, . . . the falling of the leaves, the pure virgins ascending to heaven, and the voice of the Eternal discoursing down the valleys" (28). Thus Emma reduces and assimilates her mother's death to her ordinary romantic musings.

Economically as well as socially, Emma has no productive or reproductive function. She is a pure consumer in a world where commodities tend to be reduced to counters in a largely imaginary game. And her pattern of consumption, which is more heedless and imprudent than wasteful, creates financial difficulties that adulterate the purity of "romantic" fate—the one thing she would like to attain, perhaps even in its more elevated tragic form. In fact, her financial mismanagement is itself paradoxically traditional rather than modern: she behaves like a displaced *grande dame* in her desire to give gifts, unconcerned with mere money matters, and like a good *bourgeoise* in her will to possess fully what she has bought. Yet her lack of

181

prudence is capitalized upon by those, such as Lheureux, who are more in tune with existing economic demands in their own small scale and petty fashion. Emma is less a victim of Capitalism than someone whose desires cannot be accommodated within its limits—and perhaps within any limits, even largely technical or formal ones. But the system she chooses to disdain returns to her with a vengeance, bringing her both to the verge of prostitution and to the absurdly virtuous and highly conventional affirmation that she cannot be bought. Emma is a scandal both to the traditional bourgeois family and to its modern economic setting.

Linguistically, Emma herself disrupts the code of realistic representation. Her primary use of language is incantatory. Her magical clichés and rhythmic repetitions create their object —one that can never be attained in the world of mundane realities. Indeed an "other" attains reality for her only when it may be perceived as the incarnation of a memory recast through the imagination. A perverse Platonist, she is also a small-town Proustian *avant la lettre*. Rodolphe registers as a lover only after the event of seduction when Emma may intone him into imaginary existence through an appeal to an evanescent but transcendent archetype.

> She repeated: 'I have a lover! a lover!' delighting at the idea as if a second puberty had come to her. So at last she was to know those joys of love, that fever of happiness of which she had despaired! She was entering upon a marvelous world where all would be passion, ecstasy, delirium. She felt herself surrounded by an endless rapture. A blue space surrounded her and ordinary existence appeared only intermittently between these heights, dark and far away beneath her.
>
> Then she recalled the heroines of books that she had read, and the lyric legion of their adulterous women began to sing in her memory with the voice of sisters that charmed her. [117]

Cliché and stereotype are as much the vehicles of Emma's dreams as they are the powers that help to create them. The one thing they are not is a simple representation of a preexistent reality. Emma herself is both utterly conventional and in-

sistently unconventional—so much so that it becomes difficult
to distinguish between what is and is not "ordinary" in her
behavior. Her disaffection for her child is the conventional
response of a "narcissistic" woman who would have her prog-
eny be what she is not but would like to be. But her reaction
goes beyond the limits of convention in its hyperbole. And her
various "men" always have something dubious about them:
Rodolphe is a hackneyed, hollow phallus that crudely signifies
the imaginary; Léon is her mistress; and Charles as fool and
saint is both less and more than the average man.

Emma herself is strangely above and below the level of her
time—above it, however equivocally, in the magnitude and insistence of her claims and below it, however pathetically, in her
willingness to sacrifice everything—others as well as self—in
trying hopelessly to make those claims good. I have intimated
that, in one sense, her demands cannot be fulfilled because they
are of such an exorbitant nature that nothing could conceivably
satisfy them. In another sense, they cannot be made good
because the concrete forms they take are so trite that they
coalesce confusingly with that to which they are presumably
opposed. Metaphysics turns maudlin as Emma's quest for an
absolute becomes excessively compromised by its continuous
contact with vulgar desires and realities. Her claims cave into
the same subsoil of empty repetition from which they would
escape until they are terminated—not meaningfully ended—by
death. Both the divided nature of her demands and the fact
that they subside into an order that is itself on the verge of
exhaustion prevent her suicide from attaining the grandeur of
tragic protest. To the extent that it makes a statement, that
statement is itself threatened by trivialization and cliché. Yet
the nature of her quest prevents reducing her to her milieu,
and it allegorically raises questions about its relation to the
project of pure art itself.

Charles and Homais are distinctive among the men in Emma's life for rather different reasons. Emma is the sole object
of Charles's desire, and he ends his life as a *memento mori* to her.
He is throughout life like her in ways that serve only to exacerbate their incompatibility. There is no shadow of a hope for
him with her. But he, alone among her men, keeps her vigil

and her memory with a ridiculous single-mindedness that approaches the saintly. A "stigmartyr" of emptiness, Charles dies of Emma's disease, thereby carrying his *imitatio* to its self-excavating extreme. ("Monsieur Canivet . . . performed an autopsy, but found nothing" [255].) At the end, Emma is indeed almost a pure fiction for Charles—a memory with virtually no correspondence to the reality of Emma's life, only a "purified" echo of its imaginary excesses. Emma kills herself. Charles dies. Yet, in dying, Charles remains her grotesque and ridiculous but nonetheless holy fool. In according him this death, the narrator does not break all solidarity with Charles. Indeed the narrator's relation to Charles is both simpler and more perplexing than his relation to Emma. The fact that the object of Charles's devotion—the image of Emma once dead—negates and transcends the reality of the Emma who lived, makes it a closer analogue of the ideal of pure art than Emma's own compromised quest—and, conversely, it functions as a more pointed contestation of that aesthetic ideal itself.

Homais is exceptional among the principal male characters—and in relation to minor figures such as Justin or Guillaumin—in that he has no "romantic" interest in Emma. Even his clerical *sosie*, Bournisien, seems at times to be closer to a possible intimacy with her. In fact, Homais competes with Emma for the company of Léon and the service of Justin. He is, however, like Charles in being a fool—but one unredeemed by any touch of holiness. He is a success where Charles is a failure, and he has the ability to turn potential disaster (Hippolyte's operation, Emma's suicide, his inability to cure the Blind Man) into the pretext for furthering his own interests. Yet he is, in his own self-interested way, also an imitation, caricature, or bizarrely carnivalized double of Emma. He sees the world radiating from himself as its center. His materialism has its impractical sides, and his realism borders on the "crackpot." But he drives hard to realize his ends. His very lack of interest in Emma as a "love object" may be due to their similarity. His relation to the narrator also has its less obvious sides. He is clearly the most hated character in the book—the one we never see "from the inside" and in reference to whom the "free indirect style" takes on its most ironic inflexions. Yet the hatred and irony of the narrator toward Homais shade into self-hatred and self-directed irony. I have already mentioned the fact that Homais is the only "professional" writer in the novel, the closest analogue to Flaubert in literal terms. And his technological use of language parallels in its own perverse manner the ideal of decontextualized or detached linguistic functioning in pure art. Homais may thus be seen as a parody of the pure artist. But he is also one embodiment of the reduced and distorted carnivalesque in the modern world—the unwitting self-parodist who represents the danger of what contestation and the spirit of laughter may become in certain contexts. In this respect, he is the *frère ennemi* of the Blind Man whom he finally hounds into an asylum as well as of the narrator who tries to take his distance from the pharmacist-scribe.

Three minor characters seem to be the most unproblematically "positive" figures in the novel. Justin attracted the attention of Sainte-Beuve, who otherwise echoed the prosecutor's complaint that the novel did not furnish the positive characters or the redeeming virtues one encounters in "real life." Sainte-Beuve is moved to tell the reader that he himself knew a woman in Emma's situation who nonetheless remained a good and loving *mère de famille*. And he notes that even "little Justin, who loves Emma in silence . . . the only devoted, disinterested character . . . goes by almost unnoticed" in the novel.[6]

But Justin's role seems reinforced by that of Catherine Leroux and of Doctor Larivière. What is significant, however, is that all three are indeed fleeting figures with very small parts to play. And they have their questionable sides. In addition, all the characters in *Madame Bovary* are suspended between the full-bodied portraiture one would expect in a realistic novel and the scaled-down miniatures that are most clearly in evidence in the minor characters. For characterization itself often tends toward minimalization that makes the proper name approximate the cliché or the label for an empty figure.

Justin in his adolescent attachment to Emma is moving, well intentioned, and good hearted. He is the son she never had,

6. "*Madame Bovary*, by Gustave Flaubert" in Paul de Man, ed., *Madame Bovary*, 335–36. Sainte-Beuve's article first appeared on May 4, 1857.

but neither she nor Charles recognizes him in this role. When he worshipfully visits her grave, Lestiboudois even mistakes him for the thief who has been stealing the tubers that the gravedigger has been growing in the cemetery. Justin is innocent, but his innocence is never put to the test. And he is the one who passively allows Emma to take the poison from Homais' inner sanctum. Justin may be a positive image, but—as Sainte-Beuve intimated—he is too insubstantial to provide a basis for a human type.

What Catherine Leroux and Doctor Larivière share is an altogether episodic appearance: they are almost literally one-paragraph characters. And while the one seems to transcend bourgeois stupidity from below, the other seems to transcend it from above.

Catherine of course comes into her own as Félicité in *Un Coeur simple*. But, in *Madame Bovary*, the appearance of the almost mute servant is simply too brief to allow the reader to do very much with it. In her animal-like simplicity, she is an innocent victim, but Flaubert allows Homais to get the last anti-clerical and deflationary word in with respect to her.

Doctor Larivière is in his own field the precise and competent craftsman whom Flaubert sought in the realm of art itself. He is the genuine professional, the man above considerations of petty self-interest and social status, authentically devoted to his calling. But he arrives too late—too late to save Emma and too late for more extensive characterization. Both his appearance and the consequences of his intervention seem gratuitous. He too remains a fleeting image in an otherwise barren landscape. If one were to draw an analogy between him and Flaubert's father and to credit at least in part Sartre's characterization of Flaubert's hatred of the paternal figure, his image would be rendered even more dubious. In the novel itself, it is significant that Larivière's only durable influence is suspect and superficial; indeed its position is comparable to that of romantic novels in Emma's life. His disciples, we are told, imitate his dress and manner. We are not told about the substance and spirit of their work. Larivière too seems to function as another false model—or at least a model that is used falsely—in a world of doubtful images and paradigms.

I put forth these observations to indicate that the relation between the "positive" and the "negative" in *Madame Bovary* cannot be sought simply on the level of what is represented or characterized. The quest for positive images or characters will not get one very far in the often bleakly stylized world of the novel. It will probably tend to reinforce the idea that the work is demoralizing, although there are qualifications to be made even on a conventional level—for example, Charles's saintliness, the metaphysical aspect of Emma's desire, and the mere presence of certain minor characters. But issues become more complicated when one attempts to relate what is represented to the mode of representation or narration.

The relation of the narrator to Emma is intense yet modulated. For example, the narrator seems to follow Emma closely in giving her child only a bit part to play. In fact Berthe is absent from the story for implausible lengths of time. When Emma uses the child as an excuse as she encounters Binet on one of her visits to Rodolphe, no one—including the reader—is surprised by the lack of surprise over the fact that the excuse is transparently false (because the child has been home from the wetnurse for years). Berthe even when present seems like little more than a movable prop. She reappears at the end to discover the dead Charles and to assume a "fate" one might expect in "socially realistic" melodrama. She is dispatched to work in a spinning mill.

The narrator is himself somewhat conventional in his desire to possess Emma and in his willingness to compete with her other men for her. Yet his desire takes a highly unconventional form. He does not become a character in the novel whose relation to her might be understood in more standard and straightforward terms. And the style of narration makes it difficult to personify him in any sense. But it does, as I have tried to indicate, generate possibilities that seem closed to Emma, for her mode of ambivalence holds little promise of renewal. Indeed there is a sense in which the reader's interest in the story shifts from Emma's entanglements in the "worn-out fable" to the way the narrator will relate to her in his attempt to come to terms with her and her world. It may also turn to the larger problems this attempt helps to disclose.

The model of a dissipation of romantic illusions through novelistic insight may be too simple to account for Flaubert's narrative practice in *Madame Bovary*. For Flaubert as narrator (and as author) faces problems comparable to Emma's own: how to confront a world in which viable mediations are absent or excessively weak and in which more uncanny overtures may lack a genuinely contestatory and possibly regenerative relation to existing structures. Yet Flaubert's manner of coming to terms with this problem is not identical to Emma's. Although one cannot apodictically ascribe to it a full mastery of problems or even a clear-cut superiority to Emma's response, the mode of narration deployed in the novel cannot itself be confined to the "world" it represents. Its critical reworking of that context and its relation to the possibility of transformation give it a significantly differential position. Before returning to this issue in a summary fashion, let us look a bit more closely at the way in which *Madame Bovary* relates to, or "textualizes," its literary and sociocultural contexts.

A quotation from one of Flaubert's letters is especially interesting in this regard:

> There are in me, literally [or literarily: *littérairement*] speaking, two distinct persons [*deux bonhommes distincts*]: one who is taken with bombast [*gueulades*], lyricism, great flights of the eagle, all the sonorities of the sentence and the summits of the idea; another who searches [*fouille*] and hollows out [*creuse*] the true as much as he can, who likes to accentuate the little fact as powerfully as the big one, who would like to make you feel almost materially the things he reproduces; the latter person likes to laugh and enjoys the animal side [*animalités*] of man. [January 16, 1852]

This quote plays both lexically and conceptually with ambivalence and self-directed but not altogether negative irony. The relation between Flaubert as "real" author and as narrator of fiction is suggested by the phrase "*littérairement parlant.*" And the components of his divided self are referred to, in subdued parodic fashion, as "*deux bonhommes.*" (He later referred to Bouvard and Pécuchet as his "*deux bonhommes.*") The two sides might in traditional terms be seen as "romantic" and "realistic," thereby providing some basis for two standard classifications of

Flaubert: those of covert, repressed, or frustrated romantic and of realist *malgré lui*. Or, shifting the emphasis of interpretation, one might make room for Harry Levin's understanding of realism not as an absolute but as a modifiable rectification of romanticism, which changes its point of attack with the metamorphoses of its protean adversary to bring about newer forms of disillusionment.[7] But there are qualifications in Flaubert's letter that suggest the limitations of both the realistic and the romantic labels and complicate the nature of their "dialectic." "Materially" is used in an affirmative sense to indicate the way Flaubert's style tries to evoke the very feel of things, but the term is modified by an "almost." The realist who sees truth digs for it and hollows it out—*"creuser"* is an ambivalent term. And the romantic is alluded to with somewhat roundhouse and bombastic images reminiscent of Flaubert's references to Rabelais. Nor is the romantic self univocal, for he seeks both the sonority of the sentence—with its relation to the materiality of language in terms that confound the writing-speech dichotomy: writing here sounds—and the summits of the idea (in the Platonic singular). Flaubert also attributes to the seeming realist the love of laughter and the pleasure in the ways man is an animal. But this feature, with its strong intimation of the grotesque and the carnivalesque, might be better positioned in the gaps between the realist and the romantic—gaps that also emerge in the brief characterizations of the *"deux bonhommes"* themselves. For the last qualification in the passage points to the more liminal and undecidable aspects of Flaubert and his "style," and it does so in the key of laughter.

Another quotation seems to lean more heavily in the direction of the "romantic," and it too touches on ground that should by now be familiar to us:

> The reason I am going so slowly is that nothing in this book [*Madame Bovary*] is drawn from myself. Never has my personality been of less use to me. After it is finished, I shall perhaps be able to do things that are better (I sincerely hope so). But it seems doubtful whether I shall compose anything more skillful. Everything in it comes from the *head*. [Tout est de *tête*.] If

7. *The Gates of Horn* (New York: Oxford University Press, 1966), chap. 2.

it is a failure, it will still have been a good exercise. What is natural for me is what is non-natural for others: the extraordinary, the fantastic, the metaphysical, mythological howl [*hurlade*]. *Saint Anthony* did not cause me a quarter of the mental tensions that *Bovary* does. It was a drainpipe [*déversoir*], and I had only pleasure in writing it. The eighteen months that I spent writing its 500 pages were the most profoundly voluptuous of my entire life. Think by contrast of what it means for me to enter every minute into *skins* that are antipathetic to me. [April 16, 1853]

This quote evokes the legendary *affres de l'art* and the ascetic practice involved in the writing of what Flaubert at times called his *pensum*. And it situates the ironic distance of the narrator as a sublimation of Flaubert's intensely felt hatred for his characters. It does so, however, in a forced and categorical contrast between *Madame Bovary* and *The Temptation of Saint Anthony*. The writing of the latter at least loosely framed the writing of *Madame Bovary*. In that legendary marathon reading, Flaubert declaimed the first version of *The Temptation* to his friends, Louis Bouilhet and Maxime Du Camp, and their harshly negative reaction—unexpected by Flaubert and coming as a severe blow to him—presumably helped to turn him toward a subject that would constrain him to discipline his "natural" tendencies. And after the completion of *Madame Bovary*, Flaubert returned almost immediately, as if for release, to the writing of a second version of *The Temptation*. The standard version is of course a third one composed in 1872, immediately before *Bouvard and Pécuchet* (which itself ran into impasses and was interrupted for the composition of *Les Trois Contes*). It may be noted that the first and third versions of *The Temptation* were literally positioned as memorials to the dead, for the first was written after the death of Flaubert's close friend, Alfred Le Poittevin, and the third after that of his other close friend, Louis Bouilhet. The second version might be more metaphorically seen as a memorial to Emma and Charles and perhaps to the dead—or to the death of ideals—in 1848.

One might further hypothesize that *The Temptation* in certain ways went underground in *Madame Bovary*, which is in its own manner a story of temptation, transgression, and a quest for the absolute, as is in some sense everything that Flaubert wrote. That Flaubert recognized an association between the two works is indicated in a letter of February 8, 1852: "I think that it [*Madame Bovary*] will be less lofty than *Saint Anthony* as regards ideas (a fact that I consider of little importance), but perhaps it will be more intense and unusual, without being obviously so." Conversely, those very problems Flaubert might have wished to escape in turning to more "exotic" subjects in *The Temptation* and his other more "romantic" works (such as *Salammbô*, composed after the second version of *The Temptation*) returned with distressing insistence. Flaubert had a paradoxical fascination for epochs that seemed to resonate with his own sense of decadence and belatedness, and this attraction tended to counteract the more conventional allure of the exotic. For him modernity was not unique as an age at the end of its cycle that leveled the web of similarity and difference into bland conformity, mediocre desire, boring repetition, and violence at the edge of exhaustion. The seeming alterity of remote ages and distant places gave way on closer inspection to problems perplexingly like modern ones. The exotic "other," in this sense, functioned less as a lost paradise or as an inviolate point of origin than as an indirect way of illuminating, or casting a shadow over, modern dilemmas.

In *The Temptation,* the saint is himself edged by exhaustion. His "temptations" are so bizarrely diverse that it is difficult for the reader to see how they constitute temptations in any ordinary sense. This would also seem to be the problem of the epigonal saint himself. He lives in a world of bewildering monstrosities and unspeakable excesses whose very proliferation makes them surprisingly workaday. In fact, his temptations would seem to be those of recurrent visions and words that deny the premise of temptation: the contrast between the temptation, for which one is not responsible, and giving in to it through "sin" or crime. His horribly monochromatic world is without relief. Its imaginary spaces are both excessively empty and crowded, and in them everything and nothing comes to pass. (One may recall the shock of recognition Flaubert felt in reading Balzac's *Louis Lambert* which he saw as "the story of a man who goes mad by dint of thinking of intangible things" [December 27, 1852].) The figure of approaching madness seems traced on the face of the saint. His final equivocal epiphany is undecided between merging with matter and a vision of the face of Christ in the disc of the sun. Like Emma Bovary herself, the saint would seem to be confronted with the uncanny in the form of what might be called the hysterical sublime.

In *Salammbô*, the exotic is clearly situated in a period of almost still-life decadence, and the bloody war between the Carthaginians and their mercenaries is itself on the outer margin of major historical developments. It is a war whose atrocities seem especially gratuitous because they have no lasting influence on the course of events. This war is devoid of meaningful combat or purposive goal—a very "modern" war in this respect. Indeed the "context" in general seems washed up on the shores of *post-histoire*. The "sacred" itself may be more available but it is, if anything, also more opaque than in modern times.

In addition, Flaubert's own mode of access to the "exotic" subject could only be through the mediation of massive documentation. Between him and the subject that might seem to provide a refuge from modern boredom was modern boredom in one of its privileged forms: archival research and burial in the library or the museum. The image of the exotic as the immediate and the lyrical proved illusory for modern man. The fantastic could enter only through the baroque medium of excessive documentation—a medium that was especially maddening when it persisted in turning up only fragmentary knowledge that consorted with fictive reconstruction even in the best authorities whom Flaubert consulted.[8] (To provide the lunar

---

8. For Flaubert's research on *The Temptation*, see Jean Seznec, *Nouvelles Etudes sur "La Tentation de Saint Antoine"* (London: Warburg Institute, 1949). For Flaubert's vitriolic reply to the "Orientalist," Guillaume Froehner, who questioned the adequacy of his documentation for *Salammbô*, see Albert Thibaudet and René Dumesnil, eds., *Flaubert Oeuvres I* (Paris: Gallimard, 1951), 1006–12. Flaubert's defense of his own scholarly credentials has all the pedantic and self-parodic appeal of good academic debate. See also Michel Foucault, "Fantasia of the Library" in *Language, Counter-Memory, Practice*, trans. Donald Bouchard (Ithaca: Cornell University Press, 1979), 87–109, and Eugenio Donato, "The Museum's Furnace: Notes toward a Contextual Reading of *Bouvard and Pécuchet*" in *Textual Strategies*, ed. Josué V. Harari (Ithaca: Cornell University Press, 1980), 213–38.

perspective on modern society in *Bouvard and Pécuchet,* Flaubert claimed to have perused 1500 volumes.) It should be remarked that Flaubert was perversely proud of his documentary mania, and he wrote of it with an intensity usually reserved for apostrophes to pure art. Indeed the two were, in their extreme forms, not that far apart. For the opposition between art (or fiction) and documentation, like that between the modern and the exotic, tended to undergo the same process of abysmal collapse that other oppositions of dubious merit were made to suffer in Flaubert's hands. His propensity to take documentation itself too far for scholarly comfort belied the reassuring message he himself tried to enunciate: "Nothing is as healthy as erudition. It is not the same with metaphysics and Art, higher matters where one always navigates a little in madness" (October 8, 1865).

Although works such as *Madame Bovary* and *The Sentimental Education* did not require comparable forms of scholarly research, they called upon Flaubert's documentary sense in other ways. Aside from obvious examples such as the consultation of medical works for the precise description of the operation on Hippolyte's club foot, *Madame Bovary* bears in more general ways the obvious marks of a quasi-documentary style. On one level, one can find in it a simulated use of denotative, factually painstaking, and excruciatingly accurate descriptive language. The use is simulated in that it often does not refer to empirically real people or events whose existence can be historically verified. But it does seem to conform to the expectation of lifelikeness or verisimilitude. Things, people, and events have the feel of empirical reality. The characters are types or, at times, stereotypes that amalgamate in stylized fashion characteristics of real people. And the result is a portrait of *moeurs de province* from which the social historian could learn a great deal about the "quality of life" in provincial France to supplement the data obtained from nonliterary sources. No less a commentator on politics and society in France than Albert Thibaudet has observed of Homais and Lheureux, the two ostensible victors in the novel: "The local patrician and the tradesman were the two linchpins of the French Revolution; they furnished France with the backbone of its middle class, and the Third

Republic assured the triumph of the principles and interests that they represented."[9]

Flaubert's "realism" seems prophetic, for the state of affairs epitomized by Homais and Lheureux typifies less the Second Empire than the later phase of the Third Republic which Flaubert did not even live to see. Indeed, as one moves from Stendhal to Balzac and then to Flaubert, the critical depiction of nineteenth-century French society becomes increasingly unsympathetic, until in Flaubert it often mingles ambivalently with a seemingly generalized misanthropy. One might also contend that Flaubert seized longer-term tendencies of French society that were in certain ways intensified in the early twentieth century. Even staunch defenders of the Republic, such as Emile Durkheim, could view its later phase as a betrayal of its early promise—a promise that, needless to add, did not even exist for Flaubert. Of Homais, Thibaudet writes: "In our time, he has, through a natural progression, his designated place in the general Council of the *Seine-Inférieure* and in the Senate that Gambetta called the Assembly of the communes of France. He was directly concerned by the call of Gambetta in 1872 to the *'nouvelles couches.'*"[10] The point here is not that Flaubert provided a description, analysis, or interpretation upon which all historians would agree but that he offered a reading of the times that might find its analogue in more ostensibly historical works. From this perspective, Homais and Lheureux were the incarnations of the modern variant of "home-town" virtues that could be adjusted to the needs of a commercial society with its conventional bourgeois values. The less adaptable Emma (or her "real-life" analogues who were, in Flaubert's words, crying in twenty villages of France) had to lose, but the self-assured positivism of Homais and the shrewdly calculating but small-scale financial operations of Lheureux were promised a happier future.

One could go on in a similar vein with reference to other characters and situations in *Madame Bovary*. Suffice it to note that characters, setting, and events can quite plausibly be made

---

9. *Gustave Flaubert* [1922] (Paris: Gallimard, 1935), 121.
10. Ibid.

to appear highly realistic, with the usual allowance made for the prophetic insight into developmental possibilities provided by great art. And all this is not the mere illusion that Sartre depicts in his interpretation of Flaubert's realism as a *leurre* [lure] that diverts attention from covert imaginary and nihilistic intentions. It is quite necessary for the work and play of the novel on other levels.

Indeed realism in the more ordinary sense is operative in the novel in an even more direct way, for *Madame Bovary* can be seen as making reference to real as well as simulated places, persons, or events. Flaubert, for example, refers to Rouen and Paris—quite "real" cities—as well as to the invented small towns of Tostes and Yonville l'Abbaye. And with reference to Yonville, Claudine Gothot-Mersch finds a striking resemblance to Ry where the "real-life" story of Madame Delamare—which according to Maxime Du Camp was the occasion for the writing of *Madame Bovary* itself—took place.

> The décor of the drama must, in any case, have caught the novelist's attention. Yonville is not the copy of Ry, but Flaubert gave it the same character as this rather banal village in Normandy, with its square, its single street, its river—with its market, inn, town hall, and pharmacy that one finds in a hundred small localities. He situated it, like Ry, in the immediate environs of Rouen; and the capital of Normandy exercised on these villages the fascination of the big city.[11]

Rouen itself, one may observe, is described in terms that are quite familiar to visitors to that city. One could undertake a more technical stylistic analysis of descriptions of Rouen in *Madame Bovary* and compare them with descriptions in other writings (novels, guides, documents, eye-witness reports, and so forth). But its results, however interesting for a fuller understanding of the nature of description in the novel, would not imply that "Rouen" as a real town or "external" referent had become totally virtualized in order to emerge as a "liberated signifier" internal to the language and formal procedures of

---

11. *La Genèse de Madame Bovary* (Paris: Librairie José Corti, 1966), 35.

description in the novel. Rather the results might lead one to question any rigid intrinsic-extrinsic dichotomy, and they would direct attention to the way in which the interaction between the real and the imaginary is crucial to the procedures of the novel. The dubiousness of any pure dichotomy that might lend itself either to a purely documentary understanding of the Rouen of *Madame Bovary* or to a purely formal account of it may be indicated by one simple point. If the capital of Normandy had been called "Rouen" in the novel but had been described with the characteristics of, say, Nice, significant problems in interpretation would have been created. One possibility is that *Madame Bovary* would have been a more surrealistically "experimental" novel than it in fact is.

A further point that is somewhat less obvious concerns the way in which the novel textualizes its urban "referents." The big cities—Rouen and Paris—have "real" place names while the smaller towns—Tostes and Yonville—have invented names. Emma gets to Rouen for brief visits that chart her affair with Léon (including the important scene in the cab). But she never makes it to Paris. (Flaubert did have her visit Paris in one version, but he wisely decided to eliminate this scene.) Indeed travel and love are given analogous positions in the text. Emma never actually experiences life in the escapist center of her dreams and incantations: Paris remains for her a purely imaginary "reality"—a repetition of her imaginary lover: "What was this Paris like? What a boundless name! She repeated it in a low voice, for the mere pleasure of it; it rang in her ears like a great cathedral bell; it shone before her eyes, even on the labels of her jars of pomade. . . . At the end of some indefinite distance there was always a confused spot, into which her dreams died. . . . She wanted to die but she also wanted to live in Paris" (41, 44). (Compare: "She repeated: 'I have a lover! a lover! delighting at the idea as if a second puberty had come to her" [117].) Emma's life is spent in small towns whose characteristics simulate the most typical and banal of real provincial backwaters. Their fictional reality has in fact little to distinguish it from the most boring and uneventful ordinary reality. The fact that their names are invented seems to be a distinction without a difference. By contrast, Paris, the center of France in every respect (as Tocqueville bemoaned in *The Old Regime*—a work published the same year as *Madame Bovary* and whose spirit is often rather "Flaubertian"), is the true object of her imaginary investments, but it remains out of reach.

These brief remarks about the nature of Flaubert's "realism" indicate that he practices in relation to it the "dual style" or double writing that he puts into play with reference to other features of the novel as it had become established or conventionalized at his time. On one level, he seems to conform to given demands in ways that make certain readings—including narrowly "documentary" ones—at least plausible. One might term these readings—such as the ones at the trial—relatively "naive" insofar as one realizes that they are necessary for more "sophisticated" achievements of the novel and for related readings of it. For, on other levels, these readings and the expectations they create are questioned, tested, and at times excavated. And the uncanny or hyperbolic extremes of this process come together with more critical ones. Erich Auerbach supplied this account of the critical reading of the times or of the "lived" social text in *Madame Bovary,* and, in terms of the issues it addresses, it is difficult to improve on it:

[Flaubert] wishes by his attitude—*pas de cris, pas de convulsion, rien que la fixité d'un regard pensif*—to force language to render the truth concerning the subjects of his observation: "style itself and in its own right being an absolute manner of viewing things." . . . Yet this leads in the end to a didactic purpose: criticism of the contemporary world; and we must not hesitate to say so, much as Flaubert may insist that he is an artist and nothing but an artist. The more one studies Flaubert, the clearer it becomes how much insight into the problematic nature and the hollowness of nineteenth-century bourgeois culture is contained in his realistic works; and many important passages from his letters confirm this. The demonification of everyday social intercourse which is to be found in Balzac [what might be termed Balzac's own mode of hyperbole] is certainly entirely lacking in Flaubert; life no longer surges and foams, it flows viscously and sluggishly. The essence of the happenings of ordinary contemporary life seemed to Flaubert to consist not in tempestuous actions and passions, not in demonic men and forces, but in the prolonged chronic state whose surface movement is mere empty bustle, while underneath it there is another movement, almost imperceptible but universal and unceasing, so that the political, economic, and social subsoil appears comparatively stable and at the same time intolerably charged with tension. Events seem hardly to change, but in the concretion of duration, which Flaubert is able to suggest both in the individual occurrence . . . and in his total picture of the times, there appears something like a concealed threat: the period is charged with its stupid issuelessness as with an explosive.[12]

Flaubert on this account seems to invert the orthodox Marxist picture of modernity. The times revealed not so much a socioeconomic substructure determining changes in largely illusory superstructures in ways that a revolutionary movement might seize and convert into a force for a global transformation of society. Rather the substructure itself was increasingly hollow or exhausted, and superstructures—however illusory—became lived reality. I have already indicated how Flaubert's critical practice was directed at the dominant discourses of the time—discourses of bourgeois family life, romantic love, conventional religion, and political power—which were themselves bound up with social practices. *Madame Bovary* is a powerful written "speech act" in which these discourses are reinscribed and deconstructed in intricate ways, and it is in this sense that the novel approaches what I have termed ideological crime. But the question from which Flaubert in his letters tended to turn away in dismay was that of how his novelistic practice might be related to social and cultural transformation in any larger sense. Most notably, any connection between cultural criticism and political activity seemed to be missing. There are two significant "contextual" issues related to this question: Flaubert's reaction to 1848 and the treatment of the carnivalesque in *Madame Bovary*.

The revolution of 1848 was a major event in the history of Flaubert's frustration with politics, and we have seen the role

---

12. *Mimesis* [1946], trans. Willard R. Trask (Princeton: Princeton University Press, 1974), 490–91.

'48 plays in the interpretation of Sartre. How did Flaubert respond to 1848 and what place does it have in *Madame Bovary* in comparison with his other "modern" novels, *The Sentimental Education* and *Bouvard and Pécuchet*? Flaubert's actual behavior in 1848 merits some attention. At the end of December 1847, he attended a reform banquet in Rouen with Odilon Barrot and other notables. He was thoroughly disgusted by it. In a letter written at the time, he noted: "Whatever the sad opinion one may have of men, bitterness invades your heart when you see displayed before you such delirious stupidities [*bêtises*], such hair-raising stupidities [*stupidités*]." He especially distrusted Béranger because of the cult he inspired and the uses to which he could be put. "Béranger is the stew of modern poetry; everyone can eat it and find it good."

Flaubert was in Paris only during the February days when the revolution was in its initial and less extreme phase. Maxime Du Camp notes in his *Souvenirs de l'année 1848*: "Returning home [on February 23, 1848] I found Gustave Flaubert and Louis Bouilhet, who had arrived from Rouen to see the riot 'from the point of view of art,' and who waited for me at the fireside."[13] We have no other source for this reflection on Flaubert's attitude than Du Camp's self-serving memoirs, and it seems to some extent qualified by Flaubert's own statement to Louise Colet in a letter written sometime in March:

> You ask my opinion on everything that has just happened. Well! All that is very strange [*drôle*]. There are discomforted expressions that are pleasurable to see. I delight profoundly in the contemplation of all these flattened ambitions. I do not know if the new form of government and the social state that will result from it will be favorable to Art. It's a question. One could not possibly be more bourgeois or more of a nullity [than during the July monarchy]. As for more stupid [*bête*], is it possible?

Here Flaubert speaks of the revolution as he might speak of a natural disaster such as the storm that ravaged his garden

13. (Paris: Hachette, 1876), 51.

(one finds its analogue in *Bouvard and Pécuchet*)—a storm that brought home to him the farcical side of human activity in the face of superior forces. From this perspective, political problems are "naturalized" as part of *la condition humaine* and removed from the sphere of effective human intervention. Flaubert also relies on the contrast between Art and bourgeois stupidity in judging political phenomena, but he is ironically open-minded about the possibilities of revolution.

Du Camp tells us that he was himself sympathetic to the Republican form of government, yet he experienced an inexplicable indifference to the revolution. He found the latter stupefying—a sentiment he often attributed to Flaubert. Nonetheless Du Camp joined the National Guards and was later wounded. In his *Souvenirs littéraires*, Du Camp states that in the days following the revolution of February, Flaubert "took a hunting rifle and found a place in the ranks of the company [the second battalion of the first legion] between Louis de Cormenin and myself, and for what it was worth 'acted like a good citizen,' for it was thus that we spoke."[14] (This scene was itself recalled in *The Sentimental Education* as Frédéric goes to join Arnoux and takes the latter's place in the ranks without realizing that he thereby frees Arnoux to take his own place at Rosanette's side.)

A somber series of events in his personal life helped to keep Flaubert from any further direct involvement in the revolution. His childhood friend, Alfred Le Poittevin, died on April 3, 1848. Flaubert expressed his profound sadness in a letter of April 7 to Maxime Du Camp. He spent two days keeping vigil at Le Poittevin's coffin in a scene reminiscent of Charles's response at the death of Emma. On the third day he was followed by a dog without having called it, and he believed that this dog was the one Le Poittevin had befriended. This incredible series of events seems like a case of life imitating art—a reliving of the uncanny encounter with the dog that Flaubert had described four years earlier in *The First Sentimental Education*.[15]

14. Quoted by Jean Bruneau, *Flaubert Correspondance I 1830–1851* (Paris: Gallimard, 1973), 1043.
15. Sartre sees the encounter with the dog in *The First Sentimental Education* as itself symbolizing Flaubert's near death in his crisis at Pont l'Evêque in 1844,

In a letter of April 10, 1848 (one week after the death of Le Poittevin), Flaubert wrote to Ernest Chevalier: "What a banal ship existence is! I do not know whether the Republic will find a remedy for it; I strongly doubt it. . . . My interior, old friend, is not gayer than in the past. The death of Alfred, as you know, did not lift my spirits. The farces of the true Garçon! How far away that is, and how bitter it appears to me now."

On July 4, 1848, Flaubert wrote to Chevalier telling him that Hamard, Flaubert's brother-in-law, had returned home mad as a result of the 1848 revolution. He wanted custody of his daughter and vilified Flaubert's mother. This second personal tragedy also overlaid Flaubert's experience of 1848 and helped to color it. One might hypothesize that the superimposition of personal grief upon collective crisis was a reason why Flaubert was ready to turn to an aesthetic treatment of 1848 only well after the composition of *Madame Bovary.*

The revolution of 1848 might almost be termed *l'absent* of *Madame Bovary*—the event that never takes place in it. I have intimated that Emma's suicide might be seen as a surrogate for 1848. For Emma takes her life just about when the revolution should come. Even more generally, national politics is excluded from the novel. The closest one gets to it is the anticipation of the arrival of the prefect at the *Comices agricoles*—and even he fails to arrive and must be replaced by a representative. The discourse of politics is in a sense present and viciously parodied in the *Comices* scene, but the novel focuses on the deadly repetitiveness and petty intrigue of life in the provinces where national concerns seem to be largely on the side of the stereo-

---

and he devotes 185 pages toward the end of the second volume of *L'Idiot de la famille* to an analysis of this connection. One may further note that dogs in general have a strange place in Flaubert's writings. Emma's exotically named dog, Djali, functions as a familiar and as an emblem of the imaginary. It mysteriously runs off in the move from Tostes to Yonville, and it is never heard from—or mentioned—again. Homais refers to the bizarre capers of his friend's (Bridoux's) dog as one of the more intriguing sights in Rouen, and he uses a visit to Bridoux as a pretext to lure and cajole Léon from the hotel room where Emma is waiting. In *The Sentimental Education*, Madame Arnoux, on the night before the rendez-vous with Frédéric at which she is replaced by Rosanette, has a dream. A horrible little dog is tugging at the hem of her dress. The barking of the dog turns into the coughing of her little son whose illness she sees as a punishment for her relation with Frédéric.

typical and the imaginary. The one allusion to an event of national or international importance—the 1840 insurrection in Poland—comes from the mouth of Homais.

In contrast to his procedure in *Madame Bovary,* Flaubert does incorporate 1848 into the text of *The Sentimental Education* and *Bouvard and Pécuchet.* Although his handling of the revolution in his later works defies easy summary, it may be informative to give some brief indication of his approach.

In *The Sentimental Education,* the "prostituted" revolution breaks out as Frédéric sleeps with the courtesan Rosanette in the bed he had prepared for his ideal woman, Madame Arnoux. And he is off-stage with Rosanette on an excursion to Fontainebleau while the bloody June days rage in Paris. Hearing the news that Dussardier is wounded, he feels guilt at his absence and rushes to care for his wounded friend. Before his escape to Fontainebleau, he and Hussonnet circulate among the crowds and appear at the Tuileries during its invasion and sacking by the populace. The narrator describes this scene in biting tones. But, in terms of characterization, it is significant that the more unqualified ironies come from Hussonnet rather than Frédéric. Dussardier is presented sympathetically, but this seems more because he is a good hearted but naive chap than because he is close to the workers. Indeed his own role in the events is ambiguous, for during the June days he fights in the National Guards against the workers. Frédéric's own bid at direct participation in politics is perhaps best symbolized when he presents himself for election before a "club" and, not obtaining even the support of his putative friends, is displaced by the citizen from Madrid who proceeds to give an unintelligible speech—in Spanish. After the coup d'état of Louis Napoleon, the next sixteen years of the Second Empire are skipped— or insistently made a blank—in the text until one comes to 1867–68 in the last two chapters, and these last chapters involve the role of memory. In *Bouvard and Pécuchet,* 1848 erupts in the text and seems to create a caesura in it. It has the power to disrupt the routine of rural life by evoking the passionate involvement of Bouvard and Pécuchet, and it even causes the first domestic quarrel in the hitherto blissful life of the two bachelors. But events quickly conform to the pattern of heightened expectation followed by frustration, and 1848 proves to be the biggest in a series of aborted apocalypses.

In one limited sense, Flaubert's treatment of 1848 in his later texts might be compared to that given it by Marx in *The Eighteenth Brumaire*. For both it was a revolution of false expectations—a blindly self-parodic imitation of the past or a hysterical pregnancy. Its idealism was hopelessly compromised by the objective conditions of the time and by the pettiness of certain of its actors. But Marx in contradistinction to Flaubert strained to derive lessons from 1848 (for example, the need for a worker-peasant alliance) that could serve the larger movement of revolutionary transformation in relation to which it was a momentary if significant and brutal setback. In Flaubert, the lesson—if this term can be applied to his approach at all—would rather seem to be the hellish frustrations of politics that tended to reinforce the very conditions one hoped to change. What, if anything, might constitute viable political activity was a question never raised by Flaubert.

It is nonetheless significant that, in Flaubert's reading of the "social text" in *Madame Bovary*, one dimension of collective life that is represented as drastically underrepresented or repressed and distorted in modern existence is the carnivalesque. The use of cliché in an uncritical or unself-conscious way counteracts the carnivalizing potential of linguistic self-consciousness itself. In *Madame Bovary*, the characters take their clichés either all too seriously or all too manipulatively, being preponderantly either "inside" or "outside" them. More subtle modulations tend to be restricted to the movement of the narrative itself where, as I have intimated, one has a partial regeneration of carnivalizing forces.

There are a number of scenes in the novel where the "fate" of the carnivalesque in modern society is portrayed. At the wedding of Charles and Emma, the initiative of a fishmonger-relative, who squirts water from his mouth through the keyhole of the wedding room, is suppressed by the bride's father on the grounds that it is out of keeping with the distinguished or "grave" position of his son-in-law. Given Charles's status as a petty *officier de santé*, this is of course ironic, but it is not intended as such by Emma's father.

The *Comices agricoles* is itself the provincial carnival, its ec-static "dream from 'The Thousand and One Nights,'" in Ho-mais' paradoxically apt phrase—and Flaubert's treatment of it could not be more deflationary. It is the "carnival" in which dialogue is totally absent. Rather one has a cross fire of mu-tually self-cancelling ideological monologues.

The aristocratic analogue of the *Comices agricoles* is the ball at Vaubyessard. The festivities are confined to high society and their invited guests. The common people are on the outside looking in. And Emma as guest finds only that the ball eats into her ordinary life rather than rejuvenating it: it creates a gap in her existence that is filled by a series of romantic illusions. Toward the end of her life, a masked ball in Rouen parodically recalls Vaubyessard; at it Emma is degraded to the position of near prostitute.

The Blind Man is a grotesque carnival figure out of season—a mask of death reduced to the form of a hideous beggar. And his repeated appearances to Emma culminate in his perfor-mance at her death bed. His obscene ditty mingles with the mumbled Latin of the priest and with Emma's own death rattle in a fantastic "threshold dialogue" of the deaf. His coming does not symbolize the creative struggle of life and death, and it has no regenerative force for Emma: it elicits only a shrill, hyster-ical laugh as she dies. Her suicide might also be seen as an alternative to the threat of chaotic nonentity represented by the Blind Man. Homais himself might almost be seen, in his unself-conscious and hyperbolic inanities, as the last carnival man. He shrewdly recognizes the Blind Man as a competitor, a threat to his reputation, indeed a sign of his failure, and he successfully agitates through the "media" of the day for the pathetic crea-ture's incarceration.

I shall adduce only one more scene, for it is easily subject to misinterpretation—the scene in which the Homais family is making jelly as Emma returns from a visit to Léon in Rouen (178–81). Homais has been charged by Charles to break the news of the death of Charles's father to Emma in a gentle way, and Homais has prepared a typically inflated speech on the matter which he never gets to deliver. Instead his attention—and ours—is displaced onto the grotesque and potentially ribald festivity of jelly making, with all of the Homais in ridiculous attire (a possibly carnivalesque setting). But this scene is itself displaced as Homais upbraids Justin for having profaned the pharmacist's sanctuary—the Capharnaüm—by taking from this repository of chemicals and tools of the trade a pan for jelly making. The type of comic reversal that carnival might institute is thus excluded by Homais. The double displacement (from death to jelly making, from jelly making to the Capharnaüm) enables the revelation of the place where arsenic is kept—the poison with which Emma is to kill herself. Hence a further shift is effected, and we move from the Capharnaüm full circle back to death. This entire scene is easily understood as an extraneous and overly elaborate excuse for enabling Emma to discover where the poison is kept. But this interpretation is an excessively narrow-minded one in which the only concern is the "economical" movement of the story line. The scene is a magnificent digression or detour that, through a double displacement, leads back to the ultimate "referent": death. On the level of the story told, death again seems to have no relation to rebirth. Emma's wake itself brings only the farcical recognition scene between Homais and Bournisien, the absence of Rodolphe and Léon, and the despairingly mimetic idolatry of Charles (who, after Emma's death, becomes what might be called a belated romantic—it is in this sense that Emma corrupts him from beyond the grave). But in the way in which it is told (or in its "radical of presentation"), the scene, in its burlesque style, effects a partial return of the repressed.

For the contention that I have repeatedly put forth is that, in his own narrative practice or style, Flaubert achieves a regeneration of carnivalizing forces. That a carnivalized style might itself have political implications was both sensed and sidestepped at his trial. But the nature of these implications was never drawn by Flaubert himself in his self-commentaries, and they are difficult to articulate in any case. For they bear upon the question of the relation of politics to "carnivalesque" contestation in larger processes of sociocultural transformation—processes where the "means" of activity is also part of the desired "end." One of the most blatantly self-parodic of gestures, however, would be to displace the entire problem of political and social change onto the process of carnivalization, even when the latter is understood in the broad and generous (if somewhat utopianly populistic) terms of Mikhail Bakhtin.

Indeed, to place Flaubert's "style" in relief for a final time, one might refer by way of contrast to the procedures employed in Ernest Feydeau's *Fanny*—a novel that was published two years after *Madame Bovary* and that drew upon the latter's notoriety to enjoy an even greater *succès de scandale*.[16] This novel tells a tale that seems shocking, indeed more "lascivious" or "prurient," than that of *Madame Bovary*, but Feydeau was not brought to trial for his extremely popular novel. Yet the types of reading that the trial imposed on *Madame Bovary* could more appropriately be applied to it.

The story is told from the viewpoint of Roger, the twenty-four-year-old lover of Fanny, a thirty-five-year-old married woman. Its theme is the *supplice* of the young male adulterer who reverses roles with the husband. For the husband is blissfully ignorant of his wife's affair, but the lover is haunted by the husband's superior stature, and he is intensely jealous of him: "I saw myself as a frightened sylph contemplating the statue of a giant. What kind of a man was I compared to him? It was him only and not me who was the strong and handsome expression of man!"[17]

The young lover is actually the mistress of the elegant and distant woman of the world whom he also identifies with his mother. He is like Léon who attains a quavering narrative voice and confronts a husband who is in obvious, blocklike, Olympian ways more imposing than Charles Bovary. Roger's misery reaches its peak when he realizes that Fanny, for her own purposes, has taken him only as a miserable supplement to her husband and that he is at best but half a man: "I am only an addition, an accessory! . . . Oh! horrible!"[18] When the husband is faced with financial ruin, the wife refuses to leave him. "'The household,' she said lowering her eyes, 'is the post of honor entrusted to the woman. The woman who respects herself

16. *Fanny* (Paris: Calman Levy, 1890).
17. Ibid., 39.
18. Ibid., 56.

never leaves it.'"[19] Here the adulteress, who superficially resembles Emma in assuming the "masculine" role, rallies to the hearth and reaffirms the "traditional" calling of the good *mère de famille*. Her deviation is simple: she wants to have things both ways—indeed to be like the traditional *père de famille*. She herself becomes jealous of her husband when he meets another woman on a business trip to England.

The carefully prepared and overly "plotted" climax of the novel comes in the scene when, hiding on the couple's balcony, the young lover sees Fanny seduce her husband. The scene has a "you-are-there" quality that makes it a form of indecent exposure. After it, Roger feebly tries to commit suicide by walking into the Seine and fainting! He is ill for weeks but refuses to receive Fanny. When he finally does see her, he plays the role of offended lover and reproves her in moralistic terms. Alone at the end, he feels as he did at twenty when his mother died.

Fanny does not lose much in plot summary. It is close to the bourgeois melodrama if not the soap opera. The husband is a stereotype who, unlike Charles, does not acquire other dimensions that place in question one's initial perception of him. Fanny and Roger remain rather one-dimensional figures who fit neatly into the mold of psychological and sociological explanation. The balcony scene is much more explicit than anything to be found in *Madame Bovary*. The inversion of roles is nicely effected, but the "shock effect" of the novel stays securely on a level that makes it easy to absorb. And there is nothing in the style of narration that could shock. The story is told consistently from the viewpoint of Roger, and the writing relies complacently on the most staid and conventional of rhetorical and narrative devices. The vapid reverie and the injured exclamation are just what they appear to be, and they become "camp" only in the eyes of the reader. What is significant is that, if the criteria stated at the trial were actually operative, it would be a novel like *Fanny* that should have been brought to trial. For it does convey at best but ordinary "crime" or standard deviation from the norm. The reversals effected are altogether contained

19. Ibid., 103.

and do not unsettle the norms of their context, nor do they suggest a generalized displacement of the established frames of reference. Yet in its implications for life and writing, this novel might be argued to be more "nihilistic" than *Madame Bovary*. It leads nowhere. And the impasses it generates do not motivate either the writer of fiction or the social critic to seek new ways in the face of the seemingly impossible.

9

Conclusion

> Yes, stupidity consists in wanting to conclude. We are a thread
> and we would like to know the web [*la trame*].
>
> Flaubert, September 4, 1850

> Once one has established the existence of an evil, what it
> consists of and on what it depends, when one knows in con-
> sequence the general characteristics of the remedy, the essen-
> tial thing is not to draw up in advance a plan which foresees
> everything; it is to get resolutely to work.
>
> Emile Durkheim, *Suicide* (1897)

At Flaubert's trial, there were two principal concerns which
the prosecution and the defense approached from complemen-
tary but opposed directions: those of unproblematic deviance
from, and conformity to, established norms and laws. One concern was the relation of the novel to basic categories and oppositions essential to familial and religious values. The question in
this respect might be condensed into that of the status of the
holy family in modern society. Did the novel praise marriage
and religion while condemning adultery and irreligion? Or did
it praise adultery and irreligion while condemning marriage
and religion? The conflicting conclusions of the defense and
the prosecution on this limited issue were made possible by an
unexamined consensus on the fundamentally legitimate nature
of the larger sociocultural context which was used as a standard
in judging the novel. And they both assumed the clear-cut subordination of literary to established social and religious norms.
The defense attorney argued that *Madame Bovary* was itself
more conventional in its treatment of risqué or dangerous subjects than some of the acknowledged classics of French litera-

ture. The prosecution, on the contrary, saw the novel as damaging to accepted values of the Christian West which constituted the higher tribunal for literature itself. In pursuing this tack, the prosecuting attorney at times touched upon questions that seemed to break through his own conventional frame of reference.

I have argued that both the prosecution and the defense tended to repress or avoid the way the novel represented ideological or political crime in posing challenges to established or contextualized norms that went beyond the issue of standard conformity or deviance. For, in Emma's situation, marriage and adultery amounted to much the same thing. Adultery was not a genuine temptation or a serious challenge to marriage. It was an illusory attempt at escape that brought in its wake the same problems as marriage, perhaps intensified. The deceptive clichés of romantic love substitute for the deceptive clichés of bourgeois marriage to cloak a dubious reality. Nor does the profane profanate the sacred with sacrilegious force. It resembles the sacred so much as to become its pseudo-*frère ennemi*. For the sacred in this context is a vapid nostrum. In these respects, the novel threatened to disclose that, in the world it "represented," the very norms and founding oppositions which the trial employed to judge it tended to lose their organizing power and to collapse into one another. The scandalous question it thereby raised was that of the extent to which these norms and concomitant values also had lost their viability in the social reality which the stylized world of the novel resembled enough to cause intense concern and even anxiety.

But the readings at the trial were not simply wrong. They could be substantiated enough to be rendered plausible, and they have their analogues in literary criticism. The case for the prosecution might be reinforced and refined on a literary level by an appeal to a work with the persuasiveness and sustained insight of Wayne Booth's *Rhetoric of Fiction*. The case for the defense might be bolstered by any number of conventional liberal *plaidoyers* for Flaubert. The reason for the plausibility of the arguments of the prosecution and the defense relates mostly to the second cause of concern at the trial: that of the position of the author-narrator. The defense attorney read into the novel a secure and reliable author-narrator who was largely a construct pieced together from Flaubert's biography and the testimony of absent character witnesses. Flaubert's intentions were demonstrably good. Hence the narrator, as the author's mouthpiece, could be trusted to convey them to the reader. The prosecutor found no such narrator in the text. He bore witness to an unreliable mode of narration that gave Emma Bovary her way and left one in doubt about the conscience of the author. To find a court of final appeal in condemning her and her creator, one had to look outside the text to a transcendent law that was coterminous with Western civilization.

My own argument has been that the problem of narration or mode of "representation" in *Madame Bovary* is indeed complex. It raises the question of the positions of the narrating subject as well as that of the relation between the narrator and various roles and projects of the social individual, "Flaubert." I have not denied the importance of intentions and projects, but neither have I followed the prosecution and the defense in construing the novel predominantly in terms of a *procès d'intention*. Rather I have tried to raise critically the issue of the relation of Flaubert's projects to one another and to his narrative practice in *Madame Bovary*. In these respects, I have attempted to elucidate the complexity of pure art and of muted carnivalization as they appear in Flaubert's letters and as they bear upon the functioning of the novel. One minimal point I have tried to establish is that one cannot simply take the most lapidary statements concerning pure art (or carnivalization, for that matter) from the letters and interpret the novel as their unproblematic realization. Their "incorporation" in the novel involves intricate processes of transformation.

Pure art had many functions in the thought of Flaubert, but one of its most noble forms was dedication to an ideal of spirituality and transcendence in a world marked by generalized profanation of values. That this ideal tended to coincide with a more total rejection of the world and a nihilistic revulsion at the human condition revealed the manner in which a secular surrogate for a religious vocation may—perhaps must—replicate the latter's most dubious excesses as well as its grandeur. The fact that the lost object of transcendent purity could not be

found and that the seeker had to make do with a secular replacement (a fact already threatening the status of the object of
devotion) was further complicated by the problem of carnivalization. One of the reasons why the modern world was characterized by generalized profanation and newer avatars of religious escape could be located in its very repression or noxious
distortion of the role of the carnivalesque. Flaubert himself
feared the contamination of his ideal and its subsidence into
bathos given its context. Thus he never again, after *The First
Sentimental Education,* gave it direct representation in his novels
in the form of an artist with values resembling his own. But
analogues of the quest for the absolute did appear in various
forms. They were contested but not entirely annihilated by the
more or less subdued carnivalizing forces that were transmitted
in Flaubert's irony and in his general mode of narration whose
fluctuations might at times even attain hyperbolic extremes.
The very interplay between irony and empathy as well as the
distribution of the narrative self through modulations of perspective were subtle ways in which the carnivalesque spirit continued to live in his work, and this spirit brought with it at least
a minimal hope of rejuvenation. The extent to which the carnivalesque was represented as repressed in the world of the
novel but was itself transferred or displaced to stylistic levels is
a testimony to the more "sublimated" ways it could find an
outlet in modern culture.

One might go on to argue that the fuller realization of the
carnivalesque depended upon the generation of structures and
ways of life that were more worthy of contestation and better
able to withstand its challenge, even to the extent of providing
public, institutional recognition of the necessity of contestatory
forces. For Flaubert in his novels "represents" a world that has
been familiar since modernity became a concern: one in which
structures—with the categories, identities, oppositions, and
norms that subtend them—are too rigid, fragile, or exhausted
to order life in a meaningful way that is confident enough to
allow for challenges to its very meaning. Indeed these structures are, in a viciously paradoxical fashion, combined with
modes of indeterminacy or disorientation that do not really
challenge them because they are not viably related to them in

an on-going process of exchange and renewal. The relation tends rather to be one of oscillation and possible collapse. And as order becomes hollow, excess itself veers toward the hysterical sublime which threatens to become equally hollow in that it has little of substance to engage it. Yet this is the context that Flaubert himself somehow had to "engage" in his writing.

My general contention has been that *Madame Bovary* is situated on a fascinating threshold in the history of the novel and its relation to social and literary conventions. On one level, it follows conventions to a certain point—and this too renders plausible readings such as those at the trial. But beyond a certain point, it critically sounds those conventions out, at times to the extent of excavating them. (This is what helps to account for the "ideologically criminal" and scandalous quality of the novel.) On the level of narrative practice, the vital issue is that of the shifting positions of the narrating subject in relation to characters and other objects of narration. The entire question of the so-called "free indirect style," with its inflexions of irony and empathy in the relation between narrator and narrated, should be seen in this light. For the broader question is that of tropisms in narrative perspective or "voice" that decenter the narrating subject and create a dialectic between forces of unification and dissemination in the structure of the narrative itself. Indeed a narrative that reads so smoothly that even drastic breaks, such as that between first and third person, can appear "natural" and readily pass unnoticed, poses the question of the interaction between unification and its adversaries or "others" in an especially insistent way.

The most comprehensive and possibly intractable question I have tried to broach is that of the ways in which *Madame Bovary* is symptomatic (even aggravating), critical, and potentially transformative in relation to the "contexts" it explores. To pose this question is definitely not to exclude the pertinence of a "political" reading of the novel but to render its conditions of possibility more exacting. (It is also related to an attempt to renew an older conception of politics that is not centered exclusively on the state.) There are ways in which aspects of *Madame Bovary* may be seen as symptomatic or aggravating in relation to "negative" features of society and culture. On the most inescapable level, Flaubert himself was preoccupied with the way in which an object of representation necessarily "contaminates" the medium that conveys it, however critical or ironic the medium may be. But there were also difficulties in other respects. The narrator does seem to have a predominantly hateful or resentful attitude toward certain characters in virtually all respects and to all characters in certain respects. And on an inevitable "naive" plane of reading, the "message" of the novel is one of such abject desperation that it seems to make hope of renewal appear illusory: the only idealists are misguided romantics who lose while the Homais of the world prosper and endure. In another more provocative and less decidable sense, the text works through a fascination with the hysterical, narcissistic, seductive woman—a fascination contagious enough to affect the prosecuting attorney himself.

Yet, as the last-mentioned consideration alone should make evident, the symptomatic replication of "negative" features cannot be seen as the sole or even the dominant tendency of the novel. Beyond, or alongside, it arises the possibility of a question Sartre raises: the relation of negativity and contestation to processes of sociocultural change. The novel is highly critical of the relations and contexts it discloses. The strategies of criticism are necessarily complicit with their object, notably when the form writing takes is that of ironic or parodic citation of the cliché-ridden and ready-made—a procedure that may always misfire or be misread. Yet these strategies of criticism do exist, and one often would have to be unspeakably obtuse not to recognize them. There is a pressing sense in which a sociocultural world is itself being placed on trial in *Madame Bovary*. But the workings of this critique do at times pass beyond more recognizable modes of criticism, including those radical styles of protest classifiable as political or ideological crime.

Here one enters the perplexing realm of uncanny or "unsayable" effects which were for Flaubert the dream-inducing high point of art and its ultimate *raison d'être*. These effects may seem to be a scandal to the Marxist as well as to the bourgeois, and the temptation to provide reductionistic explanations of them is strong in any case. But equally strong may be the desire to generalize rashly these effects and to discuss the novel solely in terms of their work or play, thereby obscuring or resolving prematurely the problem of their bearing on a critique of ideology, avoiding the issue of the relationships among the novel's various tendencies, and perhaps inadvertently reinforcing its symptomatic features.

Yet one is not constrained to see the more uncanny effects of the novel either as testimony to the formalistic nature of art or as an invitation to indiscriminate aporetics and the obliteration of all distinctions. (The latter emphasis would, by another path, converge with Sartre's depiction of Flaubert as a "knight of Nothingness," although it might situate itself beyond "good and evil" in the belief that it simply described both the way things linguistic are and the way Flaubert took them to be.) These effects may by contrast be argued to raise the issue of sociocultural transformation in its largest and most difficult form. For they may serve to render explicit the problem of their actual and desirable relations to structures and criticism. Indeed I have tried to suggest that, even at its most disconcerting, Flaubert's art implies an intimate sympathy for the oppressed and that it approaches the peculiar status of a higher form of "stupidity." The very mode of satire bound up with Flaubert's stylistic innovations raised critical and self-critical questions about the times while leaving open—and opening up—the question of more viable alternatives.

Flaubert's insistence upon the importance of certain issues—call them "aesthetic" or "literary"—and his resistance to the threats posed to them in modern civilization are worth reiterating whatever the abusive distortions or aberrations with which they have been associated. Flaubert shared with writers in a variety of fields—writers who came to radically different conclusions—a common conviction: modern civilization was undergoing what might be termed a far-reaching crisis of legitimacy in which freedom bordered on emptiness. Yet the response Flaubert often proferred in his letters was, in its social and political specificity, the fatalistic prerogative of the *haut bourgeois* who combined self-laceration with self-indulgence. It was also, perhaps, the necessary defense of an exceptional talent that faced the problem of how to write, given extreme doubts about one's own ability and existence in a society deemed to be unlivable.

Risking stupidity, one may nonetheless argue that Flaubert's novelistic practice provided some basis for formulating the issue of sociocultural transformation in a way that was at times broached in his correspondence. In the most general terms, the question would be how to bring about a network actively relating institutions and norms worthy of commitment, critical modes of interrogation without which commitment is mystified, and incandescently liminal overtures that, in the modern period, may be especially marked in art but escape even aesthetic classification. For Flaubert, holes in the whole were not simply transitional anomalies, and they could not be entirely overcome or rendered entirely meaningful by a "totalizing" dialectic. Yet one may insist that their position and function in culture and life vary. And whether they serve as regenerative carnivalizing forces—relating negativity and affirmation, situating a quest for the absolute, and allowing in qualified ways for processes of unification—or as primarily deadly sources of frustration and embitterment, consuming or disfiguring forces for renewal, is a political and cultural issue of the greatest magnitude. The recurrent urgency of a text such as *Madame Bovary* is that, if read in a certain way, it aids one in articulating this issue in a manner that lends itself to a number of conclusions and creates doubt about the feasibility of others.

Index

Index

Madame Bovary on Trial

Designed by Richard E. Rosenbaum.
Composed by Eastern Graphics
in 10 point Linotron 202 Baskerville
with display lines in Baskerville.
Printed offset by Thomson/Shore, Inc. on
Warren's Number 66 Antique Offset, 50 pound basis.
Bound by John H. Dekker & Sons, Inc.
in Holliston book cloth
and stamped in Kurz-Hastings foil.

Library of Congress Cataloging in Publication Data

LaCapra, Dominick, 1939–
  Madame Bovary on trial.

  Includes index.
  1. Flaubert, Gustave, 1821–1880. Madame Bovary. I. Title.
PQ2246.M3L23   843'.8   81-70714
ISBN 0-8014-01477-6   AACR2